PLEASE RETURN THIS ITEM
BY THE DUE DATE TO ANY
TULSA CITY-COUNTY LIBRARY.

FINES ARE 5¢ PER DAY; A
MAXIMUM OF $1.00 PER ITEM.

DUE DATE

201-6503			Printed in USA

A History of
Oklahoma State University
Extension and Outreach

CENTENNIAL HISTORIES SERIES

Centennial Histories Series

Committee

W. David Baird
LeRoy H. Fischer
B. Curtis Hamm
Harry Heath
Beulah Hirschlein
Vernon Parcher

Murl Rogers
J. L. Sanderson
Warren Shull
Milton Usry
Odell Walker
Eric I. Williams

Robert B. Kamm, Director
Carolyn Hanneman, Editor
Carol Hiner, Associate Editor

CENTENNIAL
1890 • 1990

A History of Oklahoma State University Extension and Outreach

by Robert C. Fite, Ph.D.

OKLAHOMA STATE UNIVERSITY / Stillwater

Published by Oklahoma State University
Centennial Histories Series, Stillwater, Oklahoma 74078

Library of Congress Cataloging-in-Publication Data

Fite, Robert C.
    A history of Oklahoma State University extension and outreach.

    (Centennial histories series)
    Bibliography: p.
    Includes index.
    1. Oklahoma State University—History.
2. University extension—Oklahoma—Stillwater—History.
I. Title.   II. Series.
LD4297.F58 1988   378.766'34—dc19   88-25320
ISBN 0-914956-35-3

Contents

Foreword

One of the most integral and exciting aspects of land-grant universities is a commitment "to put knowledge to work in the service of humankind." A land-grant university education is a very practical kind of education, with emphases on instruction, research, and extension and public service. This volume deals with the third function, extension and public service—oftentimes referred to as an institution's "outreach."

Essential to strong extension programs of a university are strong programs of instruction and research on campus. Outreach efforts must always be rooted in, and emanate from, on-campus programs. They cannot be sustained without such. Extension personnel must have strong and continuing ties to campus instructional and research personnel and programs, if they are to have available the latest and best knowledge for those whom they serve.

Oklahoma A. and M. College, very early in its history, began sharing knowledge of the campus with those engaged in service and work off the campus. Totally committed from its beginning to putting knowledge to work wherever needed, various "delivery systems" have been utilized during the century, such as correspondence study, the sending of faculty and staff to work areas, and (most recently), teleconferencing.

Oklahoma A. and M. College, and later, Oklahoma State University, has been blessed with strong leadership in the development of their outreach programs through the years. One of the "giants" in extension for some twenty-five years was Dr. Robert C. Fite who was persuaded to write *A History of Oklahoma State University Extension and Outreach.* Highly creative in his long-time leadership role in Arts and Sciences Extension, and fully conversant with outreach efforts of other colleges of the university, as well as with University Extension programs, he provides for readers insights relative to the struggles of extension, its ups and downs, its growth and development, and the people who made it all happen. The Centennial Histories Committee is indeed grateful to Dr. Fite for undertaking this responsibility and for telling "the OSU extension story" in a very readable and lively manner.

The committee is grateful to all who shared in making the volume possible. Special appreciation is expressed to former OSU Vice President for University Relations and Extension Richard Poole who, as the original coordinator of OSU's overall centennial observance, conceived the idea of a Centennial Histories Project. He, along with former president Dr. L. L. Boger, was most generous and supportive of the project, as is new President John R. Campbell. Dr. Ralph Hamilton, director of Public Information Services; Gerald Eby, head of University Publications Services; Edward Pharr, manager of University Printing Services; Heather Lloyd, reference librarian, and their respective staffs have assisted generously.

Working closely with authors of the project have been the Centennial Histories Project editors. Judy Buchholz served ably as editor early in the project. From August of 1984 through February of 1988, Ann Carlson served as editor of several of the early volumes in the series and contributed greatly in establishing procedures which will aid the entire project. On March 1, 1988, Carolyn Hanneman became editor, bringing to the position her skills and experiences as an assistant editor in the project, assuring continued excellence of volumes. On March 21, 1988, Carol Hiner, with her considerable publications experience, became associate editor, adding further strength to the editing process. Also, Dick Gilpin's dust jacket art adds much to the series.

Appreciation is expressed to Mr. J. O. Grantham, director of University Extension, who has been most helpful and supportive in the production of this volume. And, sincere thanks are expressed to Mr. Dale Ross, the executive director of the Centennial Coordinating Office, who provides enthusiastic support and encouragement for the Centennial Histories Project.

Robert B. Kamm, Director
Centennial Histories Project
President Emeritus
Oklahoma State University

February 1989

Preface

I was indeed fortunate to pick up a little brochure in Memphis, Tennessee, at the time of being "mustered out" of the Navy in January 1946. It announced that a veterans village was being constructed at Oklahoma A. and M. College to house returning married G. I.s who wished to further their education. My wife, Lucy, had been teaching at Marlow while I was overseas. She resigned her teaching job, and we hurried to Stillwater to become two of the pioneer residents of Vet Village. Both of us pursued a master's degree. Such was the scene of our second honeymoon. Shortly thereafter, I was interviewed by Dr. Edward E. Keso, Dean Raymond D. Thomas, and President Henry G. Bennett before being offered the opportunity of a lifetime—a chance to join the faculty of Oklahoma A. and M. College.

Ordinary happenings sometimes spawn events that lead to unexpected results. A cup of coffee with Robert B. Kamm, director of the Centennial Histories Project, and J. O. Grantham, director of University Extension, in the Student Union about five years ago seemed innocent enough at the time, although it is possible they already had designs on a goodly portion of the next five years of my life. They suggested that I might like to devote some of my time to preparing a story of extension and outreach for the Centennial Histories Series of Oklahoma State University. Being retired, enjoying good health, having spent more than twenty years in extension at OSU, having some writing experience, and possessing a propensity for saying "yes" to presidents, deans, and directors, I soon ran out of excuses. Before the second cup of coffee was finished, I had agreed to give it a try. It was not as easy as first surmised. For almost two years, I wrestled with the concept without getting anything on paper.

How could the OSU extension story be told? Tables and graphs could show enrollment figures and course completions and might make acceptable reading for auditors and statisticians, but they would not produce raving reviews from the average OSU alumnus. Furthermore, the data for such a statistical approach eluded me. Many records are dumped when professors retire, leaving only memories which also fade with the passage of time. It soon became apparent that statistics would play a minor role in the extension and outreach story. Instead, the story would describe the intriguing succession of programs that were invented and carried out in response to needs of the times. Creativity, ingenuity, and serendipity characterized these extension and outreach programs from the very beginning. My task would be to organize an account of these programs into paragraphs and chapters around which a binding could be fashioned to make the book.

Accounts of extension and outreach programs have been preserved on microfilm in the archives of OSU's Edmon Low Library. This provided a rich source of information for much of this story. But I found very early that my eye cataracts and the microfilm readers in the library were completely incompatible. For getting these accounts out of the archives and into a form suitable for my use, much credit must go to Carolyn Hanneman of the Centennial Histories staff for countless hours of perusing microfilm, and to Mary Helen Evans of the library staff for what seemed to be an endless number of xerox copies of newspaper articles. Also Kathleen Bledsoe, assistant reference librarian, and Greg Hines, library assistant, in Special Collections were most helpful in pursuing documents essential to the study. Without their assistance this book might never have been written, and certainly it would have been lacking in detail. Supplementing these library sources were thirty-five personal interviews over a three-year period with contemporaries who were a part of the extension scene. Each of these is referenced in the endnotes and listed in the Bibliography. Sharon Nivens, Retta Gayle Meigs, and Venisa Nasalroad of Mr. Grantham's staff in University Extension transcribed hours and hours of interviews, helped with word processing equipment, and, in general, provided logistic support whenever it was needed. Emerging from these efforts was an exciting series of stories, at least for me and hopefully for the reader, which parallels the development and growth of Oklahoma State University.

Once I began to write, my greatest problem was organization. Should one story be completed before another was started when it extended through many years or even decades, or should the events of a period be assimilated into chapters representing eras in the life of the institution. The latter approach was adopted. For this reason, the reader may choose to view each successive era in its entirety or follow a single topic through several chapters with the aid of the Index. Originally the outline contained only seven chapters. The manuscript was essentially complete when the Oklahoma College of Osteopathic Medicine and Surgery joined Oklahoma State University as the College of Osteopathic Medicine on July 1, 1988. For the price of another cup of coffee, the Kamm and Grantham duo challenged me to add another chapter to cover the event.

Chapter 8 describes this new dimension to OSU's extension and outreach mission. I recommend it to every OSU alumnus regardless of personal interests in extension and outreach. Osteopathy has proven its worth as a health care discipline, and it may prove President Emeritus Lawrence L. Boger right when he said that it was probably the biggest thing to happen during his tenure as OSU president.

I am deeply indebted to extension directors Beulah Hirschlein, Richard Jungers, Monroe Kriegel, and Clayton Millington for critically reading the first seven chapters of this book. In addition, Katherine McCollom, the daughter of Roy R. Tompkins, also read the first seven chapters. Also, I want to thank Linda Plemons, coordinator of publications for the OSU College of Osteopathic Medicine; Bob Jones, executive director of the Oklahoma Osteopathic Association; Dr. Donald Cooper, director of the OSU Student Health Center; and Dr. Boger for reading chapter 8. In addition, the entire manuscript has been read by Ralph Hamilton, director of Public Information Services; Odell Walker, liaison to the Centennial Histories Project; Mr. Grantham; and Dr. Kamm. The finished product is a richer and more complete account of extension and outreach at Oklahoma State University because of their contributions and suggestions.

I cannot speak too highly of the editorial staff for the Centennial Histories Project. First, it was Editor Ann Carlson whose encouraging words spurred me on after my first feeble attempts to put something on paper. Doubly fortunate for me was the appointment of Carolyn Hanneman as editor when Ann moved to University Personnel Services, for it was Carolyn who had gathered much of my raw data from the microfilm in the Microform and Media Room of the library and who had been assisting Ann in the editorial office. Carolyn was then fortunate to get Carol Hiner as associate editor. These two deserve much credit for the quality of this publication. It has been a joy and a privilege to work with them. Not only did they improve the format and narrative, but they personally sought out many of the illustrations for the text. In that regard, Graphic Designer Gayle Hiner helped make the story come to life by carefully laying out the illustrations to complement the text. Even with all of this expert assistance, imperfections will remain for which I am solely responsible.

As the volume took shape it became apparent that many extension personnel over the years would not be mentioned by name. Try as I might to make the narrative all inclusive, there were many who did their work faithfully yet did not receive a lot of publicity for their accomplishments. To compensate for this shortcoming, thirteen Appendices were included listing the names of extension professionals in the various colleges and special programs in so far as existing records permitted. If a certain name is not in the Index, perhaps it will be in an Appendix.

Last, but not least, I should mention Lucy's part in this publication. As in all previous endeavors, she has been supportive yet constructively critical. She waded through each chapter to make sure my grammar and spelling would not prove an embarrassment. Her patience and encouragement have been priceless, and I dedicate this volume to her.

Robert C. Fite
Professor Emeritus of Geography
Former Administrator, University
Extension

February 1989

A History of
Oklahoma State University
Extension and Outreach

1 Foundations of Extension And Outreach 1890-1920

The role of extension at an educational institution is to disseminate knowledge to people beyond the campus so as to enrich their lives. While a useful idea can be disseminated through an extension program today and be put to use tomorrow, it might require a decade to accomplish the same result by depending solely on resident instruction. Extension supplements traditional resident instruction by providing educational opportunity for non-resident students. If an educational institution is sensitive to the educational needs and wants of the people within its sphere of influence, it may satisfy those needs and wants effectively and efficiently through appropriate extension programs. There is a motto in extension which says, "If the people know enough soon enough, they can cope." Yet, the normal extension function is not an emergency operation in response to crises; instead, it is an operation to provide information, skills, and know-how which prevent crises from occurring. By providing these services, an educational institution expands its sphere of influence to greater and more distant audiences. Indeed, those same programs may serve the institution as an outreach function to expand further its sphere of influence.

The evolution of extension techniques and accomplishments during the history of the Oklahoma State University (known as Oklahoma Agricultural and Mechanical College prior to 1957) has been marked by creativity and pervasiveness but especially effectiveness and thoroughness. Automobiles and good roads, much less airplanes, have not always been available to facilitate delivery of extension programs; communication by telephone, radio, television, or satellite has not always been possible to assist the extension agent. Yet, each of these has played an important part in the evolution of the extension services provided by the university.

Perhaps an appreciation of the scope of change within the first one hundred years of Oklahoma State University can best be illustrated by comparing a few extension and outreach activities of OSU's tenth decade with extension efforts in its first three decades. In addition to Cooperative Extension which serves the Colleges of Agriculture, Veterinary Medicine, and Home Economics, in part, there is now an extension director to promote, coordinate, and supervise extension teaching by the faculty in each of the remaining colleges (arts and sciences, business administration, education, engineering, and home economics). There is no separate director for the Graduate College. Also, there is a director of extension for the university as a whole. This individual works with the college directors to coordinate overall planning as well as exert budgetary control when needed. More than one-third of the faculty members of the university participate regularly in some form of extension instruction. The number of non-traditional students enrolled in extension courses for credit approximated one-third of the resident enrollment of the university at the beginning of the tenth decade of OSU's history. In addition, tens of thousands of individuals are served each year through non-credit programs of instruction and other forms of outreach activities.

The National University Teleconference Network (NUTN) is an innovative extension project of this centennial decade (1980-1990). It is a consortium of more than 250 educational institutions banded

COURTESY ROBERT C. FITE

J. O. Grantham (*left*) and Marshall E. Allen (*right*) confer with a technician at the Educational Television Services Center. Through telecommunications, extension programs can literally be brought to millions of people.

4

together by a common desire to serve extension education needs better through the use of space and electronic technologies. The member institutions opted for NUTN's permanent home to be on the Oklahoma State University campus in recognition of the university's leadership in the field. Prior to the spring of 1982, NUTN was only a dream of J. O. Grantham, director of University Extension. Appointed director in 1975 at the time of a major reorganization of the extension services at Oklahoma State University, Grantham was quick to recognize the enormous possibilities of instruction by television. Aided by communications satellites, which hang fixed in space for long periods of time, television signals can be relayed throughout the state and nation as easily as to an adjoining county.

To facilitate this venture was the university's well-equipped Educational Television Services headed by Marshall E. Allen. Fortunately for OSU, President L. L. Boger, Vice President Richard W. Poole, and other key faculty and staff supported the idea and encouraged Grantham and Allen to proceed. The advantages of such an organization have not yet been fully explored, but two recent teleconferences suggested some of the possibilities for future extension programs.[1]

Through NUTN, thousands of participants on 200 campuses in the United States and Canada were linked simultaneously with a panel of international experts on world food problems on October 16, 1985. The occasion was the fortieth anniversary of the Food and Agriculture Organization (FAO) of the United Nations. Talk-back capabilities were available to participants at each site. In addition to those in voice contact with the panel, several million people watched the program on cable television, educational television, and Public Broadcasting Service stations.[2]

The OSU Alumni Association used NUTN connections on August 22, 1985, to host probably the largest alumni meeting ever held. The live, eighty-minute video teleconference was estimated to have reached more than 4,000 former students simultaneously. The conference was hosted by President Boger and Felicia Ferguson, 1983 OSU graduate and Miss Oklahoma for 1985. Two-way communications were established between the hosts and alumni groups around the country extending from Bethesda, Maryland, to Houston, Texas, to Seattle, Washington.[3] The effort was so successful that a worldwide alumni meeting is planned as a part of the centennial celebration in 1990.

These two conferences remain in stark contrast to the humble beginnings of extension by the Oklahoma Agricultural and Mechanical College in the 1890s. Oklahoma's land-grant college came into being under the auspices of the Morrill Act of 1862 and was authorized by the territorial legislature in December 1890. Any resemblance to the mission normally associated with a university of today was largely accidental and was forcefully denied by those in charge at the time. An editorial in the college newspaper in 1895 reminded readers that agricultural colleges "so created and assisted by Congress are limited in their nature, organization, and purpose to certain specific and enumerated lines of work . . . that they are not institutions of 'general education' in the common ordinary sense."[4] As might be expected of a fledgling college on a frontier prairie in the 1890s, there was very little extension or outreach activity of any kind during the first decade.

Outreach was generally confined to off-campus lectures by the administrators and faculty and perhaps an occasional on-campus institute for special interest groups. The *Oklahoma A. and M. College Mirror* noted that George L. Holter, a professor of chemistry and metallurgy at the college, lectured before the Oklahoma City High School on March 9, 1895. The *Mirror* also noted that an Edmond correspondent to the *Wichita Eagle* gave good marks to Oklahoma A. and M. College President Edmond D. Murdaugh for his address to the Territorial Normal Institute, labeling him a forceful speaker. Later that same year the *Mirror* reported that Edward F. Clark, a professor of mathematics, and newly-appointed President George E. Morrow had lectured before several county teacher institutes including those held at Stillwater, Perry, Oklahoma City, El Reno, and Pond Creek.[5] In December, President Morrow lectured before a farmers' institute in El Reno and "at other places before he returned."[6] It was not reported how long the president was on tour. He may have traveled by train, on horseback, or more likely in a surrey. Because improved roads and automobiles were practically nonexistent, it was important that each trip be made as productive as possible; thus multiple appearances were common.

The college newspaper observed in 1904 that bad roads constituted the greatest drawback to rural life, and it recommended that "mud holes" might be eliminated and drainage improved if furrows were plowed along the sides of the roads and bridges were built across the drainage

NEW EDUCATION

The first farm club school in Oklahoma was held at Letitia in Comanche County in 1912. The lecturers arrived at the rural school in a "topless" surrey.

channels. A further comment noted that lack of money was a hindrance in getting these things done.[7]

In general, travelers on official business in those days either went by train or furnished their own conveyances. Early in the 1900s, farm agents were sometimes hired to accelerate the dissemination of agricultural information. These were generally successful farmers who were willing to share their experiences with their neighbors on a part-time basis. They drove from farm to farm in a buggy or rode horseback. In the summer of 1909, C. H. Prinkley may have been the first farm agent in Oklahoma to use an automobile in his work near Snyder. There were complaints against Prinkley because his auto frightened the farmers' horses.[8]

Railroads of the time provided some of the most reliable transportation. There was much evidence of cooperation between the railroads and Oklahoma A. and M. College in providing transportation for agricultural specialists. The railroad companies were eager for the country along their routes to become settled. They anticipated selling land that had been granted to them, increasing passenger traffic, and developing more commerce. The railroads were known to furnish annual passes for agricultural agents to work the territory tributary to their lines.[9] Emma A. Chandler, a female agent for Oklahoma A. and M. College, worked in domestic economy and with boys' and girls' clubs. In the spring of 1915 the *Orange and Black*, the college newspaper, reported that "Emma

OKLAHOMA HIGHWAYMAN

Lack of all-weather roads was a serious obstacle to extension activities during the early decades. Although the state constitution provided for a Department of Highways in 1907, the department had no money with which to build roads. State records show 25.5 miles of hard surfaced highways and 3,445 miles of "draggable" roads.

Chandler unexpectedly added Enid, Helena, and Alva to her list of visits last week" because the Frisco Express made a change in schedule.[10]

Early in 1913, an agreement for a demonstration train was completed between the Santa Fe Railroad and B. C. Pittuck, dean of extension at Oklahoma A. and M. College. The college equipped and staffed an eight-car train to feature poultry and hogs during an extended tour of the state. Pittuck accompanied lecturers who spoke on appropriate subject matter: W. A. Linklater, hogs and silos; James A. Wilson, hogs and silos; John W. Wilkinson, boys' and girls' agricultural clubs; A. C. Hartenbower, farm crops; C. H. McElroy, hog cholera and swine plague; H. A. Bittenbender, poultry; Irma Matthews, domestic science; and Henrietta Kolshorn, boys' and girls' agricultural clubs.

While one car was filled with poultry and poultry products, another car contained tainted hogs and hog products including specimens of cholera-damaged pork; and a flatbed car was used as a lecture and demonstration platform. The remaining cars contained various other exhibits and living accommodations for the train crew and lecturers.[11] A portion of the itinerary for the Poultry and Hog Special in 1913 included these stops:

DATE	MORNING	AFTERNOON
Monday, January 20	Crescent	Enid
Tuesday, January 21	Nash	Cherokee
Wednesday, January 22	Avard	Waynoka
Thursday, January 23	Shattuck	Fargo and Woodward
Friday, January 24	Medford	Tonkawa
Saturday, January 25	Ponca	Newkirk
Sunday, January 26	(no schedule)	
Monday, January 27	Kaw	Fairfax and Skedee
Tuesday, January 28	Sparks	Meeker and Wanette
Wednesday, January 29	Byers	Pauls Valley

The Poultry and Hog Special was switched from the Santa Fe to the Frisco lines and visited Davis, Sulphur, Wayne, Edmond, Mulhall, Perry, Goultry, Helena, Blackwell, Lamont, Ames, Okeene, Thomas, Custer City, Clinton, Rocky, Cordell, Frederick, Snyder, Cyril, Cement, Tuttle, Chandler, Stroud, Bristow, Mounds, Okmulgee, Wetumka, Holdenville, and Francis before ending the tour on February 15 at Ada. Fifty-four towns had been visited, and more than 52,000 people had visited the train. The cost of the trip, including the living expenses of the lecturers, was paid by the railroads.[12]

A demonstration on the proper care and handling of chickens elicits rapt attention from this group of young people. Early extension efforts not only included programs for adults but also for the quite popular boys' and girls' clubs.

Other demonstration trains operated to serve different audiences or to disseminate information in different fields, such as fruits, truck gardening, field crops, and draft animals. Although demonstration trains were generally considered successful, they were a short-lived phenomenon. Perhaps it was the development of better roads and the increased use of automobiles, or it might have been the approaching crisis of the first world war, but demonstration trains faded from the scene as rapidly as they had appeared in the second decade of this century. These same reasons possibly prevented the extension of an interurban line into Stillwater, even after elaborate plans and surveys had indicated the venture was feasible. In 1922, an interurban line was to be extended from Guthrie to Stillwater, thus reducing the rail distance to Oklahoma City from eighty-one miles to sixty miles and reducing the one-way travel time to only two hours.[13]

Some of the earliest evidences of organized and systematic extension efforts by Oklahoma A. and M. College were through the medium of short courses. A short course could be conducted either on or off the campus. If held off-campus, it might be known as a movable school and be repeated at several locations before the instructor returned to the campus. One such movable school visited sixteen counties and registered 27,675 participants during the fifteen weeks of the tour.[14]

The short course on campus began primarily as a way to instruct young farm people who could not afford to go to college. Many of these people were able to attend a class of one to several weeks during the slack season of the winter months, usually January and February. Room and board was available from Stillwater residents for about $3 per week, and the registration fee was only $1 per student. The first short course

Demonstration trains in Oklahoma were a phenomenon of the early twentieth century. A demonstration train would pull into a railroad station in front of various audience clusters. Lecture-demonstrations were given on livestock and field crops at one location, home economics at another, and sometimes on boys' and girls' clubs at a third.

began January 3, 1900. Open to anyone at least sixteen years old, the course dealt with topics in agriculture and mechanics. This short course developed into an annual event known as the Short Winter Courses in Agriculture, Horticulture, and Mechanic Arts. Evidently out-of-state participants were soon attracted to the short courses because the *College Paper* announced in 1902 that the fee of $1 applied to anyone living in Indian or Oklahoma Territories, but for all others the fee would be $5. The age requirement disappeared. Now the only requirement was an "expressed interest in farming." Other subjects were added such as blacksmithing and domestic economy. The short course enrollment in 1903 exceeded capacity, and several applicants were denied admission. By 1908, the short course topics included American history, boilers and engines, and cost and design of farm buildings.[15]

The short course technique spread to other audiences and covered additional topics until the calendar of the winter months was dotted with scheduled events. These were announced in advance through the *College Paper*, which was distributed to newspapers throughout the area. A member of the regular faculty was designated to serve as "dean" or "director" or "principal" of short courses. John Fields was listed as dean of short courses in 1900 and perhaps was the first person to hold such a title. He was followed by A. C. Hartenbower (1913-14) and D. C. Mooring (1914-15). In 1915 Bradford Knapp became head of the Department of Short Courses. Knapp, the son of United States Department of Agriculture Specialist Seaman A. Knapp, would later become president of Oklahoma A. and M. College.[16]

The proliferation of short courses precipitated a need to consolidate many of the activities into a common schedule so a farmer could come to the campus and get all of his problems addressed in one trip. Accordingly, the second week of January of each year was designated as "Farmers Week," and a smorgasbord of short course topics was offered. This grew in popularity and participation until the attendance at farmers week in 1917 exceeded 500 people. Of these, 216 were labeled as "real farmers." Others included farm agents, government employees, county superintendents, teachers, and youth from around the territory.[17]

Fairs provided another vehicle through which information could be delivered to the public. Oklahoma A. and M. College had exhibits and maintained an information booth in 1897 at both the Payne County Fair in Stillwater and at the Territorial Fair in Guthrie.[18] President Morrow, Colonel Henry E. Glazier, John H. Bone, and John Fields represented the college at the Territorial Fair. The *College Mirror* observed that "their efforts there will undoubtedly result in great good to this institution."[19] Within a few years, more than sixty county fairs were being held each year, plus two state fairs, one at Oklahoma City and the other at Muskogee. Although the college was the principal source of judges for these fair exhibits, other states and various government agencies, especially the U.S. Department of Agriculture, supplied many. Very early in the history of fairs, Oklahoma A. and M. College provided its own exhibit

ARCHIVES, OKLAHOMA HISTORICAL SOCIETY

In the early history of Oklahoma A. and M. College, fairs were even more important to the educational process than they are today. The college maintained its own exhibit hall at the heart of the state fairgrounds in Oklahoma City. In addition to viewing the college exhibits, fairgoers enjoyed a lively series of educational lecture-demonstrations from professors and students.

hall near the center of the Oklahoma City fairgrounds. In addition to housing college exhibits, this building was the scene of many educational demonstrations by faculty and students for the benefit of fairgoers. As fairs grew in popularity, so did the prizes; and Oklahoma A. and M. College was always high on the list of winners. Just how conflict of interest was avoided between exhibitor and judge is not clear. Perhaps the classes in which Oklahoma A. and M. College competed were always judged by outsiders.[20]

Cotton was an early cash crop favorite among Oklahoma farmers. In the early 1900s the entire cotton industry of the South was threatened by the invasion of the boll weevil. Congress appropriated funds in 1904 to investigate the problem. Seaman A. Knapp was sent to Texas to begin the study. He initiated a program of education among the farmers through the use of farm agents. This earned Knapp the title, "father of extension." It was not long before agents under Dr. Knapp's direction were working with Oklahoma farmers. By 1908 Oklahoma had two area supervisors, W. M. Bamburge in the east and W. D. Bentley in the west; each was responsible for several local, part-time farm agents. Federal funding was augmented by local contributions from any source availa-

Seaman A. Knapp (*left*) is generally recognized to be the father of the extension movement. He was sent to Texas by the U.S. Department of Agriculture to seek solutions for the boll weevil problem in cotton. His efforts led to the passage of the Smith-Lever Act providing for Cooperative Extension. W. D. Bentley (*right*) worked under Knapp as a farm agent and became the first director of Cooperative Extension in Oklahoma.

Centennial Histories Series

ble including the farmers themselves. In 1912 the Oklahoma Legislature authorized county governments to cooperate in the funding.[21]

Although Oklahoma A. and M. College identified with the farm agent movement and cooperated with it, the program was administered out of Washington by the United States Department of Agriculture. Partly in response to the late Seaman Knapp's efforts, Congress passed the Smith-Lever Act in 1914 which provided increasing aid for farm and home demonstration work and caused the administration of the farm agent program to be moved to Stillwater. This act provided for a unique system of cooperative funding between the federal, state, and county governments to perform certain well-defined but restricted extension activities. This gave rise to a separately administered and comparatively well-funded extension activity at Oklahoma A. and M. College known as the Cooperative Extension Service. Bentley became the first director of extension under the new law. By the spring of 1916 he reported having sixty men agents in sixty counties as well as twenty-one women agents in the field. At that time Oklahoma had employed more agents under the Smith-Lever Act than any other state.[22] Because of restrictions placed on the use of the federal funds, Cooperative Extension could not address all of the needs of the institution. As a result, there emerged another extension service at Oklahoma A. and M. College, insignificant in the beginning but persistent through the years.

When the United States declared war on Germany on April 6, 1917, what had been a classic European struggle suddenly became a world war. Food, engineers, and soldiers were in great demand by American allies, and Oklahoma A. and M. College was in a position to help with all three needs. Agricultural efforts were intensified, especially in the

OSU AGRICULTURAL INFORMATION

E. J. Phillippi, a demonstrator-farmer from Anadarko, believes more cotton will grow on a straight row than a crooked one! By 1908, Oklahoma farmers received technical assistance through the federal government-supported farm agent system. These early efforts in farm demonstration work gave rise to the Cooperative Extension Service.

production and preservation of food. War gardens were promoted among rural and urban dwellers alike. The women students were given emergency training in food preservation techniques so they could disseminate these skills in their home communities during the summer months. New short courses, such as training radio and telegraph operators, were developed to meet emergency needs. To help cope with a shortage of sugar, a beekeeper course, possibly the first correspondence course ever offered by Oklahoma A. and M. College, was developed.[23]

Contrary to the experience at some other educational institutions, the war had a positive effect on enrollment. Although regular classes were sometimes made up exclusively of women, enrollment of men in specialized courses for the war effort, including a new Students Army Training Corps (SATC), was sufficient to cause a net increase in total enrollment. Oklahoma A. and M. College President James W. Cantwell affirmed that all men students, except those who were unfit for military service or who were below the draft age, had to enroll in the SATC. Through special programs, both on and off the campus, the college gave much to the war effort and took great pride in the victory.[24]

The recruitment value of bringing prospective students to the campus for a visit is well recognized. Interscholastic contests provided for many such visits in the early decades. In addition to track and field events, such meets included contests in debating, public speaking, instrumental music, vocal music, and sometimes proficiency in academic subjects. Medals and prizes were offered to the student winners. School systems were also recognized when their students excelled over other schools. This two-day program was held annually and attracted hundreds of high school students to the campus depending, of course, on the condition of the roads at the time and on the weather.[25]

Another way to extend Oklahoma A. and M. College's contacts and influence among people of the state was through tours of entertainment groups such as the glee club and band. Either group could attract a large audience in about any town or city regardless of the weather. The first such tour was scheduled by the glee club in April of 1915 and included concerts in Pawnee, Kaw City, Fairfax, and Ralston.[26] The band made its first tour in 1917, visiting such places as Geary, Clinton, Hobart, and Chickasha. One purpose of the tour was obvious from the following report: "A great many young fellows have signified their intention to come to A. and M. next fall—four from Hobart alone."[27]

When Oklahoma State University was founded as the Oklahoma Agricultural and Mechanical College, its mission was more simple but perhaps just as difficult to accomplish as it is now. Within a few years after the first classes were held, the college was engaged in extension activities, which helped to accelerate the dissemination of knowledge to improve the quality of life. As would be expected in this frontier land, agriculture was paramount among the occupations and commanded most of the early extension efforts. Short courses became a principal extension vehicle in which critical information was condensed and presented to those who would listen. Fairs served a good purpose, encouraging improvements in many facets of rural life.

The passage of the Smith-Lever Act by Congress in 1914 provided for the county agent system which became known as the Cooperative Extension Service. The trickle of extension activity outside the Smith-Lever domain began to increase after World War I. Many persons contributed to the great flow of educational services that would become known as University Extension. As extension reaches out to serve the larger community beyond the resident student population, it produces a symbiotic effect in which the general public profits and the institution gains support. The story that follows is the story of University Extension as it becomes a powerful and dynamic force in the operation of Oklahoma State University.

Endnotes

1. J. O. Grantham and Richard W. Poole, "New Technology for a Traditional Land Grant Mission," *Oklahoma State University Outreach*, vol. 56, no. 3 (Spring 1985), pp. 52-53; Author interview with J. O. Grantham, 22 July 1986, Stillwater, Oklahoma.

2. National Committee for World Food Day, *Report of World Food Day Conference* (Washington, DC: National Committee for World Food Day, 1986), pp. 1-2.

3. Oklahoma State University *Oklahoma Stater*, October 1985, p. 1.

4. *Oklahoma A. and M. College Mirror*, 16 September 1985, pp. 6-7.

5. *Oklahoma A. and M. College Mirror*, 5 May 1895, p. 10, 15 June 1895, p. 13, 16 September 1895, p. 12.

6. *Oklahoma A. and M. College Mirror*, 15 December 1895, p. 12.

7. Oklahoma A. and M. *College Paper*, March 1904, pp. 213-216.

8. Edd Roberts, editor, *History of Oklahoma State University Extension* (Stillwater: Oklahoma State University, Omicron Chapter, Epsilon Sigma Phi, [1971]), pp. 6-7.

9. Roberts, editor, p. 3.

10. Oklahoma A. and M. College *Orange and Black*, 3 April 1915.

11. *Orange and Black*, 15 January 1913, p. 4.

12. *Orange and Black*, 19 February 1913, p. 2.

13. *Orange and Black*, 7 January 1914, p. 4, 16 February 1922, p. 1.

14. *Orange and Black*, 10 July 1915, p. 1.

15. *College Paper*, 1 November 1899, p. 67, 1 October 1902, p. 72, 1 March 1903, p. 42; *Orange and Black*, November 1908, p. 33.

16. *College Paper*, November 1900, p. 84; *Orange and Black*, 13 May 1914, p. 2, 10 October 1914, p. 3, 16 January 1915, p. 1.

17. *Oklahoma A. and M. College Mirror*, 15 October 1897, p. 8.

18. *Oklahoma A. and M. College Mirror*, 15 October 1897, p. 8.

19. *Oklahoma A. and M. College Mirror*, 15 November 1897, p. 8.

20. *Orange and Black*, 19 September 1914, p. 3, 18 September 1912, p. 1, 1 October 1919, p. 1.

21. Roberts, editor, pp. 1-18.

22. *Orange and Black*, 30 October 1916, p. 1, 13 May 1916, p. 2. The accomplishments of the highly successful Cooperative Extension Service through the years are described in Donald E. Green's *A History of the Oklahoma State University College of Agriculture*, another volume in the Centennial Histories Series.

23. *Orange and Black*, 7 May 1917, p. 1, 16 March 1918, p. 4; Stillwater *Advance Democrat*, 22 November 1917, p. 1.

24. *Stillwater Gazette*, 16 September 1918, p. 1; *Orange and Black*, 16 November 1918, p. 1.

25. *Orange and Black*, 20 March 1913, pp. 1-4.

26. *Orange and Black*, 3 April 1915, p. 1.

27. *Orange and Black*, 17 February 1917, p. 4.

2 The Development of Correspondence Study 1920-1936

Extension and outreach activities of the Oklahoma Agricultural and Mechanical College during the Roaring Twenties and through the Depression and Dust Bowl years which followed helped to push the institutional horizons beyond the farm, thus allowing other problems and needs of society to be addressed. The Cooperative Extension Service with its network of agricultural and home demonstration agents located in every county of the state continued. The college remained involved with county and state fairs and still hosted interscholastic contests for high school students. Travel by organized groups of student entertainers such as the band and glee club was overshadowed by the interest and participation in radio broadcasts.

As a part of the post World War I thrust to take educational offerings away from the campus, James B. Eskridge, the president of Oklahoma A. and M. College, recommended in July 1921 that a correspondence school be established at the college. He saw education by mail as a viable program which could further the influence of the institution. The Oklahoma State Board of Agriculture, the governing board of the college at that time, approved the recommendation.[1]

The following month President Eskridge discussed the correspondence school objective with the board: "I recommend that correspondence courses, wherever practical in all the departments of the A. and M. College, be prepared by the person in charge of each department best qualified to outline such course or courses, subject to the approval of the president of the college, and that a fee of $10.00 be allowed for the preparation of each course, that a fee of $10.00 be charged the student for each course, that $5.00 be allowed the instructor or specialist who grades the papers, and that the remaining $5.00 be placed in the revolving fund to the credit of the correspondence school, if this can legally be done." After the board approved the recommendation, Eskridge continued: "I hereby recommend Professor J[ames] R. Campbell, Weatherford, Oklahoma, as Director of Correspondence and Associate in the School of Education of the A. and M. College for the scholastic year 1921-22, at a salary of $3000.00 a year, same to begin September 1st."[2]

In promoting the School of Correspondence Study the *Oklahoma A. and M. College General Catalog, 1921-22* noted that former U.S. President Theodore Roosevelt once remarked that he saw "instruction by mail as one of the most wonderful and phenomenal developments of the age."[3]

The stature of Professor Campbell gave credence to the newly formed correspondence school and facilitated the preparation of the courses to be offered by mail. Early in his career he had been superintendent of schools at Hutchinson and Newton, Kansas, and at Arapaho, Oklahoma. He had been the first president of Southwestern State Teachers College at Weatherford and had continued on the faculty there after retiring from the presidency. Although Campbell retired from the correspondence school assignment, he remained on the Oklahoma A. and M. College School of Education faculty until his death in 1929 at the age of eighty-one.[4]

The *Oklahoma A. and M. College Catalog, 1921-22* attested to Campbell's success in getting correspondence courses prepared by the several departments. The School of Agriculture offered thirty courses; the School of Engineering, sixteen courses; the School of Home Economics, two courses; the School of Science and Literature, fifty-four courses; the School of Education, thirteen courses; and the School of Commerce and Marketing, sixteen courses. In addition, courses had been prepared at the high school and elementary levels, bringing the total number of courses available the first year to more than 150.[5]

In 1923 George D. Moss followed Campbell as director of the School of Correspondence Study. He had been superintendent of schools at Hamblin, Cheyenne, and Sapulpa. Ruth Cox, who had been on the staff of Oklahoma A. and M. College since 1921, succeeded Moss in 1924. By this time the number of courses offered by correspondence had increased to more than 200. Within a year numbers of enrollments in correspondence study increased from 700 to 1000 students. It is not clear how many of these students were enrolled in the preparatory courses or in those given for college credit. In the fall of 1925, 15,000 copies of a correspondence school bulletin advertising over 300 courses were distributed by mail throughout the state.[6]

In July 1921, the Oklahoma State Board of Agriculture approved a motion establishing a correspondence school. James R. Campbell, former president of Southwestern State Teachers College (*left*), served as the school's first director. Ruth Cox (*center*) succeeded Campbell as director of correspondence study in 1924. A. Lawrence Crable (*right*) was named director of correspondence study in 1929. A longtime figure in the State Department of Public Instruction, Crable expanded a plan first formulated by Cox on the development of correspondence study centers.

Cox's professional career came to an early end soon after her marriage in 1925 to a young, successful Stillwater banker, Fred L. Jones. They were married September 18, 1925, and the society notes of the local newspaper showed that they left immediately by automobile for a week-long honeymoon in Oklahoma City. Cox returned to her correspondence study office and continued to promote the program and increase enrollments. Remaining as the director until 1927, she was replaced by Lucius W. Burton, Oklahoma A. and M. College registrar and secretary to the faculty. This appointment, no doubt, was intended to be a temporary one because Burton continued his duties as registrar.[7]

On August 1, 1929, A. Lawrence Crable, who had served in the State Department of Public Instruction as a school inspector for five years became the head of the correspondence school. Crable was both dynamic and personable. Perhaps no one in the correspondence school director's office since Campbell had been able to wield as much influence or command as much respect in the academic community as that enjoyed by Crable. He was in great demand as a speaker and fund raiser, and he was very active in the affairs of the Young Men's Christian Association and the Stillwater Baptist Church.[8]

Under Crable's leadership, enrollment in the correspondence school continued to grow, although the number of courses offered had been reduced and stabilized at approximately 150. Of these, 121 courses were at the college level, and the others provided an entire high school curriculum. Many college courses, particularly those requiring laboratory experience, were never offered by correspondence study. Rules were for mulated very early to limit the number of credit hours taken by correspondence to one-third or one-fourth of total baccalaureate degree requirements. Other rules prohibited simultaneous enrollments in residence and correspondence courses, enrollment in more than two courses at one time, or earning more than thirty semester hours by correspondence in any one year. Other quality controls included rules governing when lessons should be submitted and circumstances under which final examinations would be administered.[9]

Soon after joining the faculty, Crable revised and expanded a plan, initiated by Ruth Cox, to facilitate instruction by correspondence. It remained for him, however, to develop the idea into a practical, instructional methodology. The plan involved the establishment of study centers where six or more students would enroll simultaneously in the same correspondence course. An instructor or specialist would be identified and approved by the correspondence school to meet with the students, usually on a weekly basis, to assist them in their study. These instructors might be from the campus, if the study center was nearby, or be someone living in the immediate locale of the study center. In 1925, centers were functioning in Pawhuska, Chandler, and Shawnee.[10]

At this time, many public school teachers had earned only a few hours of college credit. To improve the quality of instruction in the schools, various incentives and requirements were devised to encourage teachers to seek more college education. Crable's previous experience as a school inspector and his position as director of the correspondence school placed him in a uniquely favorable position to administer to this need. He began to expand the study center plan and focused on the needs of teachers to update their credentials. Study centers were often organized and courses taught in remote locations without the aid of a correspondence study guide. These courses gave the teachers an opportunity to continue their studies and at the same time to work out the school problems which confronted them.

The classes were called "extension courses" as distinguished from correspondence courses. Prior to this time the word "extension" had seldom been used at Oklahoma A. and M. College except in the agricultural extension context. Ben C. Dyess, one of the early educational extension instructors, offered a 2-hour course in sociology for teachers of area schools. The teachers commuted to the campus; and the class met from ten to twelve o'clock on Saturday mornings. Instructors from the campus would also drive to nearby communities to conduct extension classes. Very soon, courses by extension could be taken for either undergraduate or graduate credit.[11]

When there was opportunity for a class beyond the commuting range

GRADED ROADS	4,161	MILES
GRAVELED ROADS	621	MILES
PAVED ROADS	374	MILES
TOTAL SYSTEM	5,156	MILES

Oklahoma published its first official highway map in 1925. It showed an embryonic highway network which included only 374 miles of hard surfaced roads.

of a resident faculty member, Crable would seek an adjunct instructor to do the teaching. Such a person had the qualifications required of the professor but was not on the regular teaching staff. One of the best sources for adjunct faculty members was from the faculties of the six teachers' colleges located in Edmond, Ada, Durant, Weatherford, Alva, and Tahlequah. By 1933, faculty members from each of these institutions were, or had been, employed to teach courses for Oklahoma A. and M. College. The geographical range for extension courses now included most of the state. In that same year, E. C. Baker and V. L. Maleev, both professors in the Department of Mechanical Engineering, teamed up to offer an extension class in diesel engine operation to industrial workers at Drumright.[12]

When President Eskridge had proposed the creation of a correspondence school at his board meeting in 1921, he had also recommended the employment of Charles Evans as a public relations person to provide specific liaison with the Oklahoma public schools. Evans was to work with the high schools of the state and give them information about all the departments and schools of the college. Approval of the Eskridge recommendation marked the early beginning of a high school and college relations program at Oklahoma A. and M. College. Evans was assigned the title of director of Educational Extension, but his assigned duties were more in the realm of public relations. Evans served in this capacity until 1925.[13]

By the time Bradford Knapp, the former director of short courses, assumed the presidency of Oklahoma A. and M. College, the importance of radio in communication had become well established. The technology of radio transmission and reception had been greatly enhanced during World War I. Oklahoma A. and M. College became involved in radio as a part of the war effort when the federal government asked that 15,000 radio operators be trained on an emergency basis for service in the Army Signal Corps. W. C. Lane, a civil engineering professor, organized a night course to help meet this need. It was 1922, however, before the first radio receiving station was installed on the campus. Funds to build the station were obtained by an admission charge to hear Hilton I. Jones lecture on "vibrations." Jones, the head of the chemistry department, was on leave as a lecturer with a Chautauqua company. Stillwater had no broadcasting facility, but news of the college was sometimes broadcast over a station at Yale.[14]

Whirr—Clatter, Clatter—Clang, Clang, Clang! Even though the radio audience could only hear the program, the sounds of making homemade ice cream made listeners' mouths water. By 1927, Oklahoma A. and M. College was broadcasting three radio programs a week. Comprised of short talks and musical numbers, the programs were quite popular among Oklahoma farm families.

A survey showed there were a thousand radio receiving sets in Muskogee County in 1924. From these figures, projections were made as to the effectiveness of radio communications. By 1925, Oklahoma A. and M. College had installed a remote radio control to broadcast through the station at Bristow. The first college program to be broadcast from the campus occurred during the noon hour on April 6, 1925. Telegrams of congratulations poured in and reported that no extraneous noises or undesirable sounds were observed.[15]

The potential of radio as a vehicle to reach the public caused President Knapp to name his top administrators to a committee to supervise and direct the radio operation. Serving on the committee were Knapp; C. T. Dowell, dean of agriculture; E. P. Boyd, dean of engineering; Nora Talbot, dean of home economics: C. H. McElroy, dean of science and literature; Herbert Patterson, dean of education; J. W. Scott, dean of commerce; W. H. Clendenin, commandant of military science; and Dover P. Trent, director of Cooperative Extension. Within a short time Oklahoma A. and M. College had its own 2½ hour weekly radio program. A survey in June 1925 showed that 6.5 percent of the farm families had radios, and J. T. Sanders, head of agricultural economics, predicted that three out of four farm families would have a radio by 1930.[16]

Oklahoma A. and M. College football games were first broadcast with a play-by-play description in 1926 over radio station KVOO in Bristow. By the time KVOO moved to Tulsa in 1927, Oklahoma A. and M. College was broadcasting three programs a week for 2½ hours each. A typical program was made up of short talks by various members of the faculty interspersed with both instrumental and vocal music. Radio became the dominant tool for mass communications during the 1930s. Even then there was talk that television was right around the corner. The basic technology for television had been known and demonstrated by the American Telephone and Telegraph Company as early as 1927, but like radio, television was destined to wait for a world war before it would reach fruition.[17]

When President Knapp submitted his resignation to become effective July 1, 1928, the Oklahoma State Board of Agriculture selected Henry G. Bennett as his successor. At the board of agriculture meeting on June 1-2, 1928, Knapp, Bennett, and McElroy conferred; Bennett then presented a list of the faculty he was recommending be retained for the coming year. It was moved, seconded, and approved by the board that "all members of the faculty be elected, except those to whom objections had been filed."[18] Thus, without calling any names for the record, several prominent faculty members had been fired simply by omitting their names from the approved list. Among those terminated was Henry Clay Potts, an alumnus and an agronomy staff member since 1922.[19] Had this firing been upheld, Oklahoma A. and M. College would have been

During the Depression years, short course programs boomed on the Oklahoma A. and M. College campus. Many of these courses were directed toward relieving the plight of the farm families caught up in the trials of the Dust Bowl. Both men and boys attended this terracing course.

deprived of the services of one of its most ardent ambassadors during the next third of a century.

Nine days after the firing, Bennett presented a letter to the board of agriculture from the head of the field crops and soils department praising Potts and asking for his reinstatement. Where Potts worked the following year was not clear, but President Bennett named him director of short courses in December 1929. Perhaps Bennett recognized a unique talent in Clay Potts and expanded the job description just for him. There had been other directors of short courses, but the focus had been on agriculture. Potts was to represent the whole campus. Within a few years, Potts had not only caused the short course activity to flourish as never before, but in his spare time he had developed a reputation as a fast-foods expert that would put Ronald McDonald to shame. He once claimed he got his start in the fast-foods hobby in 1928 when he helped Stillwater's Legionnaires serve a barbecue reception for the newly selected President Bennett.[20]

The smallest of details involving short courses became Potts' business. Publicity, transportation, housing, food, registration, meeting places, facilities, audio and visual equipment, communications—nothing was too small for his attention. He was wise enough to rely on the academic departments for the short course programs, but he was always there to make sure things ran smoothly. During 1930-31—his first full year as director of short courses—8,989 participants visited the campus. Despite the Depression and Dust Bowl years, the number of short course participants increased each year; 23,893 short course students registered in 1935-36.[21]

In 1930, John C. Muerman was employed as professor of rural and

John C. Muerman enjoyed immense popularity as a speaker. Not only did he call for the improvement of rural schools, Professor Muerman stressed the value of visual education when he spiced his lectures with numerous slide illustrations.

visual education. He was widely traveled and a great proponent of visual aids as a teaching device. Everyone soon learned that when Muerman was to speak, they would be treated to a slide presentation illustrating the lecture. From the beginning, he was in great demand as a speaker at school assemblies, teachers' meetings, and various professional and civic groups. He possessed about four thousand slides which he could rearrange in expert fashion to illustrate many facets of school activities and to depict landscapes at home and abroad. As his popularity as a speaker grew, so did his collection of slides. In 1934, he boasted of having six thousand slides in his personal collection. By 1936 it was not uncommon for Muerman to have out-of-town speaking engagements on four evenings in one week. The thrust of all his talks was the improvement of rural schools.[22]

The failing economy in Oklahoma in the late 1920s created a very real financial hardship for many young men and women who wanted to go to college. Jobs were scarce, and parents everywhere were having trouble making ends meet even without supporting children in college. Schiller C. Scroggs, director of administrative research, conceived the idea to maintain or even increase enrollments by establishing several industries on or near the campus to create part-time jobs for needy students. Among the enterprises tried were a broom factory, ceramics factory, hooked rugs enterprise, a cabinet shop, the college cafeteria, duplicating service, and a self-help farm. In addition to raising various crops on the farm, students were permitted to bring a producing milk cow from home. They would care for the cow, obtain her feed at cost, and sell the milk to the campus food services. These projects flourished with varying degrees of success, but were soon eclipsed by several

Because of the financial hardships faced by many young people seeking an education during the Depression, the Oklahoma A. and M. College created several self-help industries. While students could earn ten to fifteen cents an hour in the broom factory, others could show creative flair in the hooked rug enterprise.

government-subsidized programs under the New Deal.[23]

The entire program of student employment was placed under the direction of A. Frank Martin. With the impetus of the early student industries and the new federal dollars available for students through the Federal Emergency Relief Administration (FERA), many poor but academically capable students were able to work their way through college. This was especially true if the student possessed special talents in music or secretarial skills. In 1935 the National Youth Administration (NYA), another federal program, provided financial assistance. It persisted as a dominant source of funds for student aid through the rest of the 1930s.[24]

Even these noble efforts to help the nation's youth attend college during the Depression years left many unemployed and uneducated young men idle on the streets. To address this problem, still another federal program was created under the New Deal. In 1933, a group of approximately two hundred young men in the Civilian Conservation Corps (CCC) was assigned to a camp at Oklahoma A. and M. College, where they worked and studied during the height of the country's economic crisis.

Some of their accomplishments, such as the landscaping around Theta Pond on the main campus, are still in evidence.[25]

During the 1920s the farsightedness of administrators, faculty, and staff provided the basis for extension and outreach into areas that could not be addressed by Cooperative Extension. The establishment of a correspondence school and the beginnings of a high school and college relations program enjoyed immediate success. In addition, the college worked to improve the quality of instruction in the public schools.

With the development of radio into an important means of communication, the dissemination of information, culture, and entertainment from the campus community became a significant outreach function for the college. Oklahoma A. and M. College responded in a variety of ways to the problems and challenges of a changing socioeconomic climate.

Endnotes

1. Minutes, Oklahoma State Board of Agriculture, 1 July 1921, p. 2, Special Collections, Edmon Low Library, Oklahoma State University, Stillwater, Oklahoma.

2. Minutes, Oklahoma State Board of Agriculture, 1 August 1921, p. 24.

3. *Oklahoma A. and M. College General Catalog, 1921-22*, p. 289.

4. Oklahoma A. and M. College *Daily O'Collegian*, 3 December 1929, p. 1; *Stillwater Gazette*, 6 December 1929, p. 8.

5. *Oklahoma A. and M. College General Catalog, 1921-22*, pp. 289-290.

6. Stillwater *Advance Democrat*, 6 June 1923, p. 8; Oklahoma A. and M. College *O'Collegian*, 6 January 1925, p. 2, 20 September 1925, p. 1, 16 October 1925, p. 1; Oklahoma A. and M. College *Orange and Black*, 10 January 1924, p. 2.

7. *Stillwater Gazette*, 25 September 1925, p. 1; *Oklahoma A. and M. College General Catalog, 1926-27*, p. v; *Oklahoma A. and M. College General Catalog, 1927-28*, pp. v, xvi.

8. *Daily O'Collegian*, 7 November 1929, p. 1, 14 May 1933, p. 1.

9. *Oklahoma A. and M. College General Catalog, 1925-26*, pp. 291-296; *Daily O'Collegian*, 30 January 1930, pp. 1, 4.

10. *Oklahoma A. and M. College General Catalog, 1923-24*, p. 299; *O'Collegian*, 6 January 1925, p. 1.

11. *Daily O'Collegian*, 20 November 1929, pp. 1-2, 19 February 1930, p. 1, 24 January 1930, p. 1.

12. *Daily O'Collegian*, 23 September 1933, p. 1, 25 November 1933, p. 1.

13. Minutes, Oklahoma State Board of Agriculture, 1 July 1921, p. 1; *Oklahoma A. and M. College General Catalog, 1921-22*, p. 13.

14. *Orange and Black*, 10 November 1917, p. 1, 14 September 1922, p. 1.

15. *O'Collegian*, 3 April 1924, p. 4, 7 April 1925, p. 1.

16. *O'Collegian*, 16 April 1925, p. 1, 4 June 1925, p. 2.

17. *O'Collegian*, 22 September 1926, p. 4, 12 November 1930, p. 1, 4 December 1928, p. 1.

18. Minutes, Oklahoma State Board of Agriculture, 2 June 1928, pp. 52-59.

19. *Daily O'Collegian*, 5 June 1928, p. 1; *Orange and Black*, 21 September 1922, p. 4.

20. Minutes, Oklahoma State Board of Agriculture, 11 June 1928, p. 4, 3-4 December 1929, p. 30; *O'Collegian*, 19 June 1936, p. 1.

21. Phil Perdue, "Short Courses," *Oklahoma A. and M. College Magazine*, vol. 8, no. 3 (December 1936), p. 6.

22. *Daily O'Collegian*, 7 October 1930, p. 1, 6 March 1936, p. 1.

23. *O'Collegian*, 13 September 1929, p. 3, 15 February 1933, p. 1.

24. *Daily O'Collegian*, 31 October 1934, p. 1, 9 December 1936, p. 1.

25. *Daily O'Collegian*, 5 December 1933, p. 1, 27 January 1934, p. 1.

3 Impact of Depression And World War 1936-1945

As the decade of the 1940s drew near, Oklahoma A. and M. College was approaching its fiftieth birthday in a state that was younger still. Although much had been accomplished in the past, optimism abounded for the future. Oklahoma had survived crop failures yet maintained hope; it had endured the Dust Bowl yet kept its sanity; it had withstood economic crises without collapsing; and it had survived political turmoil and maintained its honor. In every case Oklahoma A. and M. College had made contributions to the solutions of these problems.

Extension and outreach at Oklahoma A. and M. College from 1936 through 1945 coincided with the first half of the tenure of Roy R. Tompkins as director of Educational Extension. "We were packed and ready to move to Tennessee. My father was going back to finish work on his Ph.D. degree at Peabody College. About three days before we were to leave for Nashville, Dr. [Henry G.] Bennett called my father and we moved to Stillwater instead," recalled Katherine Tompkins McCollom.[1] In August of 1936, Governor E. W. Marland had appointed A. Lawrence Crable to fill the unexpired term of John Vaughan as state superintendent of public instruction. Vaughan had been named president of Northeastern State Teachers College at Tahlequah. As a successor to Crable President Bennett named Tompkins, another old friend from Durant, as director of the correspondence school. The resignation of Crable and the appointment of Tompkins were made official by the Oklahoma State Board of Agriculture, August 15, 1936. Crable, nevertheless, continued to maintain a close relationship with Dr. Bennett and the college.[2]

Roy R. Tompkins (*left*) became director of correspondence study at Oklahoma A. and M. College in 1936. Soon afterwards, his title was changed to director of Educational Extension. As the tempo of World War II increased, Tompkins served as director of civil defense, armed services representative, and counselor for veterans. Henry Clay "Mr. Barbecue" Potts (*right*) continued to serve as director of short courses throughout the war years. In addition, he became director of the college food units.

A genial man of moderate stature, Tompkins was forceful and dynamic in his relations with others. He had been given his first teaching job by Dr. Bennett when Bennett was superintendent of schools at Hugo. He next moved to Boswell as superintendent of schools and then to Durant where he was school superintendent for eight years. Some time after Dr. Bennett was named president of Southeastern State Teachers College, Tompkins moved to the college as director of teacher training. Now these personal and professional good friends were together again, working on the same team at Oklahoma A. and M. College.[3] Tompkins became one of several people Dr. Bennett hired from his associates at Durant and Hugo and on whom he relied heavily for leadership and advice.

Very soon after arriving on the job in Stillwater, Tompkins was listed as director of Educational Extension, a designation not used since Charles Evans held the title in a public relations role. The new role reflected increasing use of extension teaching as a means of in-service training in Oklahoma, not only for public school teachers, but also for other professions and occupations. Extension classes for the spring semester of 1937 included courses from the Schools of Agriculture, Commerce, Engineering, Home Economics, and Science and Literature, in addition to those from the School of Education.[4]

Extension teaching followed certain guidelines which had evolved over a period of eighty years. Originating at the University of Berlin in 1856, the technique soon spread to the United States where the University of Chicago became the first major American institution to develop an educational extension program. Although some courses, especially those requiring a laboratory, were not adaptable to the extension model, others, such as school problem solving and geographical studies, were quite popular for the method. In the summer of 1937, R. W. Lynch, assistant professor of geography, recognized this advantage and organized a course for credit consisting of a Caribbean cruise with many ports of call. That same year George H. White, professor of English, conducted a historic tour of England, including attendance at Shakespearean plays and a study of the legendary lore of King Arthur.[5]

In April 1937, Tompkins announced the appointment of L. M. Hohstadt, former school superintendent at Terral, as an Educational Extension instructor at the college.[6] This appointment marked the first of several attempts in Educational Extension to employ subject-matter specialists for full-time off-campus teaching. Cooperative Extension had enjoyed this staffing arrangement in agriculture for two decades where subject-matter specialists spent most of their time in the field with county agents and in working directly with the farmers.

In the fall of 1941 Meredith W. Darlington joined Professor Hohstadt. Darlington's employment came as a result of a grant from the Farm Foundation to explore ways to upgrade the quality of rural education in America. Oklahoma A. and M. College was one of only two colleges in the country to be funded for this experiment. Okfuskee, Kay, and Delaware counties were selected to be the subjects of Darlington's efforts because they had wide cultural differences as well as significant rural school problems. If solutions were forthcoming in these counties, they could be applied in other counties in Oklahoma and throughout the United States.[7]

Clay Potts remained busily engaged in many extension activities, especially those relating to instruction through short courses. A short course seldom ended without another one or two ready to begin. Mr. Potts admonished Stillwater merchants always to display a "Welcome Visitors" sign because short course visitors were always in town. Short courses were especially prevalent in the spring and summer months. Topics ranged from band music to wildlife conservation, from cottonseed crushing to fire fighting techniques. Resident enrollment numbered less than 6,000 students. Enrollment in extension and correspondence courses totaled approximately 5,000 students. Non-credit short course enrollments numbered nearly 35,000. Even this number was dwarfed by Cooperative Extension's educational contacts where 100,000 farmers, 30,000 farm women, and 80,000 4-H Club members were enrolled in all kinds of educational programs.[8]

Soon after Dr. Bennett became president in 1928, he had announced his Twenty-Five Year Plan for expansion and development of the college. His faculty caught the vision, and almost everyone associated with the institution became goodwill ambassadors. Key faculty members developed reputations as good speakers and were in great demand throughout the state. Among these were J. C. Muerman, a professor of rural and visual education; T. H. Reynolds, a professor of history; and C. P. Thompson, a professor of animal husbandry. Students also were conscious of their image beyond the campus and were quick to reprimand any student group that tarnished it. Ten years after Dr. Bennett's plan was announced, many were surprised but greatly pleased to find construction and other improvements of the plan to be on schedule. World War II would halt building progress, but the Twenty-Five Year Plan would blossom in the late 1940s and early 1950s.[9]

By the late 1930s war clouds hung over Europe. Although a *Daily O'Collegian* survey in September 1939 found students solidly against

Al Guthrie (*standing, behind*) and Glenn L. Rucker (*standing, right*) confer with Army Air Corps personnel at Searcy Field. Manager of the airport and also a flight instructor, Guthrie organized a Civil Air Patrol as a part of civil defense. With the increased need for pilots, Guthrie's flight school soon became the largest operation of its kind in the Southwest. Rucker handled the Civil Aeronautics Administration flight training program during the war. Following the war, both men did much to expand campus extension programs through air transportation.

war, they had not objected, however, to a strong national defense—perhaps that would prevent war. Soon Oklahoma A. and M. College became immersed in the war effort. A civil aeronautics training program emerged in the interest of national defense. College and city officials were successful in obtaining federal help to enlarge and improve Searcy Airport. Al Guthrie, who was airport manager and also flight instructor, got the first flight training program underway on November 25, 1939. By June of 1940, some ten students were receiving flight certificates at the close of each ten-week session.[10]

The airport received a boost in March 1941 when Works Progress Administration (WPA) funds were provided to extend runways and to make other airport improvements. President Franklin D. Roosevelt approved the grant less than three weeks after it was proposed, suggesting there was urgency to get another aviation facility established in the country's midlands. The flying school flourished. In little more than one year 220 students had received primary flight instruction, 50 had taken secondary training, and 12 were enrolled in the advanced course. The school had 14 training planes. It had become the largest operation of its kind in the entire Southwest.[11]

National defense plans called for trained technicians in many fields. DeWitt Hunt, head of industrial arts education, geared up his department to meet these needs. Since regularly enrolled students used the facilities during the day, a schedule was devised to keep the shops open on a twenty-four hour basis. The first shift for national defense ran from 4 P.M. until midnight, and the second shift was completed before the regular classes began in the morning. Defense classes were offered in aircraft welding, combustion engine mechanics, machine shop, aircraft sheet metal work, and aircraft woodworking. About a hundred men ranging in age from twenty-two to forty-five were trained during an eight-week period at government expense. Most were recruited from WPA labor and after training were employed in industry at much higher wages.[12]

In spite of the increased tempo of activities on and around the campus, students still did not want war. When asked by an O'Collegian reporter in October 1941 if they favored going to war with Germany or Japan, twenty-eight of thirty men students answered "no." Forty percent were absolutely against sending troops overseas for any reason. Pearl Harbor changed that viewpoint. A follow-up survey on the afternoon of December 7, 1941, found no isolationists on campus.[13] In fact, on December 8, 1941, after conferring with the faculty and the board of agriculture, President Bennett sent a telegram to President Roosevelt which stated: "Oklahoma A. and M. is at your service . . . please use our college in any way which will further the American war cause."[14]

The campus was transformed almost overnight for an all-out war effort. Schiller Scroggs, dean of the School of Arts and Sciences, returned from a conference in Baltimore with plans on how to mobilize the college. Dr. Bennett named a war policy committee. Al Guthrie organized a Civil Air Patrol. Students formed an auxiliary branch of the American Red Cross.[15]

Administrators and faculty geared up for the mobilization effort as well. Dean Raymond Thomas and his faculty reorganized the business school and offered courses to meet wartime needs. The School of Home Economics designed special courses to fit the needs of women in wartime. Tompkins was given additional responsibilities as director of civilian defense. He hired John E. Arendell as a full-time Educational Extension specialist. Engineering set up an accelerated schedule to permit students to graduate in only three years. DeWitt Hunt headed a statewide program to build model airplanes. These included both U.S. and Axis planes and were used in instruction and in teaching aircraft recognition.[16]

The declaration of war on the Axis powers impacted the nature of short courses in significant ways. As soon as the emergency needs were recognized, a course was developed quickly. In February 1942, the college offered a short course for women firefighters. A new course in food preservation was begun. By April 1942, H. P. Adams, a professor in the industrial arts department, reported twenty-two national defense short courses in operation. Five more were planned to begin in June. The fed-

Oklahoma A. and M. College administrators showed solid support for the war effort by turning out to plant potatoes in a victory garden on one of the experimental plots near Stillwater Creek. From the left are Archie O. Martin, H. F. "Pat" Murphy, Roy R. Tompkins, Tom N. Harris, A. Frank Martin, and H. Clay Potts.

eral government established the Engineering, Science, and Management War Training (ESMWT) program to facilitate training for wartime occupations. ESMWT programs were administered through the School of Engineering. Dean Edward R. Stapley designated Professor Adams to head ESMWT. Under it, subsidized training was provided in such skills as aircraft inspection, engineering drawing, industrial drafting, cost accounting, production control, and industrial chemistry.[17]

Several regular short courses became temporary war casualties. Among them was the longstanding Farm and Home Week. Undoubtedly because of the gasoline and tire rationing, which had begun in 1942, President Bennett decided to take the program to the farmers by radio in the summer of 1943. Due to the temporary absence of Dr. Bennett, Tompkins, now designated as armed services representative, welcomed the farm and home people of Oklahoma to the "Farm and Home Week of the Air" over radio station KVOO of Tulsa. The format of other programs was changed or dropped for the duration, but one short course that did not fall victim to the war was Feeders Day, a one-day event held each April; throughout the war 1,200-1,300 people attended each year. The program concerned proper feeding of livestock. The noontime attraction was feeding the feeders with a Clay Potts' barbecue![18]

In February 1942, the U.S. Navy sent a contingent of 300 seamen to the campus for training in radio communication. In October of the same year, the first group of 600 Navy WAVES (Women Appointed for Voluntary Emergency Service) arrived on campus to be trained as yeomen for the homefront navy. Within a year Oklahoma A. and M. College might have been mistaken for a military school! On campus at that time were several units of the Reserve Officers Training Corps (ROTC), Army Air Corps, and the Army Specialized Training Program. The latter included a unit of the Specialized Training Acceptance and Reclassification School, basic and advanced engineering units of the Army

 *1943 REDSKIN*

During World War II, classes at the Oklahoma A. and M. College took on a decided "military" appearance as the campus made an all-out effort for victory. Engineering courses especially attracted the servicemen as they prepared for future combat duty.

Specialized Training Program, a group of A-12 students, and a group of former ROTC students under special instruction as Army Specialized Training Reserve Officers Training Corps. In addition there were Navy units studying electrical engineering. Before the war ended 7,500 WAVES, 3,500 sailors, and over 2,000 crewmen and officers for the Army Air Corps had trained on the Oklahoma A. and M. College campus.[19]

As the war in Europe approached an end, one training program after another was phased out. The last war training program assigned to Oklahoma A. and M. College was a Navy language school. The Navy sent 750 officers to the campus in 1945 to study Oriental languages.[20] Fortunately for all, the war was over before the course was finished.

Correspondence courses were more easily adapted to the regimen of war than were extension courses. Dislocation of student servicemen or civilians posed no insurmountable problems for correspondence study enrollees so long as there was a reliable forwarding address. Mail delays were common, but complete loss of contact was rare. Sometimes students could complete a course of study for credit by correspondence when war demands took them away from resident classes. Very soon, Tompkins was able to negotiate a contract with the United States Armed Forces Institute in which the federal government paid half of the costs for servicemen to enroll in the School of Correspondence Study courses. This earned Oklahoma A. and M. College the title, "foxhole university." The whole world became its campus. Soldiers, sailors, marines, and coast guardsmen on every part of the globe were able to enroll in courses, and many of them did. By 1945, 350 servicemen were studying by correspondence. In one instance a correspondence course was provided through the American Red Cross for Sergeant Russell J. Condry of Stroud while he was being held as a prisoner of war by the Germans.[21]

The war disrupted most, but not all, routine extension activities. During the 1930s, the Schools of Agriculture and Engineering, had developed an "open house" event which was held during the spring interscholastic contest and was very popular with visiting high school students. Various departments prepared exhibits and demonstrations to attract and entertain the visitors while subtly recruiting them as students for that school. Soon the Schools of Arts and Sciences, Commerce, Home Economics, and Education joined in these festivities until the whole campus became a showplace on interscholastic weekend. Open houses and, to a lesser degree, interscholastics contests and fairs became war casualties.[22]

The NYA (National Youth Administration), one of the last New Deal programs to leave the campus, was finally phased out in 1943. It might have ended sooner if not for its importance in providing student entertainers who were in demand and always ready to entertain the troops. As the war progressed, these entertainers, under the direction of A. Frank

As World War II progressed, more and more of the Student Entertainers were women. Whether offering a song, performing magic, dancing, playing a musical instrument, or even exhibiting ventriloquism, the entertainers were always in demand and were ready to entertain the troops. Getting ready to board the station wagon are (*standing, left to right*) Charles Wilbanks, Max Godfrey, Ellen Butler, A. Frank Martin (director), Don Martin, and Betty Wright. Those seated are (*left to right*) Rose Ann Smith, Doris Gregory, Ruth Helen Fischer, Elsie Mae Richter, Dorothy Daniels, and Milan Dunlap.

Martin and booking agent Tom N. Harris, became almost entirely female, and they performed almost exclusively before military personnel. Radio became more important in reaching audiences off-campus. The dissemination of farm information by radio and the frequent appearances of student entertainers on radio programs contributed significantly to the establishment of the radio services department in 1945.[23]

Dr. Bennett's educational leadership and phenomenal success as president were not to go unchallenged. On many occasions he found himself at political odds with Oklahoma's governor, Leon C. Phillips; thus, it was not unexpected that in the gubernatorial campaign of 1942, Dr. Bennett supported the candidacy of Robert S. Kerr. Just before Governor Phillips left office, he caused a suit to be brought against Dr. Bennett and several others, alleging unlawful manipulation of the textbook market in Oklahoma. Even though Mr. Kerr had been elected governor, the Oklahoma A. and M. College president fought a war of his own in the Oklahoma courts for the next three years until the last of the charges against him was finally dismissed by the Oklahoma Court of Criminal Appeals in October 1945.[24]

During this same period, Dr. Bennett fought and won another battle significant to the future of Oklahoma A. and M. College. He recognized a need to broaden the mission of the college to serve other interests, such as industry, with the same commitment as that given to agriculture. The president also wanted to reduce the political pressures coming from the Oklahoma State Board of Agriculture, the governing board of the college. Under the friendly administration of Governor Kerr, the state legislature submitted State Question 310 for a vote of the people providing a constitutional board of regents for the college. The question was approved by only the narrow margin of 9,147 votes on July 11, 1944, but it represented a major milestone in the development of the college.[25]

Even before the reverberations of World War II had subsided, Dr. Bennett named a steering committee, headed by Napoleon Conger, dean of the School of Education, to study postwar needs of Oklahoma and to plan Oklahoma A. and M. College's future in meeting these needs. Subcommittees were formed to study curriculum, educational extension, occupational training, and student housing. As early as February 1944, Tompkins, newly appointed counselor for veterans, had announced the arrival of eight disabled servicemen for rehabilitation under the federal government's G.I. Bill of Rights. Returning veterans were the primary

Even before World War II was over, the Oklahoma A. and M. College had formulated plans to help returning servicemen secure an education. Plywood hutments sprang up almost over night to provide homes for married student veterans. The creation of Veteran's Village had a positive effect on student enrollment for several years.

Centennial Histories Series

focus of these plans. Many of these men, who had been on campus during the war, now returned to complete their education under the federal government's programs. A bulletin, *What Oklahoma A. and M. College Offers the Veteran*, was widely distributed to separation centers and other places involved in the processing of returning veterans. By November 1945, Dr. Bennett announced that 282 housing units for married student veterans would be ready for occupancy the next semester, with more soon to be acquired.[26]

Events affecting Oklahoma A. and M. College just prior to and during World War II were among some of the most critical in all of the institution's history in determining what the college was to become. While certain extension activities were curtailed or even ceased forever, other programs began which strengthened the college's position in the state, nation, and world. The Oklahoma A. and M. College had strived to provide the necessary facilities and courses to aid the nation's war effort. In addition, it had worked to ease the problems of the civilian population through radio programs and special classes. Through the efforts of President Bennett and his able staff it seemed there was always a person or a program which could help ease the tensions of the national emergency. As Oklahoma A. and M. readied to take its place in the postwar era, the institution had proven it could meet pervasive challenges with intelligence, practicality, and innovation. Extension and outreach at Oklahoma A. and M. College could-- and would—only move forward.

Endnotes

1. Author interview with Katherine Tompkins McCollom, 24 January 1986, Stillwater, Oklahoma.

2. "Faculty Changes," *Oklahoma A. and M. College Magazine*, vol. 8, no. 1 (October 1936), p. 10; Minutes, Oklahoma State Board of Agriculture, 15 August 1936, p. 35, Special Collections, Edmon Low Library, Oklahoma State University, Stillwater, Oklahoma; Oklahoma A. and M. College *Daily O'Collegian*, 26 August 1943, p. 1.

3. McCollom interview; Minutes, Oklahoma State Board of Agriculture, 15 August 1936, p. 35.

4. *Oklahoma A. and M. College General Catalog, 1937-38*, p. ix; *Daily O'Collegian*, 8 January 1937, p. 1.

5. *Daily O'Collegian*, 10 January 1937, p. 3, 11 February 1937, p. 1, 16 February 1937, p. 1.

6. "Around the Campus," *Oklahoma A. and M. College Magazine*, vol. 8, no. 7 (April 1937), p. 10.

7. *Daily O'Collegian*, 3 October 1941, p. 1.

8. "Short Courses," *Oklahoma A. and M. College Magazine*, vol. 8, no. 3 (December 1936), p. 6; Stillwater *Payne County News*, 8 May 1936, p. 1; *Daily O'Collegian*, 11 August 1937, p. 6.

9. *Daily O'Collegian*, 4 November 1937, p. 1, 26 March 1938, p. 2, 5 May 1938, p. 2, 23 October 1938, p. 4.

10. *Daily O'Collegian*, 23 September 1939, p. 1, 5 January 1939, p. 2, 11 June 1940, p. 1; *Stillwater Daily News Press*, 11 September 1939, p. 1.

11. *Daily O'Collegian*, 18 March 1941, p. 1, 20 September 1941, p. 1.

12. *Daily O'Collegian*, 15 September 1940, p. 1, 12 October 1940, p. 1.

13. *Daily O'Collegian*, 28 October 1941, p. 1, 8 December 1941, p. 1.

14. *Daily O'Collegian*, 20 November 1942, p. 1.

15. *Daily O'Collegian*, 6 January 1942, p. 1, 7 January 1942, p. 1.

16. *Daily O'Collegian*, 11 January 1942, p. 1, 15 January 1942, p. 4, 12 February 1942, p. 1; Schiller Scroggs, "Cooperation for Defense," *Oklahoma A. and M. College Magazine*, vol. 13, no. 5 (February 1942), pp. 3, 4, 12-13.

17. *Daily O'Collegian*, 14 February 1942, p. 1, 10 March 1942, p. 1, 18 March 1942, p. 1, 29 April 1942, p. 1; "ESMWT Courses Offered," *Oklahoma A. and M. College Magazine*, vol. 14, no. 5 (February 1943), p. 6.

18. *Daily O'Collegian*, 31 July 1943, p. 1, 21 November 1942, p. 1, 3 August 1943, p. 1, 18 April 1942, p. 4, 20 April 1943, p. 1, 26 April 1944, p. 1.

19. *Daily O'Collegian*, 20 February 1942, p. 1, 10 October 1942, p. 1, Colonel Howard M. Yost, "Military Training Expands at Oklahoma A. and M.," *Oklahoma A. and M. College Magazine*, vol. 15, no. 3 (October 1943), pp. 8-11.

20. *Daily O'Collegian*, 18 May 1945, p. 1, 15 September 1944, p. 4.

21. *Daily O'Collegian*, 13 September 1944, p. 3, 25 July 1945, p. 4, 14 July 1944, p. 4.

22. *Daily O'Collegian*, 29 April 1938, p. 1, 28 April 1939, p. 1, 2 May 1941, p. 1, 16 October 1942, p. 1.

23. *Daily O'Collegian*, 9 July 1943, p. 1, 3 August 1945, p. 5.

24. Philip Reed Rulon, *Oklahoma State University—Since 1890* (Stillwater: Oklahoma State University Press, 1975), pp. 256-257; *Tulsa Tribune*, 1 January 1943, pp. 1, 3; *Daily O'Collegian*, 19 October 1945, p. 1.

25. Rulon, pp. 265-266.

26. *Daily O'Collegian*, 4 February 1944, p. 1, 15 February 1944, p. 1, 20 December 1944, p. 1, 10 January 1945, p. 1, 28 November 1945, p. 1.

4 New Avenues for Extension And Outreach 1945-1956

During the post World War II era, there was an increasing emphasis on technology. Because of the vast socioeconomic changes of the previous two decades, it was becoming more and more evident education could not and should not stop with the end of formal schooling. Indeed education should be a lifelong process. Colleges and universities became the focal points of new technologies. It was not uncommon for a business or industry to ask the Oklahoma A. and M. College for help to adapt a new technology to its specific needs. More common, however, the college conducted extension courses on a regular basis to update these professionals and technicians. Because institutions of higher education were now "center stage," the matter of outreach—in modern athletic parlance, recruitment—became all the more crucial. The institution needed students, especially good students, to accomplish its goals. Public image of the college was important, and favorable publicity was always welcome.

In the spring of 1945, Roy Tompkins met with J. Conner Fitzgerald and told him President Henry G. Bennett would like to see him. A meeting was arranged, and Dr. Bennett asked him to come to Oklahoma A. and M. College as an audio-visual specialist. Fitzgerald was the epitome of a home town boy who made good. The son of a Ripley druggist, Fitzgerald's reputation as a photographer and disciple of audio-visual teaching aids was first gained while he served as principal of Hillside Elementary School near Cushing and later as Payne County superintendent of schools.[1]

Although Fitzgerald would have "given his right arm" to accept Dr. Bennett's offer, he did not. Only a few days before, he had been rehired as superintendent of the Yale Public Schools and had promised that he would remain at Yale during the ensuing year. Dr. Bennett waited, and one year later made the offer again. This time Fitzgerald accepted with a clear conscience. He was given a desk in Tompkins' office and became his understudy for nine years.

Fitzgerald was civic-minded and willing to assume responsible roles. He served as president of the Stillwater Rotary Club, campus chairman of the United Way fund drive, president of the Will Rogers Council of Boy Scouts of America, and president of the Rural Education section of the National University Extension Association. In addition he often served on local, state, and national committees of professional organizations, sometimes attending two or more out-of-state committee meetings of different organizations in a single trip. Yet, he found time to conduct an occasional study tour abroad. In 1956, Fitzgerald completed his Ed.D. degree at Oklahoma A. and M. College.[2]

At first, Fitzgerald's duties involved making movies of athletic events and taking pictures for Dr. Bennett when he went on numerous business trips. It was not uncommon for the two of them to be flown by Al Guthrie to remote Oklahoma towns, where they often landed and took off as necessary from farmers' pastures.[3]

Within five years, Fitzgerald was in charge of all audio-visual materials then in use at Oklahoma A. and M. College. He had succeeded in building a sizeable film collection plus movie projectors and other photographic equipment which could be rented for a nominal fee by the various academic departments on campus and also by the public schools. The audio-visual department was housed upstairs over Swim's Campus Shop at the corner of Elm and Knoblock streets. Assisting with the audio-visual materials were J. E. Arendel and L. M. Hohstadt, both of whom were full-time Educational Extension professors.[4] A. D. Hanry also worked in the audio-visual area as a technician.

When most colleges and universities across the country were filled to capacity with returning veterans, Oklahoma A. and M. College announced room for two thousand returning World War II veterans at the new School of Technical Training at Okmulgee. Oklahoma A. and M. had received title to the 164-acre site of the former Glennan Hospital, including ninety buildings. This World War II facility was quickly converted to serve as a college campus. L. K. Covelle, an employee of Oklahoma A. and M. College, was named director of the Okmulgee school which began its first semester in September 1946. Five hundred students, only two of whom were women, enrolled for the first semester and chose from courses in agriculture, construction, commerce, dry cleaning, laundry, printing, auto mechanics, and diesel engines. The new facility would soon be filled to capacity with returning war veterans.[5]

Dr. Bennett was a tireless developer and promoter. In 1947, he found time to spend fifteen days on a booster train visiting major cities throughout the Midwest and eastern seaboard. The purpose was to extol industrial possibilities in Oklahoma. In 1949, Secretary of Agriculture Charles F. Brennan suggested that Dr. Bennett might someday become President of the United States. Later that year Dr. Bennett spent eight weeks in Europe at the request of the U.S. Occupation Forces.[6]

The decade following World War II witnessed many developments. One legacy of the war was the airport facility and widespread interest in aviation. Some thought airplanes might replace automobiles as the principal means of transportation. Tompkins promoted extension classes in "air age education." Glenn Rucker was the coordinator for civilian pilot training and was ground school instructor in the School of Engineering. The flying school was owned and operated privately by

SPECIAL COLLECTIONS, OSU LIBRARY

Following World War II, there was increased interest in aviation. Farmers especially liked the advantages of air travel for checking fences, providing emergency food to livestock, hunting coyotes, and getting from farm to market. Under the sponsorship of the Oklahoma A. and M. College, the Flying Farmers was organized in the mid-1940s. This particular group of Flying Farmers participated in a tour of southeastern Oklahoma in 1949.

Al Guthrie, who trained individuals to secure a commercial pilot's license and who contracted flight services to the college.[7]

Ferdie Deering, editor of the *Oklahoma Farmer-Stockman*, and Herb Graham, OSU agricultural extension editor, organized the Flying Farmers in 1946 under the sponsorship of Oklahoma A. and M. College. Dr. Bennett was proud of the organization and attended its annual meetings. Each year he would personally present a plaque to the oldest Flying Farmer present. In 1948 a student group called the Flying Aggies was organized. Membership was limited to students holding a pilot's license. Members could rent planes from the flight school at $3 per hour plus gas. This organization thrived and brought national recognition to the college by demonstrating superior flying skills in air shows and in winning flying competitions.[8]

In keeping with outreach programs, an A. and M. Rodeo Club was organized in 1949. It did not receive financial support from the college; but, even so, its teams ranked high in national competitions against institutionally-backed rodeo teams from other colleges. Student cowboys who earned much recognition and praise for Oklahoma A. and M. College included Buddy Reger from Woodward; Eldon Dudley from Apache; Dick Barrett from Ryan; Roy Russell from Enid; Don Fedderson from El Reno; Benny Combs from Checotah; Herbert Savage from Fairfax; Bob Walters from Claremore; Dave Miller from Okmulgee; Quintin Martin from Chattanooga; Wayne Cox from Stroud; Garland Kelley from Roswell, New Mexico; Dave McNamara from Vernon, Texas; and Bill Walker from Springdale, Arkansas.[9]

The role students played in the outreach function should not be undervalued. It was a general belief that if a high school student visited on campus two or three times before graduation, the student would likely choose that school for college. Interscholastic contests were resumed after the war with accompanying career days, engineering and science expositions, and open houses. Nonathletic events gained increasing attention, especially from the music department. Individual and group contests in voice and instrumental music brought thousands of students from hundreds of high schools to the campus each year.[10]

Another music program was the Thanksgiving Choral Festival under the direction of J. K. Long. An advisory group of music teachers would choose numbers to be sung at the festival near the end of November. Schools planning to participate would order the music and teach it to their choirs and choruses prior to the event. Early on the day of the festival, buses would roll into Stillwater from schools all over the state, and about eight thousand high schoolers would disembark for a day of vocal music under the direction of guest conductors chosen from across the nation. The climax came in the evening when all students would assemble in the fieldhouse for a rousing mass performance accompa-

Each year, high school choirs flocked to campus for the Thanksgiving Choral Festival. After daylong participation in vocal music workshops, the students gathered for a rousing mass performance in Gallagher Hall.

nied by the college symphonic orchestra.[11]

The college bands and choirs resumed touring the state on an annual basis as wartime travel restrictions were lifted. The bands were under the direction of Max Mitchell and assisted by Hiram Henry. The Men's Glee Club, under the direction of L. N. "Cy" Perkins, sometimes went out-of-state to perform for such groups as the Southwestern Music Educators Conference in Colorado Springs, Colorado.[12]

Student Entertainers under the direction of A. Frank Martin gained new life after the war and provided opportunity for hundreds of students to earn part of their college expenses by performing for various groups. In addition to the Student Entertainers, the college provided an employment service for students who needed to work. Tom N. Harris, director of student employment, estimated in 1950 that 6,000 students had found work through his office during the previous school year.[13] This amounted to almost half of the student body and reflected the financial status of the average student.

The Carnegie Foundation had presented the Carnegie Music Library to the Oklahoma A. and M. College library in 1936. Although Schiller Scroggs, dean of arts and sciences, was credited with obtaining this valuable collection, Edmon Low, who became head librarian in 1940, helped make the Carnegie collection popular among library patrons, both on and off the campus. By the end of the 1940s, H. G. Faust supervised another service feature called the package library. Any organization or group in the state could obtain the loan of a package of library materials on specified subjects and, within a reasonable time, could exchange these for additional materials.[14]

The concept of continuing education suggests that people have a need to continue to learn throughout their lives to avoid occupational obsolescence. In keeping with this philosophy the various schools of the college began taking action. The School of Education continued to rely on Tompkins. The Division of Engineering named M. L. Powers, a practicing industrial engineer, as director of Engineering and Industrial Extension in 1947. The Division of Commerce began extension services to state businesses and industries in 1953 and employed Harry Canup, a businessman with thirty-five years of merchandising experience, as the director. The School of Arts and Sciences would take similar action in 1956 when it appointed Robert Fite as the first director of Arts and Sciences Extension.[15] Fite also was given the rank of professor at the time of his appointment, having held the ranks of instructor, assistant professor, and associate professor in geography since 1947.

Under Powers' leadership, Engineering Extension provided conferences and short courses throughout the state, but especially in industrial towns like Ponca City, Bartlesville, Tulsa, and Oklahoma City. Technologies that tended to be updated annually included safety, highway maintenance, electromagnetic relays, paving techniques, fire fighting, aircraft mechanics, management of water supply and sewage disposal, industrial management, personnel analysis, and job evaluation. Powers was succeeded in this position by L. F. "Mike" Sheerar in 1953. Sheerar had been a member of the engineering faculty since 1927, except for a leave to work for the Oklahoma Planning and Resources Board.[16]

The High School Institute was one of Sheerar's innovative programs.

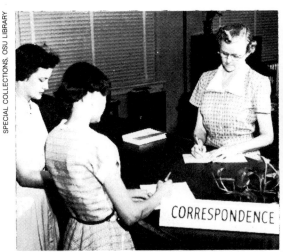

Gladys McGaugh (*left photo*), the assistant director of correspondence study, confers with Nina Coleman and Jean Raper regarding the availability of correspondence courses. The popularity of audio-visual teaching devices led to the establishment of a photographic service in 1947. Paul E. McCrary (*upper left*) headed this new facility.

It was a summer program, first offered in 1955, where advanced high school juniors were given a glimpse of professional engineering. Selected participants paid their own expenses or, in many cases, were sponsored by civic groups in their home town.[17]

The Division of Commerce for many years had offered night classes in business subjects such as typing, shorthand, and accounting for those who could come to the campus. The horizons of Business Extension were broadened to provide off-campus business courses in other towns. Mr. Canup's greatest contribution seemed, however, to be his promoting the Division of Commerce to business and industry.[18]

In the meantime, under the leadership of Tompkins, the concept of educational extension and the services provided through his office expanded. Enrollments in correspondence study courses remained strong after World War II. More than 500 students were enrolled by mail in 1947. General Byron E. Gates, commanding officer of Chanute Air Force Base, was one of the prized students. Gladys McGaugh was employed to take charge of correspondence study in 1952. When Fitzgerald was named assistant director of Educational Extension, he then employed Guy M. Pritchard to assist him in the audio-visual department. Pritchard had succeeded Fitzgerald at Hillside Elementary School and had a mutual interest in audio-visual teaching devices. Still another new member of Educational Extension's staff was Paul E. McCrary, who was hired in 1947 to head a photographic service.[19]

In response to a request from the Vance Air Force Base commander, Tompkins developed an extension program at the Enid air base known as Operation Bootstrap. This program, begun in 1951, allowed servicemen and women to complete all but one semester of work toward a bachelor's degree via extension courses at the air base. Military persons were then granted six months leave to come to the Stillwater campus to complete requirements for graduation. Raymond Caskey, a professor of mathematics, supervised the operation. The early faculty for Operation Bootstrap included Caskey and Milton Berg of mathematics, George White of humanities, Ralph Birchard of geography, Glenn Laughlin of business law, and Alfred Levin of history.[20] They would travel to the base—sometimes by airplane and sometimes by car—to teach a 3-hour class each Tuesday and Thursday night for nine weeks. They returned to Stillwater the same evening in preparation for the next day's on-campus schedule. This off-campus teaching assignment was accepted as a voluntary overload for which the instructors were paid a stipend above their regular salaries, ranging from $250 to $500 per course.

Tompkins promoted the concept that Oklahoma A. and M. College had a statewide campus. He believed services should be provided within reason regardless of location of the community. This concept led to the employment of Gerald T. Stubbs as director of public school services

Director of Public School Services Gerald T. Stubbs (*left*) responds to calls for help from public school administrators and teachers. On-site visits were often necessary to analyze the problem and arrive at a solution. Stubbs developed a plan to identify aptitudes and interests of prospective students which was implemented through the Bureau of Tests and Measurements. Harry K. Brobst (*right*), the head of the bureau, confers with students concerning test results.

in 1945. A former school superintendent in Durant for sixteen years, Mr. Stubbs served as a trouble-shooter and problem solver in the realm of high school and college relations. Upon recognizing a problem, Stubbs would initiate corrective action as the situation dictated. One problem was the lack of adequate guidance in high school for college-bound graduates. Stubbs' remedy was to establish a Bureau of Tests and Measurements which could provide the tests and evaluations necessary to identify aptitudes and interests of the students. Harry K. Brobst headed the bureau. Stubbs would counsel school officials, and, if they were willing, he and Brobst would administer standardized tests to the student body. Brobst's bureau graded the tests, interpreted the results, and assisted Stubbs in reporting back to the school.[21]

In 1950 Dr. Bennett chose Randall T. Klemme to be vice president of the college and director of an Agricultural-Industrial Development Service (A.I.D.S.). This program provided a comprehensive survey of resources of a community and projected possibilities for its development based on its agricultural and industrial attributes. First a community would request the service, then a contract would be negotiated to establish the levels of participation and cooperation between the community and the college. William Abbott was named assistant director. Other staff members included Ancil D. Simpson, E. F. Dowell, J B LeMaster, Bob Spears, and Joe Parris.[22]

The early success of A.I.D.S. drew national attention to Oklahoma A. and M. College and to Dr. Bennett. Invited to an international conference on food problems in 1945, he served as an agricultural consultant in Occupied Germany in 1949. In April 1950, he counseled with Ethiopian agricultural leaders in Abyssinia. It therefore came as no great surprise when President Harry Truman asked Dr. Bennett in November 1950 to direct the recently enacted Point Four economic program of aid to underdeveloped countries. The last speech President Bennett made on-campus was to the Southwest Regional Adult Education Association general session. He talked about the Point Four program and made a plea for continuing education.[23]

In December 1951 while on a mission for Point Four, President Bennett was killed when his plane crashed into the Elburz Mountains of Iran. Tompkins eulogized his old friend: "To those of us who knew him and loved him he was a great teacher, a prophet, a statesman, a philosopher, a Christian gentleman, and a man of stupendous courage and energy. He dreamed dreams and saw visions, and he had the capacity to make them come true."[24] President Truman paid tribute: "In the death of Henry Garland Bennett . . . I have lost a friend and the American people have lost a great teacher . . . he understood how people can work miracles in sharing knowledge to help themselves and each other."[25]

The first great experiment under the Point Four program got underway in 1952 with the development and staffing of an Ethiopian college of agriculture and mechanical arts. At about the same time Randall T. Klemme resigned to accept a position as economic advisor to Pakistan for the Ford Foundation.[26]

As the reputation of Oklahoma A. and M. College reached the Third World countries through the Point Four program and the Ford Foundation project in Pakistan, there was first a trickle and then a stream of international students seeking a college education at the Stillwater campus. The Newman Club established a scholarship program for foreign students in 1949. Glenn B. Hawkins, head of the Department of Political Science, was named foreign student advisor. Through an arrangement with the United States Lines, Dr. Hawkins became the agent for international students as they traveled to and from their homelands. The more Oklahoma A. and M. College exported its expertise to Third World countries by sending members of its faculty abroad, the more international students came to the Stillwater campus for a college education.[27]

While Dr. Bennett had worked on the international scene, others at Oklahoma A. and M. College were busy applying his philosophy at home. C. B. Loomis had been employed as director of a community development program. Even broader in scope than the Agricultural-Industrial Development Service, the community development concept included using any facet of academic expertise that might be found on the campus to treat any aspect of community life that might be experiencing problems. In all cases the object was to make the community a better place in which to live.[28]

Vice President Philip S. Donnell was the principal proponent in the establishment of the I-O-A (Individual-Opportunity-Achievement) Ranch near Perkins in 1949. The state's juvenile court system referred boys and girls to the ranch as an alternative to incarceration. The first ranch parents, Mr. and Mrs. Floyd Fry, received the first child at the ranch in March 1952.[29]

The Former Students Association began a systematic touring of the state's high schools "to encourage attendance at A. and M." DeWitt Hunt had accepted the role of safety expert on campus and, through publication of his gleanings from the media, had gained recognition as a safety specialist. Vocational counseling was provided state high schools upon request. The Reserve Officer Training Corps Rifle Team was gaining recognition for its marksmanship.[30]

Oklahoma A. and M. College was chosen by the National Science Foundation in 1956 to receive one of only two grants for an Academic Year Institute for high school mathematics and science teachers.[31] The institution had already been a pioneer for three years in summer institutes specially designed for the same target group. James H. Zant, a professor of mathematics, became the director of the program.

Highways into Stillwater were still far below average in the 1950s even though Oklahoma A. and M. was receiving credit for much improvement in the science of road building. Central Airlines came to Stillwater with the first commercial air service to Oklahoma City and Tulsa in April 1953.[32] In spite of its isolation, Oklahoma A. and M. College had become nationally and internationally known for its excellence in many academic fields.

In the early 1950s the prospect of war again loomed on the horizon. Except for the news from Korea and a few military groups being trained on campus, however, Stillwater seemed far removed from this struggle. While the administration again offered facilities for the war emergency, there was no widespread military training program as had occurred in World War II. Draft deferments were common for students, which may have had a positive effect on enrollments. Some faculty reservists were called up, including Lieutenant Elmo G. Peterson, assistant civil engineering professor, who was wounded in action by shrapnel. Major J. N. Baker was luckier. He returned to the campus from his second war in six years to resume duties as Clay Potts' assistant at barbecues and to pursue a doctoral degree in education.[33]

Potts' fame as a food wizard continued to grow. He was named director of the campus foods units in 1942, and as late as 1947 a student's

Henry Clay Potts, one of the college's best known ambassadors, caters one of his famous bar-becues to a campus crowd which includes President Henry G. Bennett. Potts served his alma mater for nearly forty years.

meal ticket was priced at only $1.07 per day. During Robert S. Kerr's gubernatorial term, Potts was honored with the title of honorary colonel. Later, in 1950, when Kerr was a United States senator, he had Potts and his crew flown to Washington to prepare a barbecue for senators and their spouses. Potts remained director of short courses and personally prepared and served the food to many of the participants. During the 1951-52 academic year, Potts counted 49,723 people through his special food lines on 138 different occasions.[34]

During the course of a year nearly a hundred short courses would routinely be scheduled and conducted for special target audiences. These originated from the various schools within the college. A sample of the titles included water and sewage management, band directing, custodial services, fire fighting, teaching music, rural electricity, safety, dairy, horticulture, first aid, newspaper editing, soil conservation, wildlife management, driver education, business course for ministers, civil defense, tax assessors, writing for publication, gardening, hotel management, community development, speed reading, school lunch program, job evaluation, audio-visual, pest control, poultry, adult educators, traffic control, rural mail carriers, insurance, aviation education, and farm and ranch buildings.[35]

Tompkins' stature loomed large in adult continuing education. He was elected a member of the executive committee of the National University Extension Association in 1952. After serving two years in this capacity, he was elected vice president in 1954 and then president for 1955-56. He also served as president of the Oklahoma Adult Education Association and hosted the Southwest Regional Adult Education Association convention on campus in 1950.[36]

All the while Tompkins was going about his job quietly, whether it was handling racial integration, establishing a graduate center, or developing Operation Bootstrap, his administrative genius was always at work.[37] Tompkins retired in the fall of 1956 after twenty years of service. A bound volume of letters from well-wishers was presented to him at that time:

"You always worked for the betterment of people." Vance Posey.

"I can still hear Dr. Bennett saying—'I will check this with Roy'." Raymond Girod.

"It was not difficult for me to know that the invitation to come to A. and M. was inspired by Roy." Jerry Stubbs.

"You belong to that very rare group of people who make life seem better than it is." John Monk.

"You have helped me with many difficult problems, and above all you have been loyal." Oliver Willham.[38]

The Tompkins' era came to a close on September 1, 1956. Fitzgerald, assistant director of Educational Extension, was named as his replacement but with a new title—director of continuing education. The title change reflected the emerging concept that learning is a lifelong process, that no one ever knows enough to satisfy his or her every need. It also reflected the need for coordination of the extension activities of the Schools of Education, Engineering, Commerce, and Arts and Sciences. Schools of the college without an extension director were considering such appointments. Although Oklahoma A. and M. College had lost some stalwarts, notably Dr. Bennett and Mr. Tompkins, from the ranks of extension and outreach, the course they had charted was clear, and their torches were caught by individuals who held them high so that the momentum of progress was not halted.

Endnotes

1. Author interview with J. Conner Fitzgerald, 28 January 1986, Stillwater, Oklahoma.

2. Fitzgerald interview; Oklahoma State University *Daily O'Collegian*, 1 October 1960, p. 8, 27 February 1964, p. 3.

3. Fitzgerald interview.

4. Fitzgerald interview.

5. *Daily O'Collegian*, 19 September 1946, p. 2; "The Okmulgee Branch College," *Oklahoma A. and M. College Magazine*, vol. 18, no. 3 (December 1946), pp. 8-9.

6. *Daily O'Collegian*, 28 June 1947, p. 1, 10 May 1949, p. 1, 10 July 1949, p. 1.

7. *Daily O'Collegian*, 17 October 1946, p. 1, 3 October 1946, p. 4, 15 February 1947, p. 1.

8. Phil Stout, "The Story of the Flying Farmers," *Oklahoma State Alumnus Magazine*, vol. 4, no. 6 (June 1963), pp. 8-10; *Daily O'Collegian*, 22 July 1947, p. 1, 16 November 1948, p. 1, 11 April 1951, p. 3.

9. *Daily O'Collegian*, 8 March 1951, p. 2, 23 February 1950, p. 1, 29 April 1954, p. 8, 28 February 1951, p. 1, 18 March 1950, p. 8.

10. *Daily O'Collegian*, 29 April 1948, p. 1, 5 May 1949, p. 1, 27 April 1950, p. 1.

11. *Daily O'Collegian*, 16 November 1950, p. 1, 21 November 1950, p. 1.

12. *Daily O'Collegian*, 30 March 1949, p. 1, 28 April 1949, p. 2.

13. *Daily O'Collegian*, 21 September 1949, p. 1, 22 September 1950, p. 8.

14. *Daily O'Collegian*, 23 February 1949, p. 8, 16 October 1948, p. 2.

15. *Daily O'Collegian*, 25 October 1947, p. 2, 10 October 1953, p. 1; Raymond D. Thomas, "The Trend of Our Times," *Oklahoma A. and M. College Magazine*, vol. 25, no. 4 (December 1953), pp. 20-22; Minutes, Board of Regents for the Oklahoma Agricultural and Mechanical Colleges, 19 October 1956, p. 1, and attachment, President Oliver S. Willham to the A. and M. Board of Regents, 19 October 1956, Special Collections, Edmon Low Library, Oklahoma State University, Stillwater, Oklahoma.

16. *Daily O'Collegian*, 13 April 1949, p. 8, 14 March 1953, p. 3; Author interview with Leonard F. "Mike" Sheerar, 27 February 1986, Stillwater, Oklahoma.

17. *Daily O'Collegian*, 21 June 1955, p. 3.

18. *Daily O'Collegian*, 13 July 1951, p. 5.

19. *Daily O'Collegian*, 27 March 1947, p. 1, 19 February 1952, p. 8; "Campus and Faculty News," *Oklahoma A. and M. College Magazine*, vol. 26, no. 8 (April 1955), p. 22; Author interview with Gladys McGaugh, 24 January 1986, Stillwater, Oklahoma; Author interview with Guy Pritchard, 27 January 1986, Stillwater, Oklahoma.

20. *Daily O'Collegian*, 3 February 1951, p. 8; "Campus and Faculty News," p. 20.

21. "Eyes, Ears, Wheels and Wings," *Oklahoma A. and M. College Magazine*, vol. 26, no. 1 (September 1954), pp. 10-13; *Daily O'Collegian*, 2 July 1948, p. 1, 15 June 1951, p. 1.

22. Minutes, Board of Regents for the Oklahoma Agricultural and Mechanical Colleges, 17 November 1950, p. 4; *Daily O'Collegian*, 25 November 1952, p. 8, 26 October 1956, p. 10.

23. *Daily O'Collegian*, 15 November 1950, p. 1, 1 March 1952, p. 8. The speech was taped and is a part of the audio-visual archives of Oklahoma State University.

24. *Daily O'Collegian*, 16 January 1952, p. 2.

25. Jerry Leon Gill, *The Great Adventure: Oklahoma State University and International Education* (Stillwater: Oklahoma State University Press, 1978), p. 8.

26. *Daily O'Collegian*, 11 July 1952, p. 1, 7 November 1952, p. 1.

27. *Daily O'Collegian*, 17 May 1949, p. 1, 30 May 1949, p. 1, 8 April 1954, p. 8.

28. *Daily O'Collegian*, 11 June 1948, p. 1.

29. *Daily O'Collegian*, 30 May 1949, p. 3, 29 March 1952, p. 8.

30. *Daily O'Collegian*, 22 February 1950, p. 6, 6 June 1950, p. 1, 21 July 1950, p. 6, 15 May 1953, p. 11.

31. *Daily O'Collegian*, 5 January 1956, p. 1.

32. *Daily O'Collegian*, 14 December 1949, p. 3, 22 April 1953, p. 1.

33. *Daily O'Collegian*, 25 July 1950, p. 1, 15 December 1950, p. 1, 10 September 1952, p. 4.

34. "Potts Sets a Good Table," *Oklahoma A. and M. College Magazine*, vol. 19, no. 2 (November 1947), p. 7; *Daily O'Collegian*, 22 March 1951, p. 3, 18 July 1952, p. 8; "Clay Potts Serves in Nation's Capitol," *Oklahoma A. and M. College Magazine*, vol. 22, no. 1 (September 1950), p. 13.

35. *Daily O'Collegian*, 17 July 1956, p. 1.

36. *Daily O'Collegian*, 10 May 1955, p. 1.

37. "Your College Extension Program," *Oklahoma A. and M. College Magazine*, vol. 18, no. 5 (February 1947), pp. 8-10; *Daily O'Collegian*, 21 December 1948, p. 1, 12 September 1951, p. 1.

38. Bound Volume of Letters from Friends and Professional Associates Presented to Roy Tompkins on His Retirement from Oklahoma A. and M. College, 1 September 1956, in personal possession of Katherine Tompkins McCollom, Stillwater, Oklahoma.

5 Unbridled Extension And Outreach 1956-1965

It was the best of times and the worst of times for extension and outreach at Oklahoma A. and M. College. Just as President Henry G. Bennett had reached his highest pinnacle of success and was prepared to bring more fame and fortune to himself and to the college, his career was cut short by unexpected tragedy. Now Roy R. Tompkins was retired. The man with the musical voice and smiling countenance had chosen to spend his retirement years as vice president of an insurance company. But business and industry had awakened to the need for continuing in-service education to keep their employees current with the rapidly changing technology in almost every field of endeavor. By 1957 the Schools of Education, Engineering, Business, and Arts and Sciences each had a director of extension on its faculty.

Oklahoma was preparing to celebrate its semicentennial in 1957. A group of forward-looking businessmen had organized the Frontiers of Science Foundation of Oklahoma to facilitate that observance. Fortunately for education, much of that organization's energy was directed toward improving the quality of education in Oklahoma. Robert Mac-Vicar, dean of the Graduate School, served for a time as its chief executive officer. Now a race was on to place an American satellite in orbit before the Soviet Union succeeded. The United States lost that race. As the first Soviet satellite went into successful orbit, the American booster rocket exploded on the launch pad. There was a general feeling of fail-

J. Conner Fitzgerald (*standing*) discusses strategy for delivering extension programs with Roy R. Tompkins, the director of Educational Extension. Tompkins believed that Oklahoma A. and M. College extension programs should be made available to any group in the state regardless of the distance from the campus.

ure and a fear that schools in the United States had become sadly deficient in teaching mathematics and science. Inadequate finances was the usual perennial problem, yet federal funding had not been accepted in principle because of the nagging fear of losing local autonomy and control of education. Congress had found ways to pump significant resources into education, however, first through the Office of Naval Research and then through the National Science Foundation. In the late 1950s and early 1960s there was a regular avalanche of federal acts providing funds for education—physical facilities, teacher training, counseling and guidance, plus laboratory equipment and supplies.

Oliver S. Willham succeeded Dr. Bennett as president and continued most of the existing policies in force, including participation in several international education projects. J. Conner Fitzgerald was appointed to succeed Tompkins in Educational Extension on September 1, 1956. His new title was director of continuing education with the rank of dean. The division included correspondence study headed by Gladys McGaugh, the audio-visual center administered by Guy Pritchard, and photographic services directed by Paul McCrary. Fitzgerald coordinated all off-campus education programs, the audio-visual center, the photographic services, and a speakers bureau.[1]

There was considerable enthusiasm in some quarters to change the name of Oklahoma A. and M. College to Oklahoma State University. The change required approval by the Oklahoma State Legislature as well as the Oklahoma A. and M. College Board of Regents. Finally in the spring of 1957, Dr. Willham suggested that extension personnel ask people over the state to encourage their representatives to vote in favor of the change. The change was approved by the legislature and implemented by the regents at their regular meeting on July 10, 1957.[2] The institution was growing in size and in stature. Everything seemed right for unbridled extension activity by every college or division within the university.

In the late fall of 1952, six staff members, including Al Darlow, Clarence Angerer, Luther Brannon, D. B. Jeffery, Hi Staten, and Everett Little, had gone to Ethiopia to begin the groundwork for an agricultural college under the Point Four Program. By January 1957, the Imperial Ethiopian College of Agriculture and Mechanical Arts had been established with an experiment station and an extension service. More than twenty-five staff members had been rotated to the project each year to make this progress possible.[3]

A Ford Foundation grant to Oklahoma A. and M. College in the mid-1950s to establish three technical institutes at Karachi, Dacca, and Rawalpindi, Pakistan, was renewed in 1959 with an additional $446,000 to train Pakistani citizens for work in factories. Henry P. Adams directed the project. Success in Pakistan led to an $800,000 grant by the Ford Foundation to provide similar educational opportunities in Brazil. By 1965, Oklahoma State University was deeply committed to international education in Ethiopia, Pakistan, Brazil, Guatemala, El Salvador, Honduras, Nicaragua, Costa Rica, and Japan. In addition, various OSU faculty and retirees participated in other international education projects in Chile, Egypt, India, and the Soviet Union. Bill Abbott served as international program coordinator. The original Point Four Program which Dr. Bennett headed had evolved into the U.S. Agency for International Development.[4]

The School of Technical Training at Okmulgee prospered. In spite of a significant recession in the economy in 1958, graduates found ready employment at attractive salaries. President Dwight D. Eisenhower's Committee on Scientists and Engineers had stressed that qualified engineering technicians were vital to the country's well being. Accordingly, Dr. Willham was able to dedicate another technical school in 1962—the Oklahoma City Technical Institute. Philip Chandler was its director.[5]

Using equipment developed in his OSU laboratory, Merle Alexander and his project director, Richard Buck, monitor the occurrence of micrometeorites in the path of *Explorer I*.

The science of rocketry, initially developed by the Germans during World War II, caused space exploration to capture the imagination of academia. Under the direction of Marvin Edmison, the Research Foundation, originally established in 1946, sought grant funds for such projects from many sources. In 1957 a microphone and amplifier designed by OSU researcher Merle Alexander was carried aboard the *Explorer I* rocket to monitor the presence of micrometeorites in outer space. There seemed always to be a need for dollars not controlled by grant documents or laws governing public funds. Accordingly, the Oklahoma State University Development Foundation was established in January 1961 to raise funds from private sources for programs that could not be funded otherwise. Robert D. Erwin was named director.[6]

This was a period of experimentation and development of communications via radio and television. The possibilities of these media being used for extension purposes seemed endless, yet no one knew how to make them most effective. KVRO was a student-operated radio station which began broadcasting locally immediately after the war. Eleven years later it was still broadcasting to a campus-wide audience through an antenna network of wire strung to campus buildings. Its purpose was to give students training in the radio field.[7]

KAMC had a more auspicious but later beginning in February 1959. It was a non-commercial FM station programmed to play classical and semiclassical music at a time when rock-and-roll was sweeping popular commercial stations. Radio-TV instructor Robert Johnson was its first faculty coordinator. Shortly thereafter the name was changed to KOSU in keeping with the name change of the institution. The initial broadcasting range had a radius of thirty miles. KOSU added stereo in 1962 to become only the third station in the state with this capacity. Because the relatively new Department of Radio-TV headed by Robert Lacy had added a new television studio, the addition of stereo equipment for KOSU incurred very little additional expense.[8]

The first live television broadcast originating on campus was a closed-circuit transmission of the February 21, 1957, basketball game with the University of Kansas, featuring Wilt "the Stilt" Chamberlain. WKY-TV provided the equipment, and admission to view the game in the College Auditorium was available to students at a dollar per person.[9]

Educational television had been established in April 1956 under the Oklahoma Educational Television Authority, which was authorized and funded by the Oklahoma Legislature. Robert C. Fite, newly-appointed director of Arts and Sciences Extension, initiated Oklahoma A. and M. College's entrance into mass teaching via television when the first of these programs was beamed over Channel 13, KETA, in November 1956. An experimental course in beginning Spanish was offered for credit in 1959, and the following year courses in Russian history, American history, and government were presented.[10] Although programs could be filmed and transported to a television station, most programs required the performers to travel to a television studio in Oklahoma City, Enid, or Tulsa.

Surface travel to and from Stillwater was no easy task. There still was no four-lane highway into Stillwater from any direction. Perhaps this helped account for OSU having the nation's largest flight school in 1958 under the direction of Tiner Lapsley. Aviation helped compensate for poor roads through an outstanding flight service provided through Airport Manager Hoyt Walkup and his staff of pilots. The Flying Aggies club flourished in membership and in winning contests nationwide. The OSU club won the Bendix Award as the top flying team in the country for the eighth time in 1964.[11]

Through Fitzgerald's efforts, Oklahoma State University offered driver education courses in cooperation with the Oklahoma Department of Public Safety, the Oklahoma Department of Education, and the American Automobile Association. Carl Tilley, who was the Stillwater High School principal, taught driver education each summer on campus. Prospective driver education teachers could earn college credit in basic and advanced courses as well as in automobile safety.[12] Credits for these courses in addition to courses in reading improvement and audio-visual techniques were granted through the College of Education, although most of the actual staffing and physical needs were met through the continuing education department.

A continuing education announcement in 1957 listed seventeen locations for adult education extension classes. These included Oklahoma City, Tulsa, Miami, Goodwell, Okmulgee, Wilburton, Hugo, Sayre, Eufaula, Woodward, Ada, Poteau, Lawton, Enid, Bartlesville, Ponca City, and Tishomingo. By 1964 the list also included Alva, Canton, Chandler, Choctaw, Claremore, Clinton, El Reno, Muskogee, Mustang, Newkirk, Nowata, Owasso, Perry, Pryor, Sapulpa, Shattuck, Vinita, and Weatherford. The Oklahoma State Regents for Higher Education desig-

Director of Engineering Extension L. F. "Mike" Sheerar (*lower left*) headed the oldest college extension service outside of agriculture. An Oklahoma City businessman, Harry Canup (*lower right*) was the first director of Business Extension. In 1963, Richard Jungers (*upper right*) became director of Education Extension.

Centennial Histories Series

nated some of these locations as graduate centers where a student might earn up to one-half of the course requirements for an advanced degree. The remainder were simply extension centers in which only one-fourth of the degree requirements could be earned. Malcom Knowles, executive director of the Adult Education Association of the United States, estimated that forty million Americans were actively engaged in continuing education pursuits in the late 1950s and the number would continue to increase.[13]

The directors of extension for the Colleges of Education, Engineering, Arts and Sciences, and Business coordinated the extension offerings from that college. Because each college usually catered to a different audience, the college director functioned independently of the others except for monthly meetings with Fitzgerald. At these meetings points of friction were identified and resolved.

Gerald T. Stubbs was formally appointed director of Education Extension in 1957, although he had been serving in an extension role as director of public school services since 1945. It was through his efforts that counseling and guidance services were emphasized in schools in order that those with special interests and abilities in the engineering and science professions might be introduced to fields where a critical shortage existed. In an effort to solve this problem nationally, Congress passed the National Defense Education Act (NDEA) in 1957. Among other things, it provided for training counselors for employment in the nation's high schools. The College of Education began receiving NDEA funds for counseling institutes in 1959, and for the next several years such a program directed by Harry K. Brobst was a regular summer feature in the curriculum.[14]

Stubbs worked closely with the school administrators organization in the state. Early in his tenure, he initiated a high school principal-student conference where principals from over the state were invited to the campus to visit with their former students, now enrolled as college freshmen. Both the principals and OSU officials watched the feedback from students to glean hints on how their respective schools might be improved.[15]

When Stubbs retired in 1963, Richard Jungers was appointed director of extension and field services in the College of Education. He had earned his doctorate at the University of Wisconsin and taught in Wisconsin and Minnesota before joining the faculty in 1957. As director of Education Extension, Dr. Jungers furthered the policies and practices established by Mr. Stubbs. Also he continued his duties as an associate professor in the College of Education. Most of the courses taught by Education Extension were designed for training teachers. As often as not, these courses were in response to legislative mandates requiring additional training for Oklahoma teachers so that they could qualify for promotions or salary increases.

Because Dr. Jungers had worked with Mr. Stubbs on many of his school service projects, he was in a position to render a much needed service to individual school districts when he became director of the program. A district would develop a problem and call for assistance in arriving at a solution. Education Extension would send a team of professors from the college to the district, study the problem, and recommend a solution. Designing optimum school bus routes, deciding which of several elementary schools to close, locating a new school site when two or more districts consolidated, or accomplishing integration were examples of the problems confronting school districts. Dr. Jungers served as advisor to several professional organizations and, in that capacity, often caused annual meetings of these organizations to be held on the OSU campus. One of the largest of these annual meetings involved the organization of superintendents and principals of Oklahoma.

Clayton Morgan headed a unique program in education designed to rehabilitate injured war veterans and other handicapped students. OSU was one of only four educational institutions in the nation selected by the U.S. Office of Vocational Rehabilitation to provide placement and vocational rehabilitation training to prepare persons as counselors for vocational rehabilitation agencies.[16]

Engineering and Industrial Extension is the second oldest at OSU, having been preceded only by the Cooperative Extension Service. Under the direction of L. F. "Mike" Sheerar since 1953, Engineering Extension sought to extend the educational resources of the college to employed engineers as its primary goal. Extension programs were of two types: graduate courses for credit and noncredit seminars were conducted by engineering faculty and other qualified personnel at graduate centers in Tulsa, Oklahoma City, Ponca City, and Bartlesville, and noncredit seminars were conducted on-campus for all qualified engineers who wished to attend. The off-campus courses for credit offered working engineers an opportunity to earn a master's degree in civil, electrical, or mechanical engineering. Many of the noncredit programs evolved into annual events which focused on recent developments in that particular field. Thus, it was not uncommon for a given participant to return year after year for updating.

Wilson Bentley, professor and head of industrial engineering, recognized the need and provided administrative support for annual seminars through Engineering Extension. Some of these "bread and butter" courses that attracted a full complement of students each year were water quality and sewage management, heating and air conditioning, thermodynamics, highway construction, soil mechanics, electromagnetic relays, and business and personnel management. An occasional guest speaker at the management institutes was J. O. Grantham, a former

A raging flame has been deliberately set on training grounds near the OSU campus to give an extension class of firemen firsthand experience in extinguishing an oil fire.

faculty member who was then vice president of Northern Natural Gas Company. Grantham later returned to OSU to become director of University Extension.[17]

The Engineering Extension director was charged with the supervision of several other programs. Among these was the OSU Technical Institute's training program for firemen. This involved conducting annual workshops for firefighters, publishing a firefighter's manual, and providing field training on demand for the fire departments of Oklahoma towns and cities. The manual was regularly updated to contain the latest technology of firefighting and was used for training firemen in all fifty states and several foreign countries. Prominent staff people in the firefighting program during this era were Everett Hudiburg, Elmer Johnson, and R. J. Douglas.[18]

The High School Institute continued to stimulate interest in science and engineering careers. Students were selected to spend six weeks on campus in a science and engineering environment before their final year in high school. Coordinated by Glenn Rucker, the program showed such promise that the National Science Foundation provided annual grants to support the costs from 1959 through 1965.[19]

Still another program was initiated in 1965 by Engineering Extension in cooperation with the Oklahoma Department of Highways to train department employees in such areas as surveying, soil mechanics, construction, and sanitation. Assisting Sheerar in these projects was Monroe W. Kriegel who was named assistant director of Engineering Extension in 1964 after Rucker retired.[20]

Late in 1957 Harry Canup resigned his position as director of Business Extension to establish his own private business consulting service in Oklahoma City. His resignation was accepted with regret by Dean Eugene L. Swearingen who praised the extension program of the past four years under Canup. Norman H. Ringstrom was named director of Business Extension effective July 1, 1958. His duties in the new part-time assignment included arranging and conducting short courses, clinics, and conferences and making trade area analyses and other economic studies. Vice Dean Edward C. Burris said Ringstrom was particularly well qualified for the position, holding bachelor's, master's, and doctor of philosophy degrees in business from the Iowa State University. The Agricultural-Industrial Development Service program, originally one of Dr. Bennett's programs for economic recovery in the late 1940s, found a new home on campus when its director, J B LeMaster, was transferred to the College of Business to become assistant director of Business Extension under Dr. Ringstom. The program continued to serve Oklahoma communities with economic surveys and counseling. In March 1959, projects were underway in Marlow, Mangum, Watonga, and Pauls Valley.[21]

City planning flourished under Ringstrom's guidance. He left, however, in the spring of 1960. On July 1, 1960, Robert D. Erwin became the new Business Extension director. He occupied the position until January 15, 1961, when he became director of the newly formed OSU Development Foundation. Clayton Millington moved into the director's office in the spring of 1961. Millington had joined the business college faculty only the year before to head up a program for the Oklahoma Council on Economic Education. He had completed all course work for the Ph.D. degree at Michigan State University, but still lacked the dissertation. Once in the office, he found the city planning operation was behind in production and, hence, in financial difficulty. Much of the budget for the full-time city planners was made up from contractual proceeds from the cities being served. Millington was able to get the city planner's program back on track, continue as director of the economic education program for public schools, establish a business extension program for professionals, and finish his degree requirements in the spring of 1964.[22]

In addition to providing extension classes for credit in such centers as Enid, Bartlesville, Ponca City, Tulsa, and Oklahoma City, Business Extension under Millington's leadership provided economic seminars for such varied groups as restaurant operators, small businessmen, clergymen, tax assessors, insurance salesmen, teachers, and industrial managers. Through his role as executive director of the Oklahoma Coun-

64

Norman Ringstrom (*left*) promoted city planning when he was named Business Extension director in 1958. Succeeding Ringstrom was Robert Erwin (*center*). After Erwin resigned to become director of the OSU Development Foundation, Clayton Millington (*right*) became director. Millington was also in charge of an educational program for the Oklahoma Council on Economic Education.

cil on Economic Education, an ambitious project was undertaken in 1965 to help integrate economic education in the social studies curriculum of Oklahoma's public schools in all grades from kindergarten through high school.[23]

Vice Dean Burris gained national fame for the College of Business in the late 1950s and early 1960s as a labor dispute arbitrator. He would frequently ''don a hard hat'' to see the problems firsthand before sitting down at the arbitration table. He served on nine cases in 1964 and would have been assigned fifty if he had had the time. Although Dean Swearingen was named vice president for development in 1964, he continued to serve as dean of business until Richard W. Poole was named as his successor effective September 1, 1965.[24]

Oklahoma State University had earned a place on the globe. With its new Student Union and active extension directors, the campus was becoming a conference and convention headquarters for many groups. Over 3,000 scientists attended the 1960 convention of the American Institute of Biological Sciences. The National Mail Carriers Association also came to the campus one or more years. Dean Scroggs initiated an annual conference for academic deans, and OSU was chosen by the deans as a permanent site for the August get-together.[25]

Because the college extension directors were finding it convenient to go directly to the Student Union to make conference arrangements, the role of the short course director had diminished. When Clay Potts retired as director of short courses on July 1, 1961, Norman F. Moore, assistant Student Union director, was named coordinator of conferences.[26]

After retirement, Potts continued to offer delicious feasts on a private basis, including serving as official chef of the Lewis Field press box where he had not missed a game since beginning the treat in 1948. OSU and the entire state of Oklahoma were saddened on December 3, 1966, when Potts died in the press box just moments after the OSU-OU football game. It was a good news/bad news situation and probably as Potts would have wanted it—the Cowboys had beaten the Sooners by a score of 15-14. No one could count the number of people who had enjoyed the famous Potts' hospitality through more than thirty-five years of service to OSU. His largest crowd of diners had numbered 17,000 at a tri-state miners convention at Miami, Oklahoma, and his most famous guest had been President Harry S. Truman, whom he served in Washington at the invitation of Senator Robert S. Kerr.[27]

The annual cheese festival continued to attract large crowds to its taste fests. At the sixteenth culinary gala in 1965, the Harley Thomas Ford agency donated the use of its showroom for the occasion. Festival visitors had the opportunity to taste two hundred brands of cheese.[28]

In 1960 Luther H. Brannon, Cooperative Extension director, announced that the U.S. Department of Agriculture had chosen Oklahoma State University for a pilot study on food distribution. George Abshier, extension marketing economist, was put in charge. Although food was often the focus of agricultural extension programs, field days

COURTESY FRED RAY

Monterey Jack, Gouda, Salami, Swiss—oh, who could resist the sights and sounds, but especially the *tastes* at the annual cheese and sausage festival.

Centennial Histories Series

at demonstration plots and annual farm equipment shows at the college farm in Oklahoma City drew many participants.[29]

Oklahoma's Flying Farmers held their twentieth annual convention on campus in 1963. The group now boasted a membership of 310. While some used their airplanes for business travel, others found them more useful for fishing trips or coyote hunting.[30]

Agriculture was plagued with a dilemma. There was a declining number of students wishing to major in agriculture so efforts were made to encourage entering freshmen to explore the many agriculturally-related career opportunities. Robert Price, head of agriculture education, estimated in 1964 that 775,000 jobs had been automated out of agriculture in the last five years; and he speculated that the trend would continue. Perhaps a new extension director could help solve this predicament. Jean C. Evans, assistant extension director at the University of Missouri, was named to head the Cooperative Extension Service effective February 1, 1965. He replaced Brannon who was appointed director of the university's educational program in Ethiopia.[31]

Home economics was experiencing problems similar to agriculture. A change in attitude was taking place regarding women's place in society. More emphasis was being placed by women on careers outside the home and less on the function of homemaking. Even though OSU's Division of Home Economics ranked third in the nation in numbers of home economics majors, there was still concern about declining enrollments. "Home Economics On Parade," an annual event held on a Saturday in the spring, always focused on the recruitment of high school students to the college. With the exception of an annual short course for school lunch cooks and the Oklahoma Homemakers' Conference, most of the college's extension activities were carried on under the supervision of State Home Demonstration Agent Norma Brumbaugh through the county extension offices of Cooperative Extension.[32]

Because Schiller Scroggs, dean of arts and sciences, believed the Soviets had outmaneuvered the Americans in claiming technological spoils of World War II from the Germans, he not only wanted to develop extension programs, he called for newsworthy extension projects. He wanted to let the public know that the college was doing something positive to correct educational deficiencies. Thus, Robert C. Fite, the first director of Arts and Sciences Extension, took on an intriguing yet nebulous assignment in 1956. Fite had completed his Ph.D. degree at Northwestern University in 1951 and was then associate professor of geography and meteorology. He had flown typhoon reconnaissance for the U.S. Navy during the war and had come to OSU to finish a master's degree in educational administration. While a student, he lived in Veteran's Village and after graduation in 1947 stayed on as a geography and meteorology instructor at the invitation of his former geography professor, Edward E. Keso.[33] Robert B. Kamm, who succeeded Scroggs as dean in 1958, continued support of extension programs in arts and sciences.

Fite inherited Operation Bootstrap, an extension program specially designed by Roy Tompkins for military personnel at Vance Air Force Base. He made educational surveys and organized extension programs to serve selected groups from education, business, and industry. He soon had as many as seventy extension courses for college credit being taught each semester—enough to keep a full-time faculty of twenty professors busy. Most of the courses were taught by the regular arts and sciences faculty members on an overload basis. A professor earned supplemental income for teaching an extension class in addition to his or her regular assignment. Arrangements were often made to hire a qualified adjunct professor for a given course with the approval of the appropriate academic department. Adjuncts were sometimes recruited from the faculties of other colleges, from industry, or from the on-campus graduate student population.[34] As many as twenty students were able to complete a doctoral degree during the early 1960s by being supported wholly or in part by teaching Arts and Sciences Extension classes.

Too many students, especially from small, rural high schools, arrived at college with little or no science. Neglect, inadequate financing, and the lack of qualified teachers all contributed to the problem. In 1957 Fite organized an experimental mobile chemistry project among twenty small high schools in Carter County. A station wagon was outfitted with chemistry laboratory equipment and supplies. Claude Gatewood, a well-qualified chemistry teacher, was hired to drive the vehicle and to visit each of the cooperating schools for a half day every two weeks. The experiment gained national attention. It was followed in the same schools by a mobile physics lab in 1958-59 that was staffed by Dale Bremmer, a physics teacher. The mobile chemistry project was continued at different schools and staffed by chemistry teacher Denman Evans. In the meantime, a grant of $3,000 was received from the Frontiers of Science Foundation of Oklahoma to help support a Traveling Science Demonstration Lecture Program which would move from school to school throughout Oklahoma to encourage interest in science as a career. Gatewood opted for this assignment and gave demonstration lectures in as many Oklahoma schools as time would allow during 1958-59.[35]

Publicity gained from these projects was directly responsible for Fite being invited by the National Science Foundation to submit a proposal to expand the mobile science lecture concept into other states. As a result OSU received a grant for $335,700 in 1959 to outfit and staff twenty labmobiles and to deploy them among the schools of an eight-state region composed of Colorado, New Mexico, Texas, Kansas, Missouri, Arkansas, Louisiana, and Oklahoma. The instructors were recruited from the same eight-state region. They received thirteen weeks of intensive training

In the late 1950s, Robert C. Fite (*upper*), the first director of Arts and Sciences Extension, administered the Traveling Science Demonstration Lecture Program. Claude Gatewood (*lower*), an instructor with the mobile chemistry laboratory, performs an experiment for some Oklahoma high school students.

at OSU during the summer of 1959 in preparation for lecturing through-out the following year in high schools requesting their services. This project was called the Traveling Science Teacher Program (TSTP). Of particular help in the TSTP training sessions were Paul Arthur in chemistry, Lee Rutledge in physics, Herbert Bruneau in biology, Roy Deal in mathematics, and C. E. Hoffman in industrial arts education.[36] The TSTP was funded again by the National Science Foundation for 1960-61 and was expanded to include the states of Arizona and Nebraska.

A report of the President's Science Advisory Committee called for increasing the number of doctoral degrees granted in engineering, mathematics, and physical sciences from 2,900 in 1960 to 7,500 per year in 1970. Clearly the need to steer more capable students toward careers in the sciences existed. OSU had already become identified with National Science Foundation institutes in mathematics and science. The university had received one of the first three summer institute grants in 1953 and one of the first two Academic Year Institute (AYI) grants for the 1956-57 school year, and these grants had been renewed on a regular basis. L. Wayne Johnson, head of mathematics, prepared the proposals for the initial grants. James Zant was named director of the AYI. When he retired in 1963, Fite became the AYI director.[37] Others also obtained and directed similar grants, including Milton Berg in mathematics and Herbert Bruneau in biology.

The National Science Foundation became involved in high school mathematics and science curricula in other important ways. Projects were funded at a number of locations involving college and high school teachers in curriculum revisions. The projects of these study groups came to be known as the alphabet soup—SMSG mathematics, PSSC physics, CHEM chemistry, BSCS biology—and in general represented a great strengthening of the text materials in these subjects. Text materials were changing so fast it was difficult for even the most proficient teachers

In the 1950s, it became increasingly apparent that there was a need for improving mathematics and science instruction. Discussing plans for the high school science teacher program are (*left to right*) Robert MacVicar, Frontiers of Science Foundation director; Wayne Johnson, head of the Department of Mathematics; and James Zant, director of the program.

Centennial Histories Series

to keep up with the latest developments. For this reason, Arts and Sciences Extension organized and conducted one-day conferences annually to update mathematics and science teachers. Brochures announcing the conference were mailed to all high schools in the state, and several hundred teachers would attend the event each year.[38]

Because the National Science Foundation welcomed innovative ideas for improving instruction, Fite conceived a plan to organize a class of advanced high school students who would be instructed for credit in one of the newly developed curricula while teachers-in-training observed the class procedures. This proposal was funded and led to the creation of a new National Science Foundation program area called the Cooperative College School Science (CCSS) program.[39]

A variation of this concept was developed in cooperation with the Oklahoma Academy of Science. High school science teachers were encouraged to have their best students perform research projects and to prepare a scientific paper on the project. These papers were submitted to Arts and Sciences Extension by mail. The best papers were selected by a committee of science and mathematics professors to be presented at an Oklahoma Junior Academy of Science meeting. OSU professors especially helpful in this endeavor included Otis Dermer, Ernest Hodnett, Ruth Gerber, Wayne Johnson, O. H. Hamilton, H. S. Mendenhall, Harold Harrington, Fremont Harris, Arlo Schmidt, Roy Jones, George Moore, Bryan Glass, Herb Bruneau, Lynn Gee, H. I. Featherly, Walter Hansen, and John Thomas. After presentation, the papers were published in a "Proceedings" to encourage the students further. The National Science Foundation also became interested in the program and provided it token financial support for several years.[40]

Also focusing on superior high school students, a summer term program called "University Preview" was sponsored by Arts and Sciences Extension. Students with high marks in their first three years of high school were given an opportunity to attend the OSU summer session, filling seats in existing classes that otherwise would remain vacant. If the student passed the course with a grade of "B" or better, he or she could obtain advanced standing credit in that course upon entering college as a freshman one year later. The "preview" students received no other special consideration except for closer supervision in the residence halls.[41]

Arts and Sciences Extension became involved in three international programs, all resulting from previous successes. Also, the U.S. Department of Defense contracted for a science improvement project for its dependents' schools in the Pacific theater. Richard Osner, a former traveling science teacher, was sent to Japan. The U.S. Agency for International Development contracted for a science materials project to be conducted for the colleges in five Central American countries. Wendall

Spreadbury, another former traveling science teacher, was sent on this mission. He was succeeded by Lawrence R. Przekop, who had a better command of the Spanish language than Spreadbury. A group of ten Uruguayan educators asked to visit the campus to see the innovative science projects they had heard about. Their visit was sponsored by the International Teacher Development Program administered by the U.S. Office of Education.[42]

The Arts and Sciences Extension office administered several routine annual events. The substance of each event was provided by an appropriate academic department. These included an industrial editors' short course, civil defense work shop, band clinic, academic deans' conference, music education work shop, and Thanksgiving Choral Festival. Interestingly, the choral festival of November 23, 1959, turned out to be not so routine. It was a cold evening in Stillwater, and several thousand high school singers were rendering the final mass concert in Gallagher Hall. About seventy buses, with motors running, were parked close to the building. Carbon monoxide fumes from the buses were drawn into the fieldhouse by the ventilation system, and 700 students rather suddenly were overcome. Fortunately no one was injured during the near panic that followed, and all victims were fully recovered the next day.[43]

During this period Arts and Sciences Extension experimented with many routines and devices for the delivery of instruction to meet off-campus educational needs. Although expensive, instructors were often flown to their off-campus teaching sites in university planes. Variations of programmed instruction were tried, including combining television instruction with correspondence lessons. The National Broadcasting Company sponsored a television course in atomic age physics in which over three hundred colleges, including OSU, participated. The master teacher was Harvey E. White, professor of physics at the University of California. Each participating school wrote its own ground rules to handle enrollments, require homework, give examinations, and collect fees.[44] The experiment, known as the Continental Classroom, was repeated several times in other subjects.

In 1957 Fite made a study of pre-enrollment counseling services being provided for entering freshmen students at the University of Indiana and Allegheny College at Meadville, Pennsylvania. OSU was already sending counselors to high schools when requested to do so. This work was coordinated by Director of Admissions Raymond Girod and assisted by Wes Watkins and others. Fite recommended that a service similar to the Indiana and Pennsylvania programs be provided for entering arts and sciences students. University-wide counseling clinics were initiated in 1958 on a voluntary basis for graduating high school seniors. The clinics were well received and became a standard requirement for entering fresh-

Ashley Alexander, director of the Student Entertainers, plays the piano for a quartet of student performers. His ever present smile was infectious to the students and to the appreciative audiences.

men at OSU. They helped to streamline enrollment procedures for all students.[45]

The OSU students also contributed greatly to outreach during this unbridled period of expansion. In addition to regular annual performance tours by glee clubs under the direction of Cy Perkins and Hoover Fisher and by bands under the direction of Hiram Henry and Stanley Green, the Student Entertainers were gaining national and international fame for themselves and OSU. Ashley Alexander succeeded A. Frank Martin as director in 1956. He was a talented, jovial, energetic individual with a great love for travel. No gathering of people was too great or too small to be entertained by the Student Entertainers. Tragedy befell when Tom Harris, an assistant dean of students, and Jean Hawkins, a coed member of the troupe, were killed and four other coeds injured in a head-on automobile crash near Pawnee. Under Alexander's leadership the Student Entertainers recovered from the tragedy and became widely renowned for their talents. In 1962 they entertained at Governor-elect Henry Bellmon's victory party at Billings. Fourteen students from the group were selected for a United Service Organizations (USO) tour in

1964 and spent sixty-one days presenting seventy-three shows in Japan, Korea, Iwo Jima, Okinawa, Formosa, the Philippines, and Guam.[46]

The 1950s and early 1960s were times of unleashed extension and outreach. Whether through the innovation of traveling science programs, the establishment of a college in Ethiopia, the popularity of the high school institutes, or the traditional choral festival, the university remained undeterred in its extension mission.

For ten years and more the federal government had moved in the direction of providing more federal aid for education. The pace had accelerated with each passing year in the administrations of Presidents Dwight D. Eisenhower, John F. Kennedy, and Lyndon B. Johnson. In addition to funding through the National Science Foundation and the U.S. Office of Education, there had been specific acts to upgrade the elementary schools, high schools, and colleges. There had been an academic facilities act, a higher education act, and an economic opportunity act. Future changes in extension and outreach were certain—the degree and direction unclear. A new era beckoned in which the state and indeed the world became Oklahoma State University's campus.

Endnotes

1. "Aggieland Roundup," *Oklahoma A. and M. College Magazine*, vol. 28, no. 2 (October 1956), p. 10; Oklahoma A. and M. College *Daily O'Collegian*, 7 February 1957, p. 7.

2. Vernon Parcher interview with L. F. Sheerar, 25 July 1983, Stillwater, Oklahoma, transcript, Special Collections, Edmon Low Library, Oklahoma State University, Stillwater, Oklahoma; Minutes, Board of Regents for the Oklahoma Agricultural and Mechanical Colleges, 10 July 1957, pp. 6-7, Special Collections, Edmon Low Library.

3. *Daily O'Collegian*, 4 January 1957, p. 3.

4. *Daily O'Collegian*, 17 January 1959, p. 1, 28 September 1965, p. 1; Oliver S. Willham, "International Extension of Education," *Oklahoma State Alumnus Magazine*, vol. 6, no. 7 (September-October 1965), pp. 30-31.

5. *Daily O'Collegian*, 23 April 1958, p. 2, 2 November 1962, p. 1.

6. *Daily O'Collegian*, 8 May 1958, p. 1, 8 January 1961, p. 4.

7. *Daily O'Collegian*, 22 February 1957, p. 3.

8. *Daily O'Collegian*, 6 February 1959, p. 1, 11 September 1962, p. 10; "A Venture into Radio's Educational Broadcasting," *Oklahoma State University Magazine*, vol. 2, no. 11 (May 1959), pp. 16-17.

9. *Daily O'Collegian*, 22 January 1957, p. 1.

10. *Daily O'Collegian*, 16 November 1956, p. 1, 17 June 1960, p. 2.

11. *Daily O'Collegian*, 25 March 1964, p. 4, 3 April 1958, p. 1, 20 May 1964, p. 1.

12. *Daily O'Collegian*, 4 October 1958, p. 5.

13. *Daily O'Collegian*, 18 January 1964, p. 3, 15 July 1958, p. 1.

14. *Stillwater Gazette*, 10 May 1957, p. 2; *Daily O'Collegian*, 9 June 1959, p. 6.

15. *Daily O'Collegian*, 2 May 1959, p. 8.

16. Author interview with Richard Jungers, 22 July 1986, Stillwater, Oklahoma; *Daily O'Collegian*, 23 October 1962, p. 8.

17. *Daily O'Collegian*, 25 January 1962, p. 4.

18. *Daily O'Collegian*, 20 July 1962, p. 10.

19. "OSU Institute for Budding Scientists," *Oklahoma State University Magazine*, vol. 1, no. 3 (September 1957), pp. 12-13.

20. "Engineering and Industrial Extension: A Tradition of Service," *Oklahoma State Alumnus Magazine*, vol. 6, no. 3 (March 1965), p. 27.

21. *Stillwater Gazette*, 18 October 1957, p. 4; *Stillwater NewsPress*, 26 June 1958, p. 1; "Serving the Needs of Business," *Oklahoma State University Magazine*, vol. 2, no. 9 (March 1959), pp. 5-7.

22. Author interview with Clayton Millington, 25 July 1986, Stillwater, Oklahoma; *Daily O'Collegian*, 10 March 1964, p. 7.

23. "'Long Arm' of Service," *Oklahoma State Alumnus Magazine*, vol. 6, no. 1 (January 1965), p. 31.

24. "Business Vice-Dean Acts as Labor Dispute Arbitrator," *Oklahoma State University Magazine*, vol. 6, no. 5 (May 1965), p. 31; *Daily O'Collegian*, 11 May 1965, p. 1.

25. "In Pursuit of Knowledge," *Oklahoma State Alumnus Magazine*, vol. 1, no. 9 (October 1960), pp. 4-7; Conference of Academic Deans, *Evaluation of Student Achievement: The Twelfth Yearbook of the Annual Summer Conference of Academic Deans* (Stillwater: Oklahoma State University Press, 1958), p. iv.

26. "Everlasting Service," *Oklahoma State Alumnus Magazine*, vol. 2, no. 6 (June 1961), p. 9; *Stillwater NewsPress*, 11 July 1961, p. 1; *Daily O'Collegian*, 11 July 1961, p. 1.

27. "OSU Ambassador H. Clay Potts Dies at Age 72," *Oklahoma State Alumnus Magazine*, vol. 8, no. 1 (January 1967), p. 26.

28. *Daily O'Collegian*, 6 November 1965, p. 1.

29. *Daily O'Collegian*, 12 May 1960, p. 8, 26 April 1960, p. 6.

30. Phil Stout, "The Story of the Flying Farmers," *Oklahoma State Alumnus Magazine*, vol. 4, no. 6 (June 1963), pp. 8-10.

31. *Daily O'Collegian*, 19 March 1964, p. 8, 14 February 1963, p. 6, 2 April 1964, p. 7; "Evans is Chosen as Director of OSU Extension," *Oklahoma State Alumnus Magazine*, vol. 6, no. 2 (February 1965), p. 19.

32. Lela O'Toole, "Strengthening of Family Life," *Oklahoma State Alumnus Magazine*, vol. 3, no. 4 (April 1962), p. 25; *Daily O'Collegian*, 24 April 1965, p. 1, 2 August 1957, p. 1.

33. Minutes, Board of Regents for the Oklahoma Agricultural and Mechanical Colleges, 6 September 1956, p. 3.

34. *Oklahoma State University Student Handbook, 1957-58*, p. 112; "Arts and Sciences Extension: A College Within a College," *Oklahoma State Alumnus Magazine*, vol. 6, no. 2 (February 1965), p. 20.

35. *Daily O'Collegian*, 17 November 1956, p. 3; *Kansas City Star*, 27 April 1958, p. 2E; "Laboratories on Wheels," *Oklahoma State University Magazine*, vol. 2, no. 4 (October 1958), pp. 16-18.

36. *Stillwater NewsPress*, 9 March 1959, p. 3; Oklahoma City *Daily Oklahoman Orbit*, 27 September 1959, pp. 1, 4-5.

37. *Daily O'Collegian*, 15 May 1963, p. 9.

38. James H. Zant, "Revolutionizing the Math Curriculum," *Oklahoma State Alumnus Magazine*, vol. 3, no. 9 (October 1962), pp. 16-17; "Nuclear Science for the Student," *Oklahoma State Alumnus Magazine*, vol. 2, no. 4 (April 1961), pp. 8-11.

39. "OSU Plans Summer Science Program," *Oklahoma State Alumnus Magazine*, vol. 4, no. 4 (April 1963), p. 47.

40. *Daily O'Collegian*, 13 May 1961, p. 8.

41. *Daily O'Collegian*, 16 May 1959, p. 6.

42. *Daily O'Collegian*, 15 September 1965, p. 3, 29 April 1964, p. 8.

43. *Daily O'Collegian*, 24 November 1959, p. 1.

44. *Daily O'Collegian*, 18 September 1958, p. 8; *Daily Oklahoman*, 5 October 1958, p. 9TV.

45. "Operations College Education: By Invitation Only," *Oklahoma A. and M. College Magazine*, vol. 28, no. 5 (January 1957), p. 9; *Daily O'Collegian*, 25 November 1958, p. 8.

46. "Maestro of Aggieland Student Entertainment Talent," *Oklahoma A. and M. College Magazine*, vol. 28, no. 3 (November 1956), pp. 5-6; *Stillwater NewsPress*, 22 November 1957, p. 1; *Daily O'Collegian*, 15 December 1962, p. 8; *Daily Oklahoman*, 15 January 1965, p. 13.

6 An Experiment Too Good to Last 1965-1975

Although resident instruction, research, and extension had always been listed as the three major functions of a land-grant institution, until now the extension function had been interpreted to mean primarily agricultural extension. Indeed, while there were those who argued many nonagricultural programs had been quite successful, these same proponents believed there was a need for more coordination. The period of unbridled expansion in extension and outreach came to an abrupt end in July 1965 when the OSU Board of Regents decided to reorganize the Division of Continuing Education and the Cooperative Extension Service into a single agency called University Extension.[1] This reorganization held promise for the varied extension activities to be integrated into a unified system under the direction of a single administrator. Now all of the extension services of all colleges of the university would be recognized as important.

It was hoped that through the reorganization of extension, all programs would receive more financial support from federal and state sources. This theory was supported by the Washington scene. The United States Congress was considering House Resolution 3420 which, if passed and fully funded, would provide a business and industrial extension service in the various states similar to the Cooperative Extension Service for agriculture. Vice President for Agriculture O. Burr Ross did not mention this possibility, however, when he explained "this is really a re-structuring of our existing extension programs on the main campus to provide for more efficient operation and better use of available funds."[2]

Ross also noted that there would be no great change in the county extension offices or in other field personnel.

Jean C. Evans, a native of Indiana, was chosen as dean of this reorganized extension service. Dr. Evans had earned his bachelor's degree at Purdue University, his master's at Michigan State University, and his doctorate at the University of Wisconsin. He had been assistant director of extension at the University of Missouri before coming to OSU as director of the Cooperative Extension Service.

When he assumed his duties in Cooperative Extension in February 1965, he arrived "on the run" and soon was dubbed the "road runner" by his associates. His energy seemed boundless. He was always enroute to somewhere or from somewhere. He began a systematic reorganization of the Cooperative Extension Service. The title of the head agent in each county was changed from county agent to county extension director; county home demonstration agents were henceforth called extension home economists. In addition, the name of each county extension office was changed to Oklahoma State University extension office, and a standard sign to that effect was displayed over each office door in all seventy-seven counties.

Other changes included moving the extension subject matter specialists from the state extension office to offices within the academic departments they represented. The district directors, who had been living in Stillwater, were moved to the districts they were to supervise. By and large these changes were accepted in good faith by those affected, being assured by Dr. Evans that they would be good for the total Cooperative Extension program.[3]

The new extension organization naturally caused changes in the way nonagricultural extension was being conducted at OSU. Dean Evans assumed fiscal responsibility and accountability for all extension funds. The college extension directors cleared budgets for extension programs with Dean Evans before new funds were committed. The directors of extension for the Colleges of Arts and Sciences, Business, Education, and Engineering met weekly with Evans to resolve problems, make plans, and generate new ideas. Extension directors from agriculture, home economics, and veterinary medicine soon joined these weekly meetings. J. Conner Fitzgerald also met with the group. He retained the title as director of continuing education but functioned until his retirement in 1969 as an assistant to Dr. Evans. His special responsibilities included supervising the correspondence study department, audio-visual department, and photographic services.

Dr. Evans announced that OSU was prepared to launch extensive educational programs for people across the state. These would range from tapestry to taxes, from soap to space, from poison to pork, from money to morality, from bathrooms to bookmobiles, and everything in

Richard W. Poole (*left*) confers with Jean C. Evans concerning the State Technical Services program. Poole was chairman of the statewide planning committee, and Evans was the program director for Oklahoma. Evans was the only individual to have the title vice president for extension. When he resigned in 1974, then Vice President for University Relations and Development Poole took on the added duties of extension.

between. The merger of extension programs under Evans' leadership was lauded editorially by some of the state's leading newspapers.[4]

In mid-September of 1965, Dean Evans and M. R. Lohmann, dean of engineering, were invited to the White House to attend the formal signing of the State Technical Services Act (House Resolution 3420) by President Lyndon B. Johnson. The act provided for industrial extension programs in the various states with federal funds amounting to $10 million in 1966, $20 million in 1967, and $30 million in 1968. The funds would be distributed by the Department of Commerce based on a formula including such things as population, business indices, technical resources, and the state's organization for administering the program. All federal payments were to be matched by nonfederal funds on a 50-50 basis. In early October 1965, Governor Henry Bellmon designated Oklahoma State University to coordinate the Technical Service Act programs in Oklahoma. In a letter to President Oliver S. Willham, the governor asked that Richard W. Poole, dean of the College of Business, be placed in charge of a planning group to develop Oklahoma's technical services extension program. The planning group was also to include Dean Evans, Dean Lohmann, two professors from the University of Oklahoma, and several people from across the state.[5]

Extension programs expanded rapidly under Dean Evans' leadership. His organizational structure was functioning well. His philosophy for continuing education for adults was catching on among extension workers and the general public. He emphasized that the major objective of extension was to help adults learn and that in today's world any society that neglected continuing education among its adults would become obsolete. He reminded his many audiences that the great milestones of progress in the development of western civilization were founded on the ability of adults to learn and to change. In his final analysis, it was the responsibility of every college, every dean, and every department head to use their imagination and ingenuity to help adults learn what they wanted and needed to know. In February 1967, on the recommendation of President Robert B. Kamm (who had succeeded Oliver S. Willham in 1966), the OSU Board of Regents changed Dr. Evans' title to vice president of extension. Dr. Kamm said the new title reflected more accurately the longtime and continuing importance of extension to a land-grant university.[6]

It is difficult to assess the impact of the reorganization of extension on agricultural extension although there were many visible evidences of positive change. William F. "Bill" Taggart was named director of agricultural extension and served within the organizational structure in a capacity parallel to the other college extension directors. He had served as a county agent and state livestock specialist. The usual extension-type activities such as the annual cheese festival, feeders day, and agriculture week continued unimpeded, but many changes could also be noted. Agricultural specialists became more prominent in the field organization, backing up the people on the front lines in the county offices. Their roles were often problem-oriented, such as an outbreak of insects in a crop or the sudden appearance of a harmful disease in plants or livestock. Basically, however, the specialists prepared research-based educational programs on an area basis for use at the county level. Several extension-type service units were developed in the College of Agriculture to serve the entire state. These included a fully equipped soil testing laboratory, swine evaluation center, beef cattle gain test station, and a plant disease diagnostic laboratory.[7]

The Oklahoma State University extension office in each county was truly beginning to function as the front door to Oklahoma State University for the people in that county. This was the way Dr. Evans had planned it. Local educational needs surveys were conducted by the county extension directors and often resulted in requests for short courses, seminars, or workshops from colleges other than agriculture or home economics. These included such varied topics as physical fitness programs for industry, supplied by the College of Arts and Sciences;

small business management, supplied by the College of Business; metrics workshop for elementary teachers, supplied by the College of Education; or earth-sheltered housing seminars, supplied by the College of Engineering. Two or more colleges would now cooperate routinely in supplying a specific need if, in fact, expertise from two or more faculties was warranted. As could be expected, some county extension directors welcomed the opportunity to enrich the educational programs offered through their offices and made use of the new organizational structure more than others.[8]

On May 9, 1969, the Oklahoma State University extension offices in all seventy-seven counties held simultaneous open houses. The concurrent scheduling was to take advantage of mass publicity throughout the state. The open house was to inform the public of the increased services they could expect through the county offices. President Kamm explained that the county offices would continue to develop strong programs in agriculture and home economics, but the new organization would allow them to serve a larger audience in a wider range of subject matter. In the same year, the first urban agent was placed in the field to address urban problems relating to education, housing, low income, transportation, local government, and economics. Jerry O. Schreiner, who had been assistant director of Arts and Sciences Extension, became the first urban agent and was assigned to the Tulsa area.[9]

Robert Fite, director of Arts and Sciences Extension, continued several extension activities abroad. In 1966 he was invited to Uruguay on a Fulbright fellowship to lecture on extension activities in the OSU

In 1968, Jerry Crockett (*left*) became director of Arts and Sciences Extension. Offering a wide variety of courses, the College of Arts and Sciences strived to meet the changing interests and needs of the public. And as these children in the Suzuki String Program indicate, no one is ever too young or too old to participate in extension.

College of Arts and Sciences. He visited a science project at the University of Sao Paulo, Brazil, for the National Science Foundation (NSF), and also the Science Materials Project in Central America which he directed for the U.S. Agency for International Development.[10] In the spring of 1967 he toured the Department of Defense schools for military dependents in the Pacific Theater of Operations where Arts and Sciences Extension was providing in-service education for teachers. Claude Jones, a traveling science teacher in 1959-60, remained on the faculty as assistant director of Arts and Sciences Extension. He kept the regular extension programs running and often was the one who responded to specific requests from county extension directors.

Fite continued to be involved in several federally-funded, local programs, including the Academic Year Institute and the Cooperative College School Science Program. He was granted a one-year leave of absence without pay in July 1967 to serve as program director of the Cooperative College School Science Program for the National Science Foundation in Washington.[11] Lavon Richardson, professor of microbiology, became acting director of Arts and Sciences Extension during Fite's leave.

Arts and Science Extension continued to sponsor the Oklahoma Junior Academy of Science program in cooperation with the Oklahoma Academy of Science. Richardson contracted with the Oak Ridge Associated Universities and the U.S. Atomic Energy Commission for OSU to sponsor "This Atomic World" in Oklahoma's high schools. The program was patterned after the Traveling Science Teacher Program, featuring lecture-demonstrations by a science teacher with special training in atomic science. It was presented on request as a public service at no charge to the receiving schools.[12]

While Richardson was acting director of extension, he was named co-director, with Kenneth Wiggins, of a newly formed Science Teaching Center at Oklahoma State University. Wiggins came to OSU in 1962 as associate professor of science education. He was named associate director of OSU's Research Foundation in 1967. His strong interest in aerospace education led to a proposal by OSU to direct a major educational project for the National Aeronautics and Space Administration (NASA). A contract was awarded to OSU in 1968 to conduct aerospace education programs in eight states on behalf of the NASA Johnson Space Center in Houston, Texas. Similar programs were administered by different universities for other NASA centers. The purpose of this effort was to bring NASA to the schools and the public in order to inform children and adults about the programs, results, and future activities planned in the fields of aeronautics research and space exploration. OSU aerospace education specialists traveled extensively to present dynamic visual programs in school auditoriums, cafeterias, gymnasiums, and anywhere else audiences, sometimes numbering in the thousands, gathered.

During 1968 NASA launched a number of preliminary Apollo missions that would lead to a manned landing on the moon in 1969. Public demand for educational programs was so great that NASA decided to coordinate regional efforts under one national contract. OSU's exemplary efforts in its regional program led to the awarding of a national contract to the university in 1969. For five years, OSU administered the Space Science Education Project and sent "spacemobiles" to all states in the union and to many foreign countries. OSU specialists gave programs to millions of school children and tens of thousands of teachers yearly. Teachers further received special, after-hour and summer, training programs to assist them in understanding aeronautics research and space exploration concepts and to provide them with "hands-on" experiences that could be translated into their classrooms. Through the project, OSU specialists appeared on thousands of television and radio programs and spoke to numerous civic and professional organizations. At the end of the five-year contract, OSU was underbid for the next contract award by California State University at Chico. OSU later regained the project in 1979.[13]

Fite returned to OSU in September 1968 to become a member of Dr. Evans' administrative staff. Jerry Crockett, a former professor of botany, returned from the University of Idaho where he was an associate dean to become director of Arts and Sciences Extension. He had worked with Fite on numerous programs when he was on campus previously and was familiar with the work of that office. Under his leadership several new programs were developed, particularly in the areas of the arts and in education for inmates of penal institutions. His new assistant director, Jerry Bayless, held a major in corrections and was active in developing programs for Oklahoma's incarcerated. Study abroad gained popularity under Crockett's leadership, particularly brief educational sojourns of one to three weeks, but also for periods of a year or more. Frances Dutreau, a Spanish instructor, was especially successful in organizing and conducting Spanish short courses in Mexico.[14]

In April 1970, William D. McElroy, head of the National Science Foundation, disclosed a grant to the Oklahoma Frontiers of Science Foundation to help Oklahoma develop a statewide policy for science planning. Fite coordinated the task force under this grant in cooperation with the Frontiers of Science Foundation of Oklahoma. In September 1970, he chaired a two-day Environmental Quality Conference at the request of Governor Dewey Bartlett for the specific purpose of developing environmental recommendations for the governor and the legislature. Fite was named co-chairman of the governing council of the Oklahoma Coalition for Clean Air in 1972 and pioneered a ban on smok-

Oklahoma State University has been involved with driver's education training since shortly after World War II. In the 1960s, the university responded to the national call for safety centers by creating the Southwest Center for Safety Education—the first such center in the region. In addition to having access to a driving range, classes can use driving simulators.

ing in public meetings for the coalition, a move not too popular at the time. One of the many problems referred to the University Extension office resulted in Fite's directing a $97,000 project for the Bureau of Narcotics and Dangerous Drugs to test a theory on how to cope with drug abusers. Richard Teague, a sociology professor, served as project leader and worked in 130 selected communities across the country. The project was known as "Operation Alternatives."[15]

A triumph for Dr. Fitzgerald in his final year before retirement was the receipt of a grant of $163,000 from the Federal Highway Administration for the construction of a driving instruction range near the north edge of the OSU campus. Its primary purpose was to train instructors of driver education. Milton D. Rhoads, director of the Southwest Center for Safety Education, was placed in charge of the new facility. Soon thereafter, the state legislature appropriated $75,000 to support the driver education program at OSU.[16]

Fitzgerald was pleased that Dr. Evans strongly advocated the use of audio-visual materials in teaching. The audio-visual department

During the Jean Evans' era at OSU, there was increased emphasis placed on the use of audio-visual equipment. Guy Pritchard (*left*), director of the audio-visual department, checks equipment with J. Conner Fitzgerald.

experienced phenomenal growth under Dr. Evans. Not only extension but also resident instruction benefited from an abundance of new audio and visual teaching aids. The first major increase came in 1966 when $120,000 of federal matching funds were channeled into new films, projectors, projection screens, lecterns, and other types of audio-visual equipment. When Dr. Evans wanted to communicate to a particular audience through his county extension directors, he would have the audio-visual department prepare a set of color slides to illustrate the message. After making the presentation to his extension directors, each director would be outfitted with a duplicate set of materials for use locally. Woodfin Harris, former director of an audio-visual center for the Oklahoma City schools, joined Guy Pritchard's staff in the audio-visual department in 1967 and later became its director when Pritchard retired. Gerald Knutson was employed as director of educational services when Fitzgerald retired.[17]

Richard Jungers was director of Education Extension throughout the Evans' era. He agreed with Evans' philosophy regarding extension—if a project had at least a 51 percent chance to succeed it should be attempted. Aided by the county extension directors in identifying educational needs among the state's school systems, Jungers sometimes had as many courses for credit in progress at one time as all of the other extension directors combined. He also served on many state school committees and was co-author of the new state-aid formula adopted by the legislature in 1969. A Community Education Center was established by the College of Education in 1974. W. D. "Deke" Johnson, professor of educational administration, was named director. Community education was a *concept* that a school system should be concerned with all things affecting the quality of life in a community, and it was also a *process* for the schools to become involved in programs to meet the needs of all segments of the community, including its adults.[18]

Soon after Dr. Evans came to OSU in 1965, he enlisted the services of George Abshier, an extension agricultural economist, to direct extension programs of an economic nature. One of the first was a work-study program to be financed by a $29,000 grant from the new, federally-sponsored Economic Opportunity Act. Abshier was named to Evans' administrative staff with the title of director of community and industry programs. OSU and Abshier's office became the focal point of political attention in the fall of 1971 when Minnesota senator and former vice president Hubert Humphrey conducted a Rural Development Subcommittee hearing in the Student Union Theater. The expressed purpose was to explore ways to improve the quality of life in rural areas.[19]

A Community Development Institute was approved by the OSU Board of Regents in 1972 "to provide aggressive leadership as people struggle to identify and solve problems that inhibit the growth of communities."[20] Abshier, who directed this project, announced that through his office a community could obtain the expertise of any department on campus to help solve its problems. No problem was too great or too small to be considered. Problems that were addressed in this manner included those resulting from the closing of a zinc smelter in Blackwell and the need for an ambulance service in Alfalfa County. At the same time the Community Development Institute was formed, the OSU Board of Regents authorized an Environmental Institute. Under the direction of Norman Durham, dean of the Graduate College, the Environmental Institute would help develop instructional, research, and extension programs in areas of environmental concerns.[21]

In 1972 J. O. Grantham joined Dr. Evans' administrative staff. Grantham had served on the engineering faculty at OSU prior to opting for a career in the business world. He spent time with the Phillips Petroleum Company and held several positions with the Northern Natural Gas Company, including vice president in charge of a subsidiary handling government grants for economic recovery. During his rapid ascension in the business world, Grantham had been an occasional guest lecturer for Engineering Extension's management institutes. After being caught in an economic squeeze within the Northern Natural Gas Company and in an unsuccessful campaign for the U.S. Congress from the state of Minnesota, he returned to his alma mater seeking employment.

Dr. Evans hired Grantham to be his grants and contracts officer and hoped that Grantham could obtain additional federal and state grants or contracts for extension programs at Oklahoma State University. One of Grantham's successes led to a four-year grant from the U.S. Department of Labor through the Oklahoma Indian Affairs Commission to provide special training for Indians. This program, which was directed by John Shearer, developed leaders and manpower specialists among the Indian participants. Another was a preliminary grant from the National Science Foundation to test the ability of the Cooperative Extension Service in Oklahoma to transfer nonagricultural environmental technology to state and local governmental officials.[22]

According to Clayton Millington, director of Business Extension, economic education had been practically nonexistent in Oklahoma's elementary school curriculum prior to 1954, the year the Oklahoma Council on Economic Education (OCEE) was organized. Soon after Millington became executive director of OCEE in 1960, he also was named director of Business Extension.

In addition to sponsoring the usual extension short courses and seminars for business, Millington developed several innovative programs and delivery systems for economic education. A popular program for Oklahoma's elementary schools was the Developmental Economic Education Program (DEEP) which started in the Tulsa schools in 1964. Other schools such as Bartlesville, Ponca City, Oklahoma City, and McAlester joined the program, which led to a significant strengthening of economics in the curriculum of all of Oklahoma's elementary schools over the next several years. Millington obtained Cooperative College School Science and summer institute grants from the National Science Foundation to help teachers adapt these new materials to their teaching routines. Director Millington was invited to serve on the National Science Foundation staff in Washington during 1971-72. Business Extension also played a major role in the community development programs directed by George Abshier. Graduate students in the College of Business served as field consultants to small business entrepreneurs while under the direct supervision of business professors on campus.

Often Dean Eugene Swearingen of the College of Business made the initial contacts for national conferences, such as Mid America Assembly's "The United States and the Middle East," which would then be coordinated by Business Extension. Swearingen's successor, Richard W. Poole, was responsible for bringing the national conference "Rural and Urban Population Shift" to campus. The hundreds of participants overwhelmed the seating capacity of the Student Union Theater, as well as the accommodations of Stillwater motels. Lodging was arranged in

Vice President for Extension Jean Evans (*left*) listens intently as U.S. Secretary for Agriculture Orville L. Freeman addresses a national manpower conference in the OSU Student Union. George Abshier, director of community and industry programs, is in the background.

neighboring towns by Millington, and buses were chartered to transport participants to and from the meetings.[23]

Millington resigned as director of Business Extension in the fall of 1974 so he could devote full-time to economics education. Earlier he had been named vice president of the Oklahoma Council on Economic Education. B. Curtis Hamm, professor of marketing, succeeded Millington as director of Business Extension. Hamm, an OSU graduate with a doctorate from the University of Texas, had worked five years with International Business Machines before joining the OSU business faculty in 1966.[24]

Engineering Extension got a new director shortly after Dr. Evans became dean. When L. F. "Mike" Sheerar retired in 1966, Monroe W. Kriegel, who had been assistant director of Engineering Extension since 1964, was named director. Among the several colleges, Engineering Extension was probably the least affected by the reorganization. The Engineering Extension audience was primarily professional engineers located in a few industrialized cities in Oklahoma and in comparable cities throughout the nation and the world. Graduate courses for credit were offered off campus only in Bartlesville, Ponca City, Tulsa, and Oklahoma City. At these four centers practicing engineers could fulfill one-half of the requirements for a master's degree before coming to the campus for residence work. No undergraduate courses for credit were offered by Engineering Extension. Other extension activities centered around conferences and seminars, usually held on campus, to inform participants of the latest technical developments in the various fields. Some of these annual programs involved electromagnetic relays, soil mechanics, industrial management, heating and air conditioning, and water quality and pollution control. Highly regarded by professional engineers, these programs attracted participants from across the United States and many foreign countries. The thrust most prevalent throughout the years was to keep professionals updated to avoid technical obsolescence.[25]

Kriegel also administered extension programs associated with the OSU School of Technology. A two-year program of the engineering college, this school was designed to provide technicians for industry. Many of the extension-type programs had continued for years. Fire service training for Oklahoma's firemen under the supervision of Harold R. Mace was probably the most notable. A highly successful technology program was specially designed for employees of the Oklahoma Department of Highways. Another was designed to train aircraft mechanics and was offered on military bases throughout Oklahoma, Texas, and Arkansas. These technical extension programs grew rapidly after Bill Cooper became supervisor of the School of Technology extension service in 1970.[26]

Extension and outreach from the College of Home Economics expanded during the Evans' years. The usual programs such as OSU Days for Women and OSU Home Economics Day were continued. More organized courses were sponsored off campus for both professionals and nonprofessionals in varied subjects such as nutrition, housing, clothing, family relations, school lunches, and hotel and restaurant management. These courses were supervised by Lora Cacy who had been appointed director of Home Economics University Extension (HEUE) in 1967. This marked the beginning of two extension programs in home economics. The traditional service through Cooperative Extension continued with a family home economist in each county working with rural families. The other service was inspired by Dr. Evans and was oriented and directed toward dissemination of knowledge from the Division of Home Economics to nonfarm audiences.

The Head Start Program was begun in 1966 with funds granted by the Office of Economic Opportunity. Head Start helped prepare underprivileged children in the four- and five-year age group for school so as to reduce the likelihood of failure. Thomas Cunningham, family life specialist, and Josephine Hoffer, head of the Department of Family Relations and Child Development, directed these programs.

In the late 1960s, a series of "firsts" occurred in OSU extension and outreach programs. Albert Malle (*left*) was appointed the first extension director for the College of Veterinary Medicine in 1966. Lora Cacy (*center*) became the first extension director of Home Economics University Extension in 1967. In 1969, Russell Conway (*right*) was named the first director of high school and college relations.

Grace L. Spivey directed the family living programs through Cooperative Extension. She was assisted by Irma Manning and Ladora Smith in an Expanded Food and Nutrition Education Program which came into existence in 1969 as a part of President Johnson's "Great Society." Spivey and staff trained 252 program aides from low income families who in turn taught other low income homemakers how to prepare nutritious meals and provide balanced diets for their families at minimum cost. Within five years, more than 15,000 low-income families in Oklahoma had been helped by the program.[27]

The most obvious users of extension from the College of Veterinary Medicine were the practicing veterinarians who faced the common problem of keeping abreast of the rapidly changing technology in the various fields and specialties. The extension office, under the direction of Albert L. Malle, had the responsibility of keeping the professionals professional. Film strips, sound tapes, and teleconferences were just some of the ways Veterinary Medicine Extension communicated with the veterinarians. But all the work was not with professionals. A farmer could request an analysis of the nutritional value of his hay crop and expect to receive a prompt reply regarding what feed supplements, if any, were needed to provide a suitable diet for his livestock. Animal breeders and animal feeders could expect rapt attention from the College of Veterinary Medicine regarding any outbreak of disease or other health problem.[28]

While Dr. Evans was busy reorganizing extension and proclaiming far and wide that "the state is our campus," several other activities were

Selecting a route for a tour of visits to Oklahoma high schools are Debbie Cavett and Dwight Helt. Offering information on all aspects of university life, these employees of the Office of High School and College Relations affirm: "OSU is number one!"

reaching out and attracting attention to the institution. President Kamm recruited Russell Conway to direct the Office of High School and College Relations in May 1969. Conway had been a field representative for the American Fidelity Insurance Company in charge of teacher enrollment and most recently had served as associate executive secretary of the Oklahoma Education Association. He knew Oklahoma schools from many perspectives, and he knew most teachers and school administrators. It was not surprising, therefore, that the high school and college relations office took on new significance under his direction. He and his staff contacted 14,000 to 16,000 high school seniors each year, telling them about OSU and what the institution offered. He kept up with the changes that might affect entering freshmen. He began to make regular contacts with the graduating classes of the state junior colleges and often served as an OSU liaison officer to the junior colleges. Within five years after Conway became director of high school and college relations, the OSU main campus exceeded 20,000 students and was recognized as the largest educational institution in the state.[29]

Ashley Alexander's Student Entertainers continued to gain fame and popularity. The military bases in Oklahoma City, Lawton, Altus, Clinton, and Enid were frequent clients. A second United Service Organizations (USO) tour in the fall of 1967 took Alexander and a troupe of seven women to Newfoundland, Labrador, Greenland, and Iceland, with a side trip to Europe. Because of the trip the seven enrolled only in a single course in photography during the fall semester. This may have caused some to wonder if this type of activity was proper for students, since the Student Entertainers supposedly existed to help students pay for their college education. Still a third USO tour was made to U.S. military bases in the Caribbean area during 1971. A wide range of student talents was used to entertain television audiences and to cut records which were sold under the Student Entertainers label. In 1973 Alexander reported more than three hundred students had received part-time jobs as Student Entertainers.[30]

The Flying Aggies of OSU celebrated their twenty-fifth anniversary in 1973 and had many achievements of which to boast. The club had been self-supporting all the while, albeit enjoying reduced plane rental rates from the OSU flying school. Started in 1948 by Hoyt Walkup, the club had been judged the outstanding flying club in twelve of those years, and each time received the Grover Loening Silver Cup for making the greatest contribution to collegiate flying. On six occasions the nation's most outstanding male student pilot was a Flying Aggie, and on four occasions the club claimed the outstanding female student pilot award.[31]

The Evans' era coincided with a national trend of student unrest. On many college campuses, students disrupted the normal functioning of the institution, usually in protest to research efforts that supported the war in Vietnam. OSU students also felt a need to get involved with the social unrest during this period, but thanks to OSU's administration, their energies were generally channeled into more constructive outlets. The OSU Student Association executive committee initiated a multifaceted educational effort called Stillwater Tutoring and Educational Project (STEP). It involved tutoring, group discovery, head start, day nursery care, and adult education. Because so many students volunteered their services in one or more of these areas, a clearinghouse became necessary in 1971 to coordinate the volunteer services. Karen Irey, assistant dean of women, served as advisor. The services were expanded in 1972 to include aid for Stillwater's elderly and participation in the newly formed Payne County Sheltered Workshop, an organization which provided training and employment opportunities for handicapped persons.[32]

Because OSU faculty members were already at work in Ethiopia, Pakistan, Costa Rica, Guatemala, Brazil, and Japan, the often repeated phrase, "the state is our campus," was now paraphrased to raise the question, "Is the world becoming our campus?" One of President Kamm's first official acts was the appointment of William S. Abbott in 1966 to be coordinator of international programs.[33]

Dr. Kamm was a strong advocate of OSU's involvement in interna-

"Is the World Becoming OSU's Campus?" Since the 1950s, OSU has been involved in many international programs. Ben Jackson, an agronomist, and two students examine some wheat in a research plot at the Imperial Ethiopian College of Agriculture and Mechanical Arts (*upper*). President Robert B. Kamm continued this international assistance during his administration. Three weeks after he visited Thailand, Thai officials were finalizing an agreement for technical aid. Shown from the left are: Sdradej Vissessurakarn, Bangkok education dean; President Kamm; Bhongs Sakdi Varasundharosoth, Thai education ministry; and Franklin Miller, U.S. Agency for International Development.

Oklahoma State University

tional projects to help underdeveloped countries. In the summer of 1967 he visited several of these sites, including those in Ethiopia and Pakistan. While in Bangkok, Thailand, he followed up efforts by Dean Helmer Sorenson and Maurice Roney of the College of Education and met with ministry of education officials regarding OSU's willingness to help with technical education in that country. Three weeks later Thai officials were in President Kamm's office to finalize a long-term working relationship which also involved OSU's School of Technical Training at Okmulgee. Dr. Kamm remained active in international projects throughout the term of his presidency. His international travels took him to forty-two different countries, most of which had OSU ties, either through outreach programs of technical assistance or through enrollment of students at Oklahoma State University. He served for many years as a member of the board of trustees of World Neighbors, Inc., an Oklahoma City-based self-help program, and was chairman of the board for two years.

In 1976 President Gerald R. Ford named Dr. Kamm as the United States representative to the executive board of the United Nations Educational, Scientific, and Cultural Organization (UNESCO) headquartered in Paris, France. During this assignment he was a member of the staff of the U.S. State Department with the rank of ambassador. He chaired the United States delegation to the UNESCO World Conference in Nairobi, Kenya, in 1977.[34]

In February 1969 OSU was honored by the Readers Digest Foundation with its Distinguished Service Award for outstanding educational work abroad. Later that same year Dr. Kamm accepted an invitation for OSU to affiliate with World Campus Afloat and designated Hugh F. Rouk as campus advisor.[35] It was also in 1969 that the Oklahoma State University Board of Regents approved a new position of vice president for university relations and development. The position was not filled, however, until 1972 when Richard W. Poole, dean of the College of Business Administration, was appointed.

The Evans' era was a time for experimentation in extension delivery systems. Technologies from atomic energy research and the space program were becoming available at a rapid pace, but no one could foresee exactly how everything would fit together. One of the early attempts to reduce travel for the instructor yet provide person-to-person contact between student and instructor was via the Victor Electrowriter Remote Blackboard (VERB). Two telephone lines permitted the projection of the instructor's voice and the image of his blackboard to a remote classroom site. The system allowed the students at the remote site to talk to the instructor. The Oklahoma State Regents for Higher Education (the coordinating board for all of Oklahoma higher education) soon favored the new system of talk-back television to VERB. Talk-back television

The Victor Electrowriter Remote Blackboard (VERB) permitted the projection of the instructor's voice and the image of his blackboard to a remote classroom site. Although talk-back television was soon favored over VERB, the system was a further example of the many benefits of technological breakthroughs that extension and outreach programs have enjoyed. Professor Daniel D. Lingelbach (*upper*) teaches an electrical engineering course using VERB to a class (*lower*) at Phillips Petroleum Company in Bartlesville.

replaced the telephone lines with a microwave relay system which projected not only the chalkboard but also the instructor's image to the students. Originally intended primarily to serve industry, talk-back television was eventually expanded to reach all areas of the state, and its uses became numerous.[36]

The ability to originate and to telecast quality television programs from the OSU campus began with the creation of Educational Television Services in 1967. Marshall Allen was employed to head the department. Within a year there was experimentation with closed circuit television in teaching resident classes on campus. A preliminary survey by Robert Gumm of the University Computer Center showed that 800 students taking basic computer programming by closed circuit television did as well as those with a live lecturer. Thirty-seven percent of the students indicated a preference for the television lectures. Instructors in other departments soon tried the new media because it showed promise of stretching instructional budgets. The history department reported much success with television teaching, but the enthusiasm for closed circuit television instruction soon faded in 1974 when the department converted all of its televised courses back to live lectures.[37]

"Candid Campus" was another early experiment in communicating with television. It was begun in 1972 as a seventeen-program series to inform the public about higher education. Produced in the OSU television studio, it was aired over public television stations KETA-TV in Oklahoma City and KOED-TV in Tulsa. Several commercial television stations, observing the viewer interest and program quality, began showing the weekly feature as a public service. This encouragement caused "Candid Campus" to be extended indefinitely.[38]

The OSU extension program under Dr. Evans' leadership seemed highly successful. The entire April 1974 issue of the *OSU Outreach* magazine was devoted to OSU's extension story. Each program in each college was explained in detail. Based on the magazine articles some concluded that Cooperative Extension was only a small part of the total picture. Yet the extension budget that year totaled nearly $10.5 million of which about 81 percent was earmarked for Cooperative Extension, 15 percent for general university extension, and 4 percent for grants and contracts. Dr. Evans had the very difficult, if not impossible, task of integrating the extension programs but separately accounting for the funds. His job was further complicated because the 81 percent earmarked for Cooperative Extension came from many sources, each with its own accounting requirements. Federal funds made up 36 percent of the budget, state appropriations accounted for 30 percent, and each of the seventy-seven counties provided a portion which collectively amounted to 15 percent of the Cooperative Extension budget.

Notwithstanding the many success stories, there were those who thought agriculture was not receiving as much attention as it should in this extension mix. Although opposed by President Kamm and many others on campus, an ad hoc advisory committee to the OSU Board of Regents recommended on April 25, 1974, that the Cooperative Extension Service be separated administratively from University Extension and again placed back under the direct administration of the dean of agriculture.[39]

our campus the state is our campus the state is our
state is our campus the state is our campus the state
te is our campus the state is our ca
us the state is our campus the state
he state is our campus the state is o
ate **the state is our campus** the
pus the state is our campus the state
r campus the state is our campus the
he state is our campus the state is ou
us the state is our campus the state is
r campus the state is our campus t
our campus the state is our cam
r campus the state is o

It was Roy Tompkins who first voiced the concept, "The State is Our Campus," but it remained for Jean C. Evans to make the concept a reality. He often used this symbolic map to "sell" the concept to others.

Other clouds were gathering over the extension program. Sister colleges and universities in the state complained of OSU's aggressive nature in providing extension services. Various government agencies and sub-state planning districts also felt threatened by the projected image of University Extension being able to solve any problem.

In the fall of 1974 Dean of Agriculture James A. Whatley was scheduled to retire. It looked to the OSU Board of Regents to be an appropriate time to return Cooperative Extension to agriculture. A public announcement was made in October that the Cooperative Extension Service would be moved from the Office of the Vice President for Extension to the Division of Agriculture in order to "accent" agriculture-related extension. "We wanted to give the dean [of agriculture] a better image over all," Regent Ronald Ford said. The regents thought the state should look to the dean of agriculture for answers to agricultural problems and that extension was getting too far away from agriculture under the integrated system.[40]

Within days of the regents' startling announcement, Dr. Evans accepted an offer to become chancellor and vice provost of the University of Wisconsin's extension service, effective November 15, 1974. He said he was leaving OSU reluctantly, as he liked the institution and was proud of the extension organization he had led. He conceded, though, that he would be less than honest not to admit that the transfer of Cooperative Extension from his office contributed to his decision to leave.[41]

At its November 1974 meeting the OSU Board of Regents, upon President Kamm's recommendation, changed Dr. Poole's title from vice president for university relations and development to vice president for university relations, development, and extension. Marvin T. Edmison, assistant vice president for academic affairs and director of the Research Foundation, was named interim director of University Extension with responsibility for all of the institution's extension programs except

Cooperative Extension.[42] Dr. Poole named an advisory committee to help identify qualified persons for the position of University Extension director. He hoped to have a recommendation within two or three months.

Vice President Poole was ready at the January 1975 board meeting with a recommendation for a new director of extension. J. O. Grantham received the nod and was officially approved to become the new director of University Extension effective January 15, 1975.[43] Grantham's varied experiences in academic, business, and political pursuits proved to be excellent credentials for his new assignment. He had not always been treated kindly in his previous endeavors, but had shown phenomenal resilience in every instance to rebound with much enthusiasm and vigor.

Extension and outreach during the Evans' era of unification and coordination reached new heights at Oklahoma State University. Whether the programs were too successful to survive might not be the issue. Both Cooperative Extension and University Extension profited from the interchange of ideas. Although there were those who lamented the separation, others pointed with pride to the accomplishments and to the programs of cooperation that survived the separation. This era was a time of experimentation, of discovery of new methods. It was a period of learning for both Cooperative Extension and University Extension. Reorganization of what had been deemed a strong program was not an easy task; it remained for the administrators and staff of extension and outreach programs at Oklahoma State University not to falter but to regroup, redefine, and most importantly to continue to move forward.

Endnotes

1. *Stillwater NewsPress*, 18 July 1965, p. 1.

2. Oklahoma City *Daily Oklahoman*, 18 July 1965, p. 6A.

3. "Extension Services Reorganized by University Regents," *Oklahoma State Alumnus Magazine*, vol. 6, no. 7 (September-October 1965), p. 17.

4. *Daily Oklahoman*, 13 August 1965, p. 5, 9 October 1965, p. 10.

5. Oklahoma State University *Daily O'Collegian*, 15 September 1965, p. 1, 8 October 1965, p. 12.

6. J. C. Evans, "Extension is Expanding," *Oklahoma State Alumnus Magazine*, vol. 7, no. 7 (September-October 1966), pp. 26-27; *Stillwater NewsPress*, 5 February 1967, p. 10.

7. "Specialists Play Major Role in Ag Extension," *Oklahoma State University Outreach*, vol. 15, no. 4 (April 1974), pp. 26-27.

8. Mary L. Turner, "Changing Times are Challenge to Extension," *Oklahoma State University Outreach*, vol. 15, no. 4 (April 1974), pp. 28-29.

9. "Extension Centers Plan Open House," *Oklahoma State Alumnus Magazine*, vol. 10, no. 5 (May 1969), p. 5; *Daily O'Collegian*, 24 September 1969, p. 2.

10. *Daily O'Collegian*, 29 March 1966, p. 5.

11. *Daily O'Collegian*, 25 July 1967, p. 7.

12. *Daily O'Collegian*, 5 September 1972, p. 13.

13. *Daily O'Collegian*, 13 October 1967, p. 1, 2 October 1969, p. 1; Author interview with Kenneth Wiggins, 21 September 1987, Stillwater, Oklahoma.

14. "Extension Administrative Personnel Action," *Oklahoma State Alumnus Magazine*, vol. 9, no. 6 (June-July 1968), p. 19; *Daily O'Collegian*, 5 February 1969, p. 2, 4 July 1972, p. 1.

15. *Daily O'Collegian*, 29 January 1970, p. 12, 2 April 1970, p. 2, 22 September 1970, p. 1, 22 April 1972, p. 7, 13 April 1972, p. 11.

16. *Daily O'Collegian*, 9 October 1969, p. 1; *Daily Oklahoman*, 20 March 1970, p. 24.

17. *Daily O'Collegian*, 5 November 1966, p. 3, 4 March 1967, p. 7, 8 July 1969, p. 8; Author interview with J. Conner Fitzgerald, 28 January 1986, Stillwater, Oklahoma.

18. Author interview with Richard Jungers, 22 July 1986, Stillwater, Oklahoma; *Daily O'Collegian*, 20 November 1969, p. 8, 6 October 1974, p. 12.

19. *Daily O'Collegian*, 10 September 1971, p. 1.

20. *Daily O'Collegian*, 11 May 1972, p. 6.

21. "Extends a Helping Hand in Community Problems," *Oklahoma State University Outreach*, vol. 15, no. 4 (April 1974), pp. 10-11; *Daily O'Collegian*, 11 April 1972, p. 8.

22. Author interview with J. O. Grantham, 22 July 1986, Stillwater, Oklahoma; *Daily O'Collegian*, 23 July 1974, p. 3; J. C. Evans to M. Frank Hersman, Director, Office of Intergovernmental Science and Research Utilization, National Science Foundation, Washington, 7 March 1974, Personal Files of the Author.

23. *Daily O'Collegian*, 11 July 1969, p. 3, 8 June 1971, p. 7; "CBA Extension Covers Three Major Areas," *Oklahoma State University Outreach*, vol. 15, no. 4 (April 1974), pp. 30-31.

24. *Daily O'Collegian*, 20 October 1974, p. 7.

25. *Stillwater NewsPress*, 12 June 1966, p. 1; "Engineering Extension Programs are Varied," *Oklahoma State University Outreach*, vol. 15, no. 4 (April 1974), pp. 34-35; Monroe Kriegel, "Attacking Technical Obsolescence," *Chemical Engineering*, vol. 70, no. 9 (29 April 1963), pp. 134-138.

26. "Engineering Extension Programs are Varied," pp. 34-35.

27. *Daily O'Collegian*, 26 January 1966, p. 1, 10 June 1966, p. 1; "Helping with Family Living Needs," *Oklahoma State University Outreach*, vol. 15, no. 4 (April 1974), pp. 7-9.

28. "Veterinary Medicine's Role in Extension," *Oklahoma State University Outreach*, vol. 15, no. 4 (April 1974), p. 36.

29. *Daily O'Collegian*, 6 July 1972, p. 7; Author interview with Russell Conway, 28 September 1987, Stillwater, Oklahoma.

30. "Coeds Entertain Troops for USO," *Oklahoma State Alumnus Magazine*, vol. 9, no. 3 (March 1968), pp. 12-14; *Daily O'Collegian*, 18 September 1971, p. 2, 11 September 1973, p. 9.

31. "The Flying Aggies—Color Them Silver," *Oklahoma State University Outreach*, vol. 14, no. 7 (September-October 1973), pp. 18-19.

32. *Daily O'Collegian*, 26 September 1968, p. 1, 29 January 1972, p. 2, 3 March 1972, p. 9.

33. William S. Abbott, "Is the World Becoming Our Campus?" *Oklahoma State Alumnus Magazine*, vol. 7, no. 7 (September-October 1966), pp. 44-46.

34. Author interview with Robert B. Kamm, 28 March 1988, Stillwater, Oklahoma.

35. *Daily O'Collegian*, 20 February 1969, p. 1, 21 March 1969, p. 2.

36. "Extension Teaching by Long Distance Hookup," *Oklahoma State Alumnus Magazine*, vol. 9, no. 5 (May 1968), p. 30; *Daily O'Collegian*, 15 May 1970, p. 8.

37. *Daily O'Collegian*, 13 June 1967, p. 7, 11 October 1968, p. 3, 7 December 1972, p. 3.

38. Bill Ellis, "'Candid Campus' Educational Series," *Oklahoma State University Outreach*, vol. 14, no. 8 (November 1973), pp. 6-7.

39. The entire *Oklahoma State University Outreach*, vol. 15, no. 4 (April 1974) concerned extension at OSU. Jean C. Evans, "University Extension Covers Wide Range of Activities," *Oklahoma State University Outreach*, vol. 15, no. 4 (April 1974), pp. 4-6; Minutes (as amended), Board of Regents for the Oklahoma Agricultural and Mechanical Colleges, 3-4 May 1974, Special Collections, Edmon Low Library, Oklahoma State University, Stillwater, Oklahoma. See Minutes, Board of Regents for the Oklahoma Agricultural and Mechanical Colleges, 4-5 April 1975, pp. 38-39 for verbage of amendment.

40. *Daily O'Collegian*, 26 October 1974, p. 1.

41. *Stillwater NewsPress*, 7 October 1974, p. 3; *Daily O'Collegian*, 11 October 1974, p. 1.

42. *Daily O'Collegian*, 19 November 1974, p. 5.

43. *Stillwater NewsPress*, 12 January 1975, p. 3.

7 Horizons Pushed to the Sky 1975-1988

The reorganizational tasks facing University Extension Director J. O. Grantham and Vice President Richard W. Poole were magnified by the successes of the system that had just been abandoned. The college extension directors, in general, had been pleased with the integrated system under Jean Evans' leadership. Yet, there was no time to dwell on the past. Existing extension and outreach programs needed to be maintained and new activities proposed and developed.[1]

Discussions began immediately between Director Grantham and Frank Baker, new dean of agriculture and director of Cooperative Extension Service, as to how the two services would interface in the future. Various memoranda of understanding were negotiated and signed regarding responsibilities, financial obligations, and the sharing of personnel. These negotiations set the stage for President Robert B. Kamm to make the following recommendations at the April 4-5, 1975, meeting of the board of regents. These recommendations were adopted and became policy:

"The county extension office will continue to be the door to Oklahoma State University for the public in each county. All employees of Cooperative Extension and University Extension will be so informed by the Directors of Cooperative Extension and University Extension and the

President of Oklahoma State University. Furthermore, there is a public relations function to be performed by county extension offices. The President of OSU and the Directors of Cooperative Extension and University Extension consider the effective conduct of this public relations function to be a high priority. Serving as a contact point and information center for Oklahoma State University will be a part of the role of the county extension offices. This includes being a contact point on workshops and short courses even though the subject matter and conduct of the course are outside of the area of responsibility for the Cooperative Extension Service. It is understood that costs incurred in special arrangements for work outside the Cooperative Extension responsibility will be considered in budgetary relationships with University Extension.

"In counties or areas where the University Extension program activity justifies it, county directors or other county or area personnel can have joint appointments between University Extension and Cooperative Extension. The number of such appointments and the percentage of time involved in each will be determined by need as assessed by the two directors and in keeping with the guidelines established by the OSU Board of Regents at their May 3-4, 1974, meeting.

"The District Directors can be joint appointees between University Extension and Cooperative Extension and administration of field programs involving the field staff will be through these District Directors. Variations in this administrative procedure for specified field personnel (such as urban agents who are full-time employees of University Extension) can be developed through memorandums of understanding between the Directors of University Extension and Cooperative Extension.

"All surveys, mass communications, or general large scale contacts with county extension offices must have prior approval from the Director of Cooperative Extension.

"There will be an annual review of activity and accomplishments to indicate necessary adjustments."[2]

While negotiations between University Extension and Cooperative Extension Service which led to the above policy were in progress, Vice President Poole was helping to reestablish University Extension as a separate administrative unit. On March 7, 1975, he addressed a special meeting attended by George Gries, dean of the College of Arts and Sciences; Vergil Miller, dean of the College of Business Administration; Donald Robinson, dean of the College of Education; Jerry Crockett, director of Arts and Sciences Extension; B. Curtis Hamm, director of Business Extension; Richard Jungers, director of Education Extension; Monroe Kriegel, director of Engineering Extension; and Grantham. First he emphasized the policy statement on relationships with Cooperative Extension which soon would be presented for regents' approval. Next, the manner in which the University Extension Council was to function was given high priority. The college extension directors were charged to participate with candid and open minds, to keep their respective deans fully informed, and to be responsible for providing input from the deans to the council.

Thirdly, Dr. Poole reemphasized the role of the urban agent and how he expected the person in this position to function as a University Extension employee who would be stationed in an urban center and be dependent in some measure on Cooperative Extension for logistic support. Fourthly, a time schedule was established for the accomplishment of certain objectives, such as budgets and reports. Finally, Dr. Poole emphasized the importance of being fully accountable. He charged each dean and director to use a quote from *The Future Executive* by Harland Cleveland as a guide in his or her day-to-day extension management activities. "If this action is held up to public scrutiny, will I still feel it is what I should have done, and how I should have done it."[3]

Robert Fite was in a position to appreciate the expedient and efficient negotiations of Vice President Poole and Mr. Grantham. As a member of Evans' administrative staff, he had been director of programs for professionals, and as such was the director of a federally-funded, multi-

CENTER FOR LOCAL GOVERNMENT TECHNOLOGY

Members of the Center for Local Government Technology oversee a geotextile application to a dirt road. A project of the Federal Highway Administration and a county government in northeastern Oklahoma, this "fabric procedure" allows roads which tend to hold water to become passable in a short time.

year project designed to demonstrate the ability of Cooperative Extension to transfer nonagricultural, environmental technology to state and local officials. Its thesis contended that the desired informational transfer could be accomplished by the Cooperative Extension field staff at least as effectively and probably more economically than by any alternate system. The project thrived under the new administrative regime, even though Fite was a part of University Extension while the system being tested was Cooperative Extension. In a 1978 report to the U.S. Environmental Protection Agency, Fite praised the state Cooperative Extension office for its reassurances to the disseminators in the field, thus strengthening their confidence in the job they were doing.[4] Fite phased out several grants and contracts to coincide with his retirement from University Extension at the end of December 1980.

Another evidence of need for specialized technology transfer was demonstrated by the success of the Center for Local Government Technology (CLGT), developed by Engineering Extension in 1974. James E. Shamblin became its director and guided its efforts toward supplying technical information to county and local governments in Oklahoma. He observed that county and small municipal governments often did not have access to technical information needed to solve their problems, such as road maintenance, bridge building, and police deployment. The College of Engineering through the CLGT made these technical resources available to Oklahoma's county and municipal governments at minimal

As OSU approaches its Centennial birthday, the Flying Aggies continue to soar and bring national recognition to the campus.

Centennial Histories Series

costs. By 1987, the CLGT was employing nine full-time professionals to supply these needs.[5]

It has been observed that "the more things change the more they remain the same." It might be added that some do and some do not. The Flying Aggies continued into the tenth decade of OSU history as newsmakers and award winners. In the thirty years prior to 1986, OSU's Flying Aggies were recognized nineteen times by the National Intercollegiate Flying Association as the top aviation club in America. In contrast, the OSU Student Entertainers gradually faded into oblivion after the retirement of Ashley Alexander in the late 1970s. Other people attempted to provide the leadership for this once dynamic organization, but without much success.[6]

The Audio-Visual Center continued to grow, offering more than 4,500 films and 2,700 albums. It provided graphic arts, photographic, and sound recording services to the various academic units on campus. The center moved from the university library to new quarters in the north wing of refurbished Cordell Hall in April 1987. When Woodfin Harris retired as director of the center effective October 1, 1986, he was replaced by Ron Payne. Payne, a native Oklahoman with a doctorate from OSU, had several years' experience as manager of OSU's Audio-Visual Center.[7]

John Jobe, professor of mathematics, was named interim coordinator of the correspondence study department upon the retirement of Gladys McGaugh in April 1975. He had been actively providing mathematics correspondence study courses and was now charged with supervising a massive updating and revision of existing courses in the department. The plan involved a new concept for the department. Resident students who had scheduling difficulties for a particular course, or those who merely liked the freedom of independent study, could enroll in a course through this department and complete the assignments at their own pace. The name of the department was changed to Independent and Correspondence Study (I&CS). The new concept was implemented in the spring semester of 1977. Peggy Gardner was named director of I&CS effective July 1, 1977. Two years later Phyllis Luebke was named assistant director. Luebke became associate director in 1984. When Peggy Gardner resigned in 1981 to accept a position as director of continuing education for a hospital in Wichita, Kansas, she was replaced as director by Charles E. Feasley from West Virginia.[8]

The I&CS department won national awards for its innovative courses in 1978 and 1979. Enrollments doubled to include more than 3,500 students annually, about half of whom were from the Stillwater campus. I&CS remained dedicated to serving students on an individual basis. It allowed one stop shopping for the student by providing the required text materials along with the enrollment credentials from its office in the Classroom Building. In 1987 OSU became one of seventeen univer-

OSU's Independent and Correspondence Study has continued to offer innovative courses. After the university became a member of the Electronic University Network, students could receive and send correspondence courses via their personal computers. From 1977 to 1981 Peggy Gardner served as director of Independent and Correspondence Study. She was succeeded by Charles Feasley.

sities to join American Telephone and Telegraph in an experimental Electronic University Network. In this program a course was downloaded to the student's personal computer by electronic mail. When the student completed the assignments, he or she uploaded the work to the master frame from which it was delivered to the supervising instructor for critique and grading. The student usually had the instructor's response within hours instead of days or weeks as was the case with regular correspondence courses. Feasley believed the university should offer an external degree program by correspondence study which would permit a student to fulfill all requirements for the degree without leaving his or her home community.[9]

In the turbulent 1960s when students across the land were engaging in civil disobedience in protest against authority, OSU students generally channelled their energies into more constructive projects. This trend continued into the 1980s when various campus groups and organizations engaged in philanthropy and other acts of service to the community. One of these outlets was known as University for Experience (UFE), sponsored by the Residence Halls Association. Persons with unique experiences were recruited to teach free, informal classes to anyone in the Stillwater community wishing to learn more about a particular topic.[10]

Robert B. Kamm stepped down as president of Oklahoma State University in 1977 and was succeeded by Lawrence L. Boger. When Kamm had come to the campus in 1958 as dean of the College of Arts and Sciences, the total university enrollment had been approximately 9,000 students; but in his final year as president, OSU, for the first time in its history, became the largest institution of higher education in Oklahoma. The fall enrollment in 1976 totaled 21,129 students.[11] Much of the credit for the increased enrollment was due to an active Alumni Association under the direction of Murl Rogers and to the Office of High School and College Relations under the leadership of Russell Conway. The euphoria of exceeding the University of Oklahoma in the numbers game lasted only briefly. In the early 1980s, OSU's enrollment began a gradual decline.

"Candid Campus" continued to thrive during the tenth decade of OSU's history. Begun in 1972 under the leadership of Vice President Poole, the program was sponsored by the Higher Education Alumni Council and the Oklahoma College Public Relations Association. It was produced on the OSU campus by the university's Educational Televi-

During a break from filming a segment of "Candid Campus," Marshall Allen (*left*) explains some of the equipment in the Educational Television Services Center to U. S. Chamber of Commerce President Richard L. Lesher (*center*) and Vice President Richard W. Poole (*right*).

sion Services. "Candid Campus" was unique in the 1980s as the only continually successful television series in the nation to deal with the various problems of higher education.[12]

The quality and quantity of programming for KOSU-FM, OSU's national public radio station, was greatly enhanced in February 1980, when a downlink satellite dish was activated to connect KOSU-FM to WESTAR 1 satellite. The event was considered significant enough to hold a public ceremony to commemorate the occasion. Speakers for the event were Larry Miller, manager of KOSU-FM; George Gries, dean of the College of Arts and Sciences; Harry Heath, director of the School of Journalism and Broadcasting; and President Boger.[13]

President Boger's interest in recent developments in electronic communications was further demonstrated by his appointing a campus-wide committee in the spring of 1980 to study the possibilities of an on-campus facility for using electronic media in the whole realm of continuing education. Dr. Boger had worked in a radio station for four years while he was in school at Purdue University. The committee included Grantham as chairman; Marshall Allen, director of Educational Television Services; Charles Bacon, head of the School of Electrical Engineering; Bill Halley, director of architectural services; Pat Hofler, assistant vice president for student services; William Segall, professor of curriculum and instruction; and Bill Taggart, associate director of Cooperative Extension. The committee planned its work in three phases: investigation, reporting, and final planning. By September 1980 the first phase was essentially completed. The committee concluded that such a facility was feasible and should be constructed. Cost estimates were vague, but estimated to be around $10 million.[14] Subsequent reports placed the price tag at more than $20 million.

In the meantime, Grantham had other responsibilities. He served as chairman of the OSU Energy Conservation Committee, which was charged with finding ways to cut energy costs. He also chaired the University Extension Council, which still struggled with the problems created by the reorganization of the extension services. He could not be unaware of the threat to the local economy if, indeed, the electronic age made off-campus learning more feasible. More than 50,000 people visited the campus annually to participate in short courses, conferences, and other types of extension activities. These visitors contributed significantly to Stillwater's economy. Grantham was assisted in his varied activities and responsibilities by Sharon Nivens, coordinator of OSU's many types of extension services, credit courses, conferences, workshops, and seminars.[15]

In 1981 an extension faculty award was initiated and presented at the president's annual faculty convocation in the fall. Its purpose was to recognize outstanding faculty service in extension. The first recipient of this honor and cash award was John Jobe, professor of mathematics. Subsequent extension faculty awards were made to Lee Manzer, associate professor of marketing, 1982; James Seals, professor of applied behavioral studies in education, 1983; Russell Dobson, professor of curriculum and instruction, 1984; Harjit Sandhu, professor of sociology, 1985; William Johnston, professor of housing, interior design, and consumer studies, 1986; Judith Dobson, professor of applied behavioral studies in education, 1987; and Larkin Warner, professor of economics, 1988. OSU's University Extension received recognition from the National University Continuing Education Association in 1984 for outstanding extension programs in home economics, arts and sciences, and engineering.[16]

Not one of the least problems facing Grantham during this period was the restriction being imposed on offering credit courses over the state through University Extension. Objections had been raised by other colleges in the state, including junior colleges, that OSU and OU were offering courses by extension in direct competition with their local resident offerings. E. T. Dunlap, chancellor of the Oklahoma State Regents for Higher Education, ruled that in the future all extension courses for credit had to have prior approval from the state regents each semester or summer term before being announced publicly. He established an advisory committee, called the Council on Educational Outreach, which was composed of one representative from each higher educational institution wishing to participate. This committee met periodically to consider the suggested offerings by extension and generally recommended denial of a proposed course if a single college raised an objection. The

OSU PUBLIC INFORMATION

Although Engineering Extension offered fewer extension courses for credit during the 1980s, total numbers of participants increased. When Monroe Kriegel (*left*) retired as director of Engineering Extension in 1978, he was succeeded by Dean E. Griffith (*center*). Since 1982, Bill Cooper (*right*) has served as director.

net effect was to deny OSU the "state is our campus" concept for credit courses, an idea which had been vigorously promoted by Vice President Evans. As a result, there was a gradual reduction in the number of courses being offered for credit by the various colleges over the next several years.[17]

Engineering Extension offered forty-seven extension courses for credit in 1977 and only nine such courses in 1986, although the total number of participants increased. The annual University Extension report for 1977 showed a total of 11,852 participants in Engineering Extension programs, while the report for 1986 indicated 17,685 took part. Monroe Kriegel retired as director of Engineering Extension in 1978 and was replaced by Dean E. Griffith. Griffith, a native of Nebraska, had come to OSU from the University of Texas Engineering Extension. In January of 1981 Griffith resigned and was replaced by Bill Cooper. Cooper was a native Oklahoman but had worked in the aircraft industry in Wichita, Kansas, and Marietta, Georgia, before joining the OSU staff in 1970 as coordinator of engineering technology programs. Under Cooper's leadership and during the acute energy shortage of the early 1980s, architecture extension got a big boost through its program on earth sheltered housing. A national teleconference was conducted for a thousand participants at thirty locations across the nation in March 1983. This national seminar was led by architecture professors James F. Knight and Walter Grondzik. In September 1987, a one-day teleconference was led by professor Jim Bose on research he had been doing on ground-coupled heat pumps. Twenty-eight thousand people at six hundred sites around the United States and Canada participated.[18]

Fire Service Training, coordinated by Harold Mace, continued to grow in stature and service. Firefighting manuals produced and updated on the OSU campus by editor Jerry Laughlin and a staff of eighteen were the official training manuals for fire departments in all fifty states, six U.S. government agencies, and forty foreign countries.

Another unique research, extension, and outreach resource of this period was the development of a remote sensing laboratory. The laboratory was first initiated by Stephen Walsh, a geographer, whose prior contacts, training, and experience equipped him to lead this endeavor. The laboratory was managed as a joint project between arts and sciences and engineering until Walsh left the campus for another job. It was then taken over administratively by the Department of Geology. Mark Gregory, who had served as an assistant under Walsh, became the resource coordinator and laboratory manager. The facility offered a program known as the Oklahoma Geographic Information Retrieval System which was of much interest to departments of state government, but it also had the capability of processing similar information from satellite photography on a worldwide basis.[19]

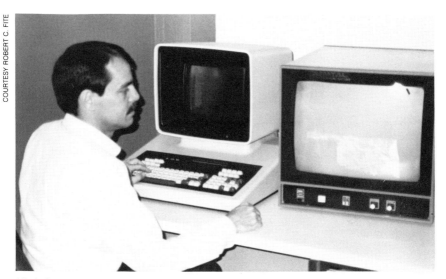

Mark Gregory manages the remote sensing laboratory through the Department of Geology. Images of the earth produced by remote sensing have applications in many areas including land use, conservation, minerals exploration, and military operations.

Extension in the College of Education was impacted severely by the restrictions imposed by the state regents. Courses for credit had been offered to teachers throughout the state whenever a sufficient number of enrollees became available to make a course feasible, but the Council on Educational Outreach changed all that. The number of credit courses in education dropped from 137 to 103 from 1981 to 1986, and this decrease would have been even greater except for recent legislation requiring all school teachers and administrators to have a certain amount of education in dealing with the "exceptional child." Tom Smith, who had succeeded Richard Jungers as director of Education Extension when Jungers retired July 1, 1979, observed that the concept of "the state is our campus" shrunk until it was more like "Payne County is our campus."[20] Smith had served twenty-two years in the Oklahoma City school system, including service as the superintendent of the Oklahoma City school system for three years just prior to coming to OSU.[21] Like other colleges, OSU's College of Education found alternative ways to serve its publics through noncredit activities. Among these were community education, education for the space age, and teleconferencing.

An initial grant from the Mott Foundation of Flint, Michigan, helped W. D. "Deke" Johnson to organize the Community Education Center at OSU in 1975. Subsequent support through the U.S. Office of Education caused the concept to grow and to become established as an integral part of many school systems in Oklahoma. The goals of the program were

Kenneth Wiggins, director of the Aerospace Education Services Project, confers with Barbara Morgan, the teacher-in-space designate, concerning lessons she will teach to the nation's school children from space.

to make maximum use of the community's school facilities to benefit not only the school children but also the other social groups living in the community. In keeping with these goals, the OSU Community Education Center held a conference in February 1987 to focus on helping local decision makers promote business at the local level rather than to wait for outside assistance. Featured speakers included Wes Watkins, U.S. Congressman from Oklahoma; Francis Tuttle, state director of vocational technical training; Robert McCormick, president of Stillwater National Bank; and Larkin Warner and Kent Olson, both professors of economics.[22]

The first contract with the National Aeronautics and Space Administration (NASA) to conduct a national spacemobile project was awarded to OSU in 1969. Kenneth Wiggins served as director. After five years the next contract was awarded to California State University at Chico, but in 1979 the multimillion-dollar program was returned to OSU, to be administered through the College of Education as the Aerospace Education Services Project. It continued to be funded and remained at OSU throughout the 1980s. The purpose of the project was to help interpret the developing technologies of the space program to the public.[23]

NASA is one of the few government agencies that deliberately makes its research information public in order that it might be put to use in the civilian sector almost immediately. OSU was privileged to be the disseminator of this valuable knowledge through lectures and demonstrations to teachers and students in all fifty states, as well as through audio-visual material and computer software development. A typical day for a lecturer began with a general school assembly at which models of the space shuttle and space suits were shown, followed by visits to various classes where space technologies were explained more fully.

By 1987 the Aerospace Education Services Project had been expanded to provide thirty professional lecturers in the field and a support staff of thirty to thirty-five people on the OSU campus and at regional NASA centers. At that time it was estimated the program had reached 53 million public school students and 300,000 teachers over the years!

The entire space program, including the OSU educational project, was shocked and saddened on January 28, 1986, by the explosion of the space shuttle *Challenger*. This tragedy took the lives of the entire crew, including Christa McAuliffe who had been selected and trained to be the first public school teacher in space. Wiggins and his staff had participated in designing the teacher selection criteria, in training McAuliffe and her backup, Barbara Morgan, and in preparing the lessons they would teach to the nation's school children from space.[24]

Another Education Extension project of the 1980s was the production and distribution of a periodical called *CHIME* (Clearinghouse of Information on Microcomputers and Education). Teachers often find their classrooms equipped with computer hardware for teaching purposes without adequate means to keep up with new developments in software. Recognizing this need, Education Extension began to publish *CHIME* in 1983 and in 1985 conducted a national teleconference on microcomputer software. Connie Lawry was managing editor of *CHIME*, which in 1987, according to Tom Smith, boasted an international list of subscribers. Smith was also proud of a new project called the Academic Bowl, which was coordinated by Deborah P. Allen. In the bowl, students from different high schools competed for academic honors by answering questions about specific subjects at a public forum. Thirty-two schools were involved in the competition in 1987, and the winner, Tulsa Washington, went on to place fourth in national competition. As is the custom in athletic tournaments, the top schools in 1988 will be assigned to different brackets in the 1989 competition.[25]

Part of Smith's energy was diverted from extension in the fall of 1982 when he was asked to coordinate OSU's courses being offered at the University Center at Tulsa (UCT). The Tulsa community wanted the state legislature to establish a free-standing, four-year state-supported college in that city. The issue was finally compromised by the passage of legislation in April 1982 which provided for the Oklahoma State Regents for Higher Education to establish a center in Tulsa similar to centers then functioning in Ardmore and Idabel. Wannette Pegues was employed to

Thomas Smith (*left*), director of Education Extension, confers with Dean of the College of Business Administration Robert Sandmeyer regarding OSU courses to be given at the University Center at Tulsa. Sandmeyer represented OSU on the committee that designed this cooperative venture for Tulsa while Smith coordinated the courses OSU offered at the center.

direct the center, which would open in the fall of 1982 in temporary quarters in downtown Tulsa. Dean Robert Sandmeyer of the College of Business Administration had represented OSU in the negotiations. Oklahoma legislators and OSU had opposed a free-standing, state-supported university in Tulsa on the premise that it would detract from OSU. At the same time OSU was already involved in programs to serve the educational needs of the Tulsa area.

Courses for the UCT, as provided by the law, were offered by the University of Oklahoma, Langston University, Northeastern Oklahoma State University, and OSU. It was decided by negotiation which school would offer which courses, but the student had the option of choosing the institution from which a degree might be granted. UCT enrolled 1,800 students the very first semester. By 1986 the enrollment had reached 2,760.[26]

Courses for credit through Business Extension became a complete casualty in the 1980s. The cause might be attributed partly to the creation of the University Center at Tulsa, but more particularly to restrictions imposed by the Council on Educational Outreach. In 1977 eighteen courses were conducted, but this number gradually dwindled to zero in 1986. Perhaps a third force contributed to the casualty. Business Extension had been hampered in offering extension courses for credit by rules imposed by its national accrediting agency, the American Assembly of Collegiate Schools of Business (AACSB). Also there was a general consensus among the resident faculty that participation in extension activities might provide supplemental income but would not assist in gaining promotions and salary increases. Although B. Curtis Hamm became director of Business Extension in the fall of 1974, Clayton Millington retained directorship of the Oklahoma Center for Economic Education (OCEE) until 1981, when he turned it over to Larkin Warner. Warner was succeeded as director of OCEE in 1983 by Kent Olson. Since 1987, Donald Bumpass has directed the program.[27]

Director Hamm discovered a growing market for Business Extension, particularly in the area of executive development, but also found a faculty reluctant to provide the desired services. A solution to this dilemma was offered by Penton Learning Systems, a New York firm that provided quality seminars in the name of cooperating educational institutions. While Penton provided the staff, did the promotion, and conducted the training, the local institution was responsible only for obtaining a meeting place and hosting the instructor when he came to town. After Hamm had successfully hosted several of these seminars in the name of Okla-

During 1974-1980, B. Curtis Hamm directed Business Extension. Professor Hamm (*right*) visits with James Hromas, then assistant director but later the successor to Hamm as director. During Hamm's tenure, courses for credit offered through Business Extension enjoyed continued popularity. Although hampered in a variety of ways in the 1980s, Business Extension personnel have sought new ways through teleconferencing to provide quality service to the public.

homa State University, the business faculty became concerned and even angry over outsiders teaching in the name of the university.[28] The Penton connection was soon discontinued, but the lasting effects were significant. The administration designed ways to ensure that academic control of Business Extension programs would rest with the deans and academic departments and that participating faculty would be recognized appropriately. The business faculty suddenly became excited about teaching in extension programs.

Director Hamm left Business Extension in 1980 to return to teaching and research. He was replaced as director by James Hromas. Hromas was a graduate of OSU, having received a bachelor's degree in accounting in 1967 and a master's degree in business administration in 1970. He had spent some time with Amoco in Tulsa and with the Johnson Spacecraft Center in Houston. Upon receiving his MBA degree he became assistant director of Business Extension under Millington and later served under Hamm as associate director. Hromas regretted the separation of University Extension from Cooperative Extension Service in 1974 for he had found the county staffs helpful in organizing Business Extension programs, especially in such population centers as Oklahoma City, Tulsa, Lawton, Enid, and Muskogee. He noted, however, that the Business Extension budget from appropriated funds doubled in the first two years after the separation. Mark Vincent was hired as program coordinator, and a short time later Mary Roberts was added to the professional staff. Programming tripled in three years. The Oklahoma economy was booming, and businesses everywhere were interested in more training for their employees.[29]

Although the demand for programs lessened with a weakened economy following the oil industry decline, Business Extension managed to maintain a strong extension effort which served some 10,000 registrants per year. This was made possible partly by more efficient operations, including computerized office management. Under the old system, a registrant's name and address was typed about seven times to produce the enrollment form, a participant list, name tag, record of deposit, and other necessary information; now the information was typed only once, and the computer did the rest. Another development was teleconferencing, both in originating programs locally for satellite distribution and by using quality programs from other members of the teleconferencing network.

Lora Cacy opted to return full-time to the classroom in 1975 rather than to devote more time to Home Economics University Extension (HEUE) as requested by Beverly Crabtree, the new dean of home economics. Dean Crabtree had been in home economics extension at the University of Missouri prior to coming to OSU. Beulah Hirschlein became the new HEUE director on September 1, 1975. Home economics was unique among the OSU colleges in that the college had programs in both University Extension and Cooperative Extension Service. Home economics was also unique in being able to continue expanding its courses for credit in spite of the close scrutiny by the Oklahoma State Regents for Higher Education Council on Educational Outreach. Sixteen extension courses were taught for credit in 1977, and the number increased to thirty-seven in 1986. Home economics received its share of challenges from the twenty-six other colleges in the state with home economics programs, but with the addition of a Ph.D. program in home economics in 1978, OSU had a unique advantage over the other colleges at the graduate level.[30]

To promote extension programs in HEUE further, various faculty members were designated to head centers for special interests within the college. William Johnson was named director of the Center for Consumer Services in 1976. This center has received recognition for its work in consumer affairs. In 1982, Dr. Hirschlein became the head of the Center for Community Services and Voluntarism; and Kathryn Greenwood directed the Center for Apparel Marketing and Merchandising (CAMM). These centers conducted programs both on and off the campus and also participated in the newest marketing technique of teleconferencing. The Center for Community Services focuses on enriching the quality of life through public service and sponsors workshops on volunteer management. CAMM offers workshops and consulting services to retailers to improve sales and merchandising techniques. CAMM received awards from the National University Continuing Education Association for creative programming in 1979 and 1980.[31]

In 1986 one teleconference was held in clothing and textiles and another in hotel and restaurant management. Six teleconferences were conducted in 1987. The first program was picked up by only twelve sites, but the last one was received at fifty sites, some of which were in Canada. The increasing participation and follow-up requests for tapes and information suggested that teleconferencing would prove both practical and profitable in reaching certain target audiences.

When Professor Johnson retired in February 1987, Margaret Weber became director of the Center for Consumer Services; and due to the retirement of Professor Greenwood at about the same time, Linda K. Good became director of the Center for Apparel Marketing and Merchandising. Legislative mandates were instrumental in promoting the programs of the centers and of home economics extension in general. One such law required certain improvements and staff training in the public schools, and subsequent legislation required additional training for people employed in residential care facilities. Dorothea Danel headed a program in staff development, and Michael Hopkins headed a program for residential care employees, both in response to new state legislation.

Beulah Hirschlein, director of Home Economics University Extension, displays some of the special features in the bedroom of the Independent Living Laboratory. Dubbed "Independence Hall," the facility has equipment as well as architectural features to allow the physically challenged to live on their own.

The home economics faculty was dedicated to HEUE as well as to research and resident instruction. Without this dedication, HEUE could not have conducted 502 extension programs in 1987 with a total enrollment of over 16,000 participants.[32]

Separation of Cooperative Extension Service from University Extension did not accomplish all that had been anticipated, although Cooperative Extension Service seemed none the worse for its marriage and annulment. It had weathered many storms, financial and otherwise, during its long history. Early in 1987, Cooperative Extension received a jolt when incoming Governor Henry Bellmon proposed, in the interest of economy, to transfer some of the Cooperative Extension programs to the forty-one vocational technical centers of the state. As in other challenges, this one was successfully defended, and Cooperative Extension remained a viable agricultural extension service. One of the most significant developments for the Cooperative Extension Service during the 1980s was the receipt of $870,000 from the Kellogg Foundation to enhance televised program capabilities from the College of Agriculture.[33] Although these facilities were designed primarily to benefit the Cooperative Extension Service, they represented an extension of the overall Educational Television Services and were available to the entire university community.

The College of Veterinary Medicine holds the distinction of being the first college to originate a teleconference via satellite from the OSU

In 1981, OSU's College of Veterinary Medicine not only became the first college of veterinary medicine in the world to offer a teleconference via satellite, but it was also the first college to host a teleconference on the Stillwater campus.

campus. Occurring on August 21, 1981, it was accomplished largely with borrowed and rented equipment. One of the objectives of the teleconference was to demonstrate the feasibility of teleconferencing before any large investments were made to purchase equipment for this purpose. This teleconference on surgical procedures and diagnostic techniques, beamed primarily to veterinarians, demonstrated conclusively that teleconferencing held great possibilities for effectively communicating technical information to selected audiences over great distances.[34]

Arts and Sciences Extension felt the full impact of the restrictions on credit courses imposed by the Oklahoma State Regents for Higher Education. The College of Arts and Sciences had traditionally been the largest and most diversified of the colleges and thus had offered the greatest number and variety of extension courses for credit. Its courses became the target of many challenges from the other educational institutions around the state. In 1978, Arts and Sciences Extension offered 143 courses with a total enrollment of 2,472 participants. In 1986 there were 47 courses with 906 enrollees. In contrast, participation in arts and sciences conferences and short courses went from 828 in 1978 to 9,600 in 1986.[35]

Jerry Crockett elected to return to full-time teaching and research in botany in the summer of 1977. Stanley Green succeeded him as director of Arts and Sciences Extension on July 1, 1977. Green arrived on the Stillwater campus in 1953 as an instructor of music and progressed through the academic ranks of assistant, associate, and full professor. In 1974 he accepted a part-time assignment in Arts and Sciences Extension. The following year, he was named coordinator of all off-campus programs in Arts and Sciences Extension. Very soon Green's influence was reflected in new and innovative extension programs, particularly in the arts. Among these innovations were annual tours to New York City to study the current Broadway plays and other cultural events.[36]

The OSU Filmathon, a brainchild of Peter Rollins, professor of English, was begun in 1974 and flourished as an annual cultural feature during this period. Each filmathon included the study of a variety of film-related topics and the screening of more than twenty movies. Usually a noted film writer or producer served as a guest consultant during the long filmathon weekend. Another series of programs, which focused on the handicapped, included sign language, wheelchair sports, cardiac rehabilitation, and speech pathology.[37]

Under Green's leadership, Arts and Sciences Extension built many study programs around tours which could be local, national, or international in scope. Geography professor Jerry Croft led tours covering the geography of the state of Oklahoma as well as the geography of Tulsa. Anthropologist Marjorie Schweitzer led a two-week study tour to explore the prehistoric ruins of the Anasazi Pueblos in Chaco Canyon, New Mexico, and the Mesa Verde National Park, Colorado. Art professor Richard Bivins led tours to major art galleries in Washington, D.C., and New York City. Some of the international tours included Mexico, led by language professor Frances Dutreau; London, led by theater professor Jerry Davis; and the Soviet Union, one trip led by language professor Dan Wells and another led by history professor Bernard Eissenstat. Harry Wohlert, a professor of German, helped introduce the International Cooperative Education (ICE) program to OSU in 1983. Twelve students who participated in the ICE program the first year gave glowing reports on their educational experiences in German homes during their normal summer vacation period.[38]

Elderhostel, an educational program for people over sixty years of age, owes its origin to a professor at the University of New Hampshire in 1975. It was introduced to Oklahoma through Arts and Sciences Extension by sociology professor Ed Arquitt in 1980. The program remained popular through the 1980s, and Arquitt continued as the coordinator for OSU and for the entire state of Oklahoma. Participants apply for admission and are selected on a national basis, which assures an interesting cultural mix at each program location. Registration, limited to a predetermined number based on the accommodations available, generally permitted forty-five people at OSU's elderhostels. Each participant

Stanley Green (*right*), director of Arts and Sciences Extension since 1977, discusses some of the finer points of extension teaching by satellite with Dean of the College of Arts and Sciences Smith Holt. Dean Holt believed that offering courses via telecommunications would not only improve a high school's curriculum but would be economically feasible as well.

took three courses during a one-week stay on campus while living in a college dormitory which otherwise would have been empty during school vacation periods.

Over the years a variety of courses have been offered. A partial list of elderhostel instructors at OSU included Ed Arquitt, of the sociology department; George Carney, of the geography department; Larry Perkins, of the sociology department; Joe Stout, of the history department; James Smallwood, of the history department; Jeff Moon, of the humanities department; A. B. Harrison, of the health and physical education department; Gerald Frank, of the music department; Donald Brown, of the sociology department; and Gary Simpson, of the finance department.[39]

George Gries was succeeded by Smith Holt as dean of the College of Arts and Sciences in 1980. Dean Holt earned his doctorate at Brown University and had accumulated a host of other academic credentials. Early in his tenure as dean, Dr. Holt recognized true professionalism in the quality of videotapes being produced for advertising by students under the direction of Paul Couey, professor of journalism and broadcasting.[40]

With the addition of uplink equipment on campus to permit broadcasting television programs via satellite in late 1983, Dean Holt began to envision a whole new realm of extension teaching via electronic media. In the Department of Foreign Languages, Harry Wohlert already

In the 1980s, the Arts and Sciences Teleconferencing Service was offering courses via satellite to high schools around the state and region. Soon the program drew national attention and recognition. Four professors who have pioneered teaching by satellite at OSU include (*from the left*) John Jobe, trigonometry; Harry Wohlert, German; Peter Shull, physics; and Jim Choike, calculus.

Sporting "German By Satellite" shirts, students from the Cleveland High School enjoy a visit to the OSU Telecommunications Center.

was experimenting with teaching German by telephone and computer programs to high school students at Beaver. A pilot class of "German by Satellite" was organized at Beaver and taught by Wohlert during the spring semester of 1985. It proved to be the next best thing to having a highly qualified German teacher on the Beaver school faculty and at considerably less cost. Within three years an Arts and Sciences Teleconferencing Service had developed which offered high school courses in German I, German II, physics, calculus, and trigonometry to all schools wishing to participate.

Dean Holt recognized that the curriculum of any school, large or small, could now be enriched by offering quality courses via satellite teleconferencing that would not otherwise be economically feasible. The only requirement of the subscribing school was that it provide its own television receiving dish. An 800 telephone number allowed the students in each subscriber school to talk directly with the instructional staff on the OSU campus. There were 172 schools subscribing to the service in January 1988. Of these, 108 were in Oklahoma, and the remaining 64 schools were scattered over 13 states from New York to Arizona and from Montana to Tennessee. Robert Spurrier introduced the College of Arts and Sciences to yet another teleconferencing technique in November 1983 when he hosted a four-hour teleconference on inexpensive justice in the small claims courts. This program was received by thirty member institutions of the new National University Teleconference Network (NUTN) and was the forerunner of dozens of arts and sciences teleconferences delivered to professionals and other special interest groups. Spurrier reported two teleconferences in the fall of 1984, and fifteen more were planned for 1985.[41]

On April 1, 1983, President Boger spoke at the dedication of a new 12,000-square-foot building to house the expanding Educational Television Services. He explained that this multimillion-dollar project was an investment in the future and "the future begins now." He told his audience that the new facility would be useful for the next forty years and suggested that the large, white, concave dish just outside the building, called a downlink, be viewed as a visible sign of the future. He concluded his remarks by observing that sometime in the future it might be feasible to add an uplink dish to transmit knowledge directly from OSU by satellite to all parts of the world. Very soon after the dedication ceremony, Dr. Boger asked Marshall Allen, director of the new center, to investigate the cost of an uplink facility. This was done by Allen's staff, and a $600,000 uplink dish was installed and ready for operation before Christmas of the same year (1983).[42]

Aided by dynamic extension programs in all of the colleges at OSU, a surge of teleconferencing activities followed. That surge continued to amplify through 1987. On September 21, 1988, U.S. Congressman Wes

Watkins announced that OSU had been awarded a $5.5 million federal grant to be used for programs, equipment, and training in satellite education. According to Watkins, "This award proves that OSU has the technical expertise to lead the nation in satellite education.[43]

The surge of OSU telecommunications by satellite was accentuated by the creation of NUTN, a consortium of more than 250 institutions of higher education in the United States bonded together by common interests in teleconferencing as a tool to market or to receive knowledge. NUTN began in July 1982, when representatives of sixty-six colleges and the Smithsonian Institution agreed to establish an experimental consortium on the OSU campus. Grantham was designated to direct the experiment, for it was he who had called for a conference earlier that year in Kansas City to explore the possibilities of such a network. Grantham recruited Marie Oberle to help plan and coordinate the project. She had recently completed her doctorate in higher education and adult continuing education at OSU and soon proved to be a natural for this assignment. Working through OSU's University Extension and taking advantage of the $7.5 million investment in Educational Television Services, NUTN soon became the largest and strongest higher education teleconferencing network in the country. OSU became its permanent home by mutual agreement of the membership on October 1, 1984. Oberle replaced Grantham as director of NUTN in October 1985, but

In the fall of 1982, OSU hosted the Second Governor's Conference on Health Care Cost Containment. Beamed via satellite to businessmen, physicians, insurance personnel, and others across the state, the teleconference was further proof of OSU's continuing role as a leader in telecommunications. Shown left to right are Marie Oberle, coordinator of the teleconference and later the director of the National University Teleconference Network; J. O. Grantham, director of University Extension; Ralph Rhoads, president of Blue Cross and Blue Shield of Oklahoma; Jim Bernstein, president of General Health, Incorporated; Dale Stratton, assistant director for Du Pont Employee Benefits; and C. J. Roberts, member of Oklahoma State Chamber of Commerce Action Committee.

Grantham continued to serve as chairman of the advisory board.[44]

NUTN is dedicated to administering "high touch to high tech." It makes possible the pulling together of the brightest and most resourceful minds within the member institutions in programming and marketing educational materials. Most of the teleconferences to date have been noncredit programs for professionals. When a member institution announces a desire to conduct a teleconference, the NUTN office goes to work immediately in notifying other institutions of the upcoming event and helping in the marketing procedure by identifying potential market groups. This preliminary work must be done in advance of the actual teleconference to permit participating institutions to market the program locally. Each institution has the option not to participate in the teleconference, but those that do commit pay a fee assessed by the originating institution to cover the cost of the teleconference. They in turn will charge a fee of the participants at their respective sites to recover the program fee and perhaps even show a profit. About sixty of NUTN's members have teleconference originating capabilities. The remaining members are primarily interested in receiving and marketing high quality programs produced by others.[45]

A major role of NUTN is to help its members market their educational products, but if a member institution does not choose to participate in a given teleconference, NUTN may sell the program to a nonmember institution in that geographical area for a higher fee. Under these rules the potential audience for a teleconference is astronomical. The 1987 World Food Day teleconference was received at more than 350 sites in all fifty states and Canada, with a total participation numbering in the tens of thousands.[46]

Although there was curtailment of some extension programs at Oklahoma State University, University Extension found new life under the leadership of Vice President Poole and Mr. Grantham. Continuing education remains a viable mission of the university and has inspired the various college directors of extension and outreach programs to use their talents to develop and implement new programs. With the massive technological breakthroughs, the means for extension seem almost unlimited. Now a state of the art educational television facility can access over thirty communications satellites positioned around the earth. A vast nationwide university telecommunications network has increased the popularity and ease of teleconferencing. No longer are areas of the country content to do without the benefits of new and innovative courses in education. It seems almost unfathomable that less than a century ago, faculty and staff of the Oklahoma A. and M. College took trains or drove cars over unimproved roads to bring the educational message to the people. Always, however, administrators and staff of the Oklahoma State University have strived to further the extension and outreach mission of the institution. For this progressive group of people, it has not been enough to rest on past accomplishments or to dwell on missed opportunities. Extension and outreach require continual renewal and uplifting. Yes, when it comes to extension and outreach at Oklahoma State University, truly the horizons have been pushed to the sky.

Endnotes

1. Author interview with Jerry Crockett, 27 September 1987, Stillwater, Oklahoma; Author interview with Richard Jungers, 22 July 1986, Stillwater, Oklahoma; Author interview with Monroe Kriegel, 24 July 1986, Stillwater, Oklahoma; Author interview with Al Malle, 27 September 1987, Stillwater, Oklahoma; Author interview with Lora Cacy, 14 October 1987, Stillwater, Oklahoma; Minutes, Board of Regents for the Oklahoma Agicultural and Mechanical Colleges, 3-4 May 1974, Special Collections, Edmon Low Library, Oklahoma State University, Stillwater, Oklahoma.

2. Minutes, Board of Regents for the Oklahoma Agricultural and Mechanical Colleges, 4-5 April 1975, pp. 37-38.

3. "Summary of Comments made by the Vice President for University Relations, Development and Extension at a meeting on March 7, 1975," and Personal Memorandum on University Extension, in Files of the Office of the Vice President for University Relations and Extension, Oklahoma State University.

4. J. C. Evans to Dr. M. Frank Hersman, Director of Intergovernmental Science and Research Utilization, National Science Foundation, Washington, D.C., 7 March 1974, Personal Files of the Author; Robert Fite, *The Transfer of Environmental Information via the Cooperative Extension Service. A Report to the U. S. Environmental Protection Agency* (Stillwater: Oklahoma State University, January 1978), Appendix G, p. 9.

5. Oklahoma State University *Daily O'Collegian*, 16 December 1975, p. 2; Author interview with Bill Cooper, 15 October 1987, Stillwater, Oklahoma.

6. *Daily O'Collegian*, 10 September 1986, p. 11, 15 September 1979, p. 6, 11 February 1983, p. 14.

7. *Daily O'Collegian*, 6 November 1980, p. 7, 15 October 1986, p. 1, 14 April 1987, p. 4.

8. Author interview with Gladys McGaugh, 24 January 1986, Stillwater, Oklahoma; *Daily O'Collegian*, 13 October 1976, p. 4; Author interview with Phyllis Luebke, 23 January 1986, Stillwater, Oklahoma; *Stillwater NewsPress*, 6 December 1981, p. 1D.

9. *Daily O'Collegian*, 15 June 1979, p. 3, 21 April 1987, p. 7; Author interview with Charles Feasley, 15 December 1987, Stillwater, Oklahoma.

10. *Daily O'Collegian*, 12 July 1979, p. 2.

11. *Daily O'Collegian*, 29 March 1978, pp. 1, 9, 28 March 1978, p. 1.

12. *Daily O'Collegian*, 4 April 1981, p. 12.

13. *Daily O'Collegian*, 15 February 1980, p. 3.

14. *Daily O'Collegian*, 11 September 1980, p. 1.

15. *Daily O'Collegian*, 10 November 1978, p. 1, 2 July 1982, p. 1, 4 November 1983, p. 16.

16. *Daily O'Collegian*, 25 August 1981, p. 3, 8 June 1984, p. 2.

17. Author interview with J. O. Grantham, 14 December 1987, Stillwater, Oklahoma; *Annual Reports, Oklahoma State University Extension, 1977-1986*, Files of the Office of University Extension, Oklahoma State University. E. T. Dunlap was a doctoral graduate of Oklahoma State University as noted in "Dunlap Appointed State Chancellor of Higher Education," *Oklahoma State Alumnus Magazine*, vol. 2, no. 2 (February 1961), p. 21.

18. *Stillwater NewsPress*, 25 June 1978, p. 5, 11 January 1981, p. 3A; *Daily O'Collegian*, 25 September 1984, p. 13; Cooper interview.

19. *Daily O'Collegian*, 13 October 1978, p. 11, 17 November 1982, p. 10. For more information on extension and outreach programs in the College of Engineering, Architecture and Technology, see James V. Parcher's *A History of the Oklahoma State University College of Engineering, Architecture and Technology*, another volume in the Centennial Histories Series.

20. Author interview with Tom Smith, 12 October 1987, Stillwater, Oklahoma.

21. *Daily O'Collegian*, 6 March 1979, p. 6.

22. *Daily O'Collegian*, 22 July 1975, p. 5, 8 July 1976, p. 2, 12 February 1987, p. 18.

23. Author interview with Kenneth Wiggins, 21 September 1987, Stillwater, Oklahoma; *Daily O'Collegian*, 2 April 1986, p. 5.

24. *Stillwater NewsPress*, 29 January 1986, p. 5.

25. *Daily O'Collegian*, 10 April 1985, p. 7; *Stillwater NewsPress*, 15 January 1988, p. 2.

26. *Stillwater NewsPress*, 11 April 1982, p. 13D; Oklahoma City *Daily Oklahoman*, 25 February 1982, p. 12; *Daily O'Collegian*, 27 August 1982, p. 1, 21 January 1986, p. 5.

27. *Annual Reports, Oklahoma State University Extension, 1977-1986*; Author interview with Jim Hromas, 13 October 1987, Stillwater, Oklahoma; *Daily O'Collegian*, 20 October 1974, p. 7.

28. William M. Kincaid, Jr. *A History of the Oklahoma State University College of Business Administration* (Stillwater: Oklahoma State University, 1987), pp. 147-148.

29. Hromas interview.

30. Cacy interview; *Annual Reports, Oklahoma State University Extension, 1977-1986*; Author interview with Beulah Hirschlein, 14 January 1988, Stillwater, Oklahoma.

31. *Daily O'Collegian*, 14 June 1977, p. 7; Lorene Keeler-Battles, *A History of the Oklahoma State University College of Home Economics* (Stillwater: Oklahoma State University, 1989), Chapter 12.

32. Hirschlein interview.

33. *Daily O'Collegian*, 3 February 1987, p. 7; Author interview with Marshall Allen, 15 December 1987, Stillwater, Oklahoma.

34. *Stillwater NewsPress*, 23 August 1981, p. 6A. For more information on extension and outreach programs in the College of Veterinary Medicine, see Eric I. Williams, *A History of the Oklahoma State University College of Veterinary Medicine*, another volume in the Centennial Histories Series.

35. *Annual Reports, Oklahoma State University Extension 1978-1986*.

36. *Daily O'Collegian*, 25 September 1975, p. 5, 16 December 1978, p. 5, 16 January 1979, p. 6, 1 November 1980, p. 12, 30 October 1981, p. 10.

37. *Daily O'Collegian*, 7 February 1979, p. 7, 11 January 1983, p. 2, 29 September 1981, p. 7, 7 February 1984, p. 5, 21 November 1985, p. 11.

38. *Daily O'Collegian*, 6 May 1982, p. 14, 17 March 1983, p. 10, 6 April 1977, p. 2, 21 January 1983, p. 3, 23 October 1985, p. 15, 5 December 1984, p. 20.

39. *Daily O'Collegian*, 26 June 1980, p. 1, 12 December 1985, p. 10, 22 April 1987, p. 4.

40. *Daily O'Collegian*, 1 July 1980, p. 1, 2 October 1980, p. 11.

41. *Daily O'Collegian*, 4 December 1984, p. 19, 15 November 1983, p. 15, 4 December 1984, p. 11, 1 January 1987, pp. 1, 6; Unpublished Materials from the Arts and Sciences Teleconferencing Service, Personal Files of the Author.

42. *Stillwater NewsPress*, 3 April 1983, p. 1D; *Daily O'Collegian*, 30 June 1983, p. 1; Allen interview.

43. *Daily Oklahoman*, 22 September 1988, p. 12.

44. Author interview with J. O. Grantham, 22 July 1986, Stillwater, Oklahoma; *NUTN Annual Report, 1986-87*, p. 4, Special Collections, Edmon Low Library; Author interview with Marie Oberle, 17 December 1987, Stillwater, Oklahoma.

45. Becky Duning, "Reaching Out With NUTN," *Teleconference Magazine*, vol. 6, no. 1 (January-February 1987), pp. 16-21.

46. E. Marie Oberle, "The National University Teleconference Network," *Teleconference Magazine*, vol. 5, no. 1 (January-February 1986), pp. 12-15; Oberle interview.

8 A New Dimension To OSU's Service Mission 1988

On April 19, 1988, the Oklahoma Legislature passed a bill transferring the Oklahoma College of Osteopathic Medicine and Surgery (OCOMS) to Oklahoma State University. The legislation passed the house of representatives 88-12. Only minutes later the senate approved the measure 44-0. Later that same day Governor Henry Bellmon signed the bill into law.[1] The merger of the institutions became effective July 1, 1988.

The OCOMS was unique in that it was the first free-standing, state-supported osteopathic college in the country. Established in 1972 to meet a need for physicians in rural Oklahoma, the OCOMS projected a philosophy which seemed in accord with the function of a land-grant university. Today, the institution is one of fifteen osteopathic colleges in the United States and one of three in the western part of the country.

The training of doctors in the science of medicine was not a new experience for OSU. Veterinary science became a part of the then Oklahoma A. and M. College curriculum as early as 1891. In addition to the College of Veterinary Medicine, OSU has had a strong academic program for students aspiring to become medical doctors. Also, OSU was already familiar with the educational scene in Tulsa through the Cooperative Extension Service, programs offered by University Extension, and

COLLEGE OF OSTEOPATHIC MEDICINE

The courtyard at the College of Osteopathic Medicine of Oklahoma State University features the statue *Affinity*, a gift of the auxiliary of the Oklahoma Osteopathic Association. It represents the goals of the profession to provide holistic health care and portrays the father, mother, and child in a spirit of strength and unity.

courses taught through the University Center at Tulsa.[2] The merger of OCOMS with OSU not only added "greater visibility and recognition" for the osteopathic college, it also "strengthened OSU's services to Oklahomans through added expertise in the health field."[3] To help understand the future of Oklahoma State University's newest college, a history not only of the college prior to its merger with OSU but also an understanding of the history of osteopathy is necessary.

Andrew Taylor Still (1828-1917), a licensed frontier physician, was the first individual to articulate and use osteopathic principles. The son of an itinerant Methodist minister who also was a licensed medical doctor (M.D.), Still moved with his family to the Missouri frontier in 1837 when he was only nine years old. He became interested in medicine, and with the help of his father as preceptor, became a licensed M.D. in 1854. When the Civil War broke out, Still enlisted on the Union side and saw action in Missouri and Kansas. Unscathed by the war itself, he returned home to experience tragedy in his own family. Three of his children were stricken by spinal meningitis and died. Still was inspired to begin questioning many of the medical remedies prescribed at this time.[4]

Perhaps it was Still's own questioning attitude or maybe the influence of other practitioners who were seeking cures outside of *materia medica*, but he began to abandon conventional medicine in favor of drugless substitutes. In 1874 he severed his ties to regular medicine in favor of "laying on of hands." Many of his friends and relatives questioned his sanity. His minister believed he was an agent of the devil and had him "read out" of the Methodist church.[5] Ostracized in his home town of Baldwin, Kansas, Still began touring the state as an itinerant healer, finally locating his family in Kirksville, Missouri, where he had had success in treating certain influential members of the community.

Kirksville did not possess a sufficient population base to support Still in his profession of healing so he continued to visit outlying communities periodically after distributing handbills and otherwise advertising his coming. During this time he developed a reputation for setting bones, thus enhancing his skills and success with manipulative therapy. He had an uncanny ability to choose some afflicted person from an impromptu audience for whom he could provide almost instant relief or even a cure for an obvious ailment. Visual evidence and raving testimonials helped Still develop a practice in these communities. In 1889 Still established an infirmary in Kirksville to facilitate his practice. He had become a charismatic figure. People, often whose cases had been pronounced hopeless by other physicians, came from far and wide. Still was able to cure enough of them to convince himself that he had discovered a new science of healing. He called his new science osteopathy.[6]

Osteopathy had been coined from two words, *osteo* (bone) and *pathy* (disease). Osteopathy literally means bone suffering. Osteopathic manipulation is a hands-on technique that uses palpation and manipulative procedures of the musculoskeletal system to diagnose illness and treat patients. Dr. Still philosophized that the human body is a machine run by the unseen force called life, and for the machine to run harmoniously each of its parts must be free to function properly. An obstruction in one part of the machine could cause symptoms of malfunction in a distant part. It was the task of the doctor of osteopathy (D.O.) to find the obstruction and remove it. The basic philosophy of osteopathy is that through the nervous and circulatory systems, the musculoskeletal system interacts with all body organs and systems in both health and disease.

Dr. Still decided it was time to tell others about his newly defined science so he opened the American School of Osteopathy in Kirksville in 1892. After a few months of instruction, students were awarded certificates stating they were diplomates in osteopathy, or D.O.s. Still was fortunate in attracting a few M.D.s to his program. Often in lieu of tuition, the M.D. would teach a class while learning as much as he could of Still's manipulative techniques.[7]

Graduates from Still's school in Kirksville began to move across the country in search of their own places to practice. They were influenced by many things, especially state laws, some of which were more friendly

Andrew Still (1828-1917) is recognized as the father of osteopathy. He was a licensed physician from Missouri during the Civil War and was often confronted by ailments which were not responsive to medical treatments of the day. Dr. Still's observations and manipulations of the musculoskeletal system to effect cures provided the foundation from which modern osteopathic medicine has developed.

to D.O.s than others. As a general rule the new osteopathic physician found one or more medical doctors already established in the community. The organized M.D. profession tried to limit or even exclude D.O.s from practicing in some states. Confrontations in the courts and legislative halls focused the need for the D.O.s to organize. A small group of alumni met at the American School of Osteopathy in Kirksville in 1897 and collectively formed the American Association for the Advancement of Osteopathy, which later became the American Osteopathic Association (AOA). During this same period, some of Still's graduates were establishing colleges of their own. In 1896 the Pacific School of Osteopathy was formed in Los Angeles, and the Northern Institute of Osteopathy was formed in Minneapolis. Additional schools followed in Boston, Philadelphia, San Francisco, Des Moines, Milwaukee, Chicago, Denver, and several other places.[8] The AOA needed also to standardize osteopathic training and reduce the competition that erupted among the many colleges.

The AOA ruled in 1899 that new members must be graduates of an approved college, and it established guidelines of proper conduct and curriculum. On-site surveys were initiated in 1903. All colleges were required to adopt a compulsory three-year course in 1905. A code of ethics in 1904 established standards for proper professional conduct among the D.O.s. Perhaps the most pressing issue facing the AOA during this period was the range of therapeutic modalities that should be used by D.O.s and the types of diseases they should treat. Two groups were competing for support of the majority of practitioners. While one group favored structural diagnosis and manipulative therapy without resort to drugs, the other envisioned the D.O.'s role as being a complete physician able to deal with any case whether it required manipulative therapy or materia medica in the treatment process.[9] The AOA chose the latter role.

The M.D.s, being larger in number and more firmly entrenched than D.O.s, were critical of osteopathic training and in general considered D.O.s incompetent as physicians. In 1937 only twenty-six states recognized D.O.s as equal to M.D.s as practicing physicians. This brought more pressure on the osteopathic profession to increase training standards in its colleges, thus causing many of the colleges to close their doors. The crowning blow to the osteopathic profession—a blessing in disguise—came with World War II. In general, D.O.s were exempt from the draft and were declared ineligible to volunteer for the military medical corps. As a result they found themselves caring for the civilian population whose M.D.s had been drafted into service. Existing hospitals, largely controlled by M.D.s, sometimes discriminated against D.O.s, thus giving reason to establish osteopathic hospitals across the country. There were 260 osteopathic hospitals operating in 1945, and these in turn provided training grounds for graduating seniors and permitted higher standards to be enforced.[10]

Having been unsuccessful in stopping the D.O.s in the courts or in the halls of the state legislatures, at least some M.D.s decided on a new tactic—absorption. More D.O.s were practicing in California than in any other state. It was estimated that in 1960 D.O.s constituted 10 percent of the practicing physicians in California and enjoyed 15 percent of the general practice. Negotiations between the California Medical Association and the California Osteopathic Association had continued for several years. Finally in 1961 the two organizations merged, and 2,000 D.O.s gave up their D.O. status to become instant M.D.s. Further, the College of Osteopathic Physicians and Surgeons became the California College of Medicine and in the future was to grant only M.D. degrees.[11]

The aftermath of the California merger was far-reaching. Although some believed that losing the strongest state in terms of practicing D.O.s would be followed by other states in succession until the osteopathic profession would no longer exist, the opposite occurred. Led by delegates from Michigan, the AOA strengthened its definition of osteopathy and at the same time helped to define more clearly the differences between osteopathy and allopathy (a term used to describe the practice of conventional medicine). Proponents of osteopathy argued that the events in California provided sufficient evidence that osteopathy was equal to allopathy. The AOA moved quickly and effectively to remove the last vestiges of discrimination against the D.O.s in the fields of insurance, service in the Armed Forces medical corps, use of hospitals for patient care, and in state licensing requirements. The last state to grant full licensure privileges for practicing D.O.s was Mississippi in 1973.[12]

Equity with M.D.s is not the only objective of D.O.s. They want also to maintain their identity. Where allopathic physicians tend to treat the disease of a patient, the osteopathic physician treats the patient as a whole person, recognizing that the musculoskeletal system interacts with all other systems of the body. Osteopathic physicians acknowledge and practice all phases of medicine and surgery as practiced by allopathic physicians, but they wish to maintain their separate identity in order to develop and perpetuate their unique system of manipulative therapy of the musculoskeletal system.[13] Another distinction may be the trend of M.D.s to specialize early in their careers while the very philosophy of D.O.s demands that they first become generalists, although they may specialize later. This characteristic has encouraged D.O.s to practice in smaller cities and towns where a complete range of specialists is unavailable.

In the late 1960s a crisis developed in Oklahoma in the field of health care, especially in rural communities. Entire counties often lacked a physician of any sort. Too many M.D.s were choosing to specialize in some narrow phase of medicine or surgery and not enough were selecting a general practice. The specialists tended to gravitate towards the population centers. At the same time the Tulsa County Medical Society asked the Oklahoma State Regents for Higher Education to consider establishing a medical college in the Tulsa area. The regents made a brief study, but pronounced the plan unfeasible. Not satisfied, the Tulsa County Medical Society pressed for a more in-depth study. Senator Finis Smith and others sponsored legislation through the state legislature which directed the state regents to supervise the new study of medical college needs in the Tulsa area. The Tulsa County Medical Society supported the study which was made by an out-of-state consulting firm. This study did not recommend a medical school in Tulsa, but did suggest that better use of Tulsa hospital facilities for student training by the University of Oklahoma College of Medicine would permit the college to increase the number of doctors trained in each class. The state regents responded by setting aside funds for developing such a plan, but the medical college was not happy with the plan and resisted taking any action toward its implementation.[14]

The legislators became impatient with the lack of action on the proposed plan to utilize the hospitals in Tulsa as clinical facilities. With the support of President Pro Tempore of the Senate Finis Smith and Speaker of the House of Representatives Rex Privett, new legislation was introduced in 1971 setting aside $25,000 for the Legislative Council to

This aerial view of the main campus of the College of Osteopathic Medicine shows its position relative to downtown Tulsa. Campus architecture features energy-saving devices including earthen berms around the ground floor. The Eleventh Street Bridge across the Arkansas River (in the upper left of the photo) connects the campus with the Oklahoma Osteopathic Hospital.

study the matter. The council would continue to examine the feasibility of a medical school or branch of a medical college in the Tulsa area but also consider the needs for a college of osteopathic medicine and surgery in the region. Ironically, both studies produced positive results. The Legislative Council reported back to the legislature that there was a definite need for more medical training in the Tulsa area to take advantage of the hospital facilities there and that there was also a need for an osteopathic college to provide doctors for rural areas in Oklahoma.[15]

Two bills were introduced in the Oklahoma Legislature in 1972. One provided for the establishment of a branch of the University of Oklahoma College of Medicine in Tulsa. The other, co-authored by Smith, James Hamilton, George Hargrave, Gene Howard, and Robert Medearis in the senate and William P. Willis and Mike Sullivan of the house of representatives, called for the establishment of a college of osteopathy in the Tulsa area to be known as the Oklahoma College of Osteopathic Medicine and Surgery. It further designated the Oklahoma State Regents for Higher Education to establish, maintain, and operate the college as a free-standing institution in the state system of higher education. The legislators were convinced the shortage of doctors in rural areas might best be solved by producing more osteopathic physicians and surgeons since, historically, they tended to locate in smaller communities than allopathic physicians and surgeons. Both bills were passed by the legislature and were signed into law by Governor David Hall on March 10, 1972. Steps were taken immediately by the University of Oklahoma College of Medicine and the state regents to implement the respective laws.[16]

Chancellor E. T. Dunlap apprised his board of the enacted legislation to establish a college of osteopathy on March 27, 1972. The state regents sought counsel from the American Osteopathic Association and requested the Oklahoma Osteopathic Association (OOA) to set up a local advisory committee. The committee was composed of Edward A. Felmlee, R. G. Gillson, Robert D. McCullough, James F. Routsong, Walter L. Wilson, Geron Meeks, LaMoyne Hickman, all osteopathic physicians, and Bob Jones, the executive director of the OOA. Within a year planning had progressed to the point of seeking a chief administrator for the institution. A national search was initiated with the help of the AOA. After several candidates were interviewed, John Barson (Ed.D., Wayne State University), who was the associate dean of the College of Osteopathic Medicine at Michigan State University, was appointed to the position of president on November 26, 1973.[17]

With the help of his advisory committee and governing board, President Barson was able to hire a faculty, recruit the first class of students, and develop a temporary home for OCOMS in time for classes to begin in the fall of 1974. A temporary facility at Ninth Street and Cincinnati Avenue in Tulsa was renovated to house the college. Recognizing the urgent need for a permanent home, a proposal for a grant of $4.5 million was prepared and submitted in April 1974 to the U.S. Public Health Service. This amount was granted in full and was supplemented by a state appropriation of $1.5 million to purchase a sixteen-acre site at the west end of the Eleventh Street Bridge, just across the Arkansas River from the Oklahoma Osteopathic Hospital.

The first class was made up of thirty-six students, only four of whom were from out-of-state. All had bachelor's or master's degrees with an overall grade point average of 3.1 on a 4.0 scale. Since urgency for new doctors was an underlying motivation for establishing the college, the curriculum was a three-year program which operated year-round on a trimester plan which in effect cut one year off the four-year program.[18] Thirty-four of the thirty-six students survived the rigors of the classroom, laboratory, and clinical experience and were graduated on August 14, 1977. They all subscribed to the Osteopathic Oath (given in part): ''I do hereby affirm my loyalty to the profession I am about to enter. I will be mindful always of my great responsibility to preserve the health and the life of my patients, to retain their confidence and respect both as a physician and a friend who will guard their secrets with scrupulous honor and fidelity, to perform faithfully my professional duties, to

136

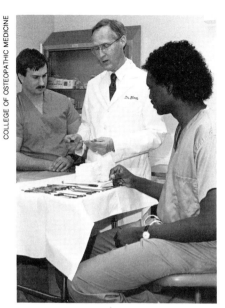
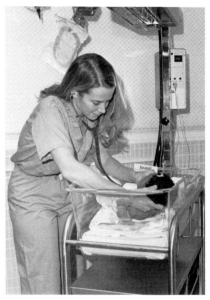

Students Charles A. Featherly and Harold Wagner, both graduates of the class of 1988, receive instruction from Warren E. Finn, associate professor of physiology. Anne Murphy, D.O., works in the nursery of the Oklahoma Osteopathic Hospital in Tulsa. The college has prepared Dr. Murphy for general practice. She has hopes of specialization later to become a pediatrician or neonatologist.

employ only those recognized methods of treatment consistent with good judgement and with my skill and ability, keeping in mind always nature's laws and the body's inherent capacity for recovery."[19]

Thirteen state and local officials turned out December 10, 1975, for groundbreaking ceremonies for the new campus of OCOMS on the west bank of the Arkansas River in Tulsa. Chancellor Dunlap said: "The State Regents are proud the school is in its second year and is establishing a permanent campus."[20] Although the campus was projected for completion in two years, the contractor took advantage of favorable weather and had the facility ready for occupancy during the Christmas holidays of 1976. Included in the 103,000 square foot campus complex is a 6-story laboratory-administration building, a 2-story education learning-resources center, and a 356-seat auditorium. Built during an acute energy crisis, the campus architecture boasts of energy-saving devices including earth-sheltered ground floors, special window placements, and an "energy wheel" to preheat or precool air before it enters the circulation system. In 1978 the three buildings were named in honor of the three stalwarts who had contributed so much in bringing the institution to fruition. The auditorium was named for Chancellor Dunlap in recognition of his guiding role. The clinical sciences building was named for

Edward A. Felmlee, D.O., a prominent Tulsa physician and one of the principal supporters in founding and developing the OCOMS. The administration building was named for President Barson.[21]

Clinical experience is important in training osteopathic physicians. Even before the establishment of OCOMS, osteopathic colleges in other states sent advanced students to Oklahoma for clinic experience under professional D.O.s. In September 1976 the college opened the first of several rural primary care clinics in Vici. These clinics not only provided students the necessary clinical training, they also encouraged students to set up their practices in rural areas. From the beginning, these clinics were established with the understanding that the host community could eventually control them. Thus, rural areas had an added incentive to support the endeavor. The clinics in Helena and Salina were later taken over by general practitioners.[22]

After a while, the rural clinic program was phased out in favor of a teaching clinic which was established in west Tulsa. The site of the clinic was in an area which had an indigent population that could be served, and it was in close proximity to the campus to facilitate student use and faculty supervision. This clinic, built at Twenty-third Street and Southwest Boulevard, was named for Senator Smith in recognition of his sponsoring legislation to establish the college in 1972. Now known as the College Clinic, it serves approximately 18,000 people a year. Four licensed physicians, including a full-time pediatrician, supervise students. While students are the primary care physicians for patients, all diagnoses and treatments are reviewed with the supervising staff physicians.[23]

In 1980 the Oklahoma Legislature passed a bill creating an independent governing board for the OCOMS. The OCOMS Board of Regents consisted of seven regents appointed by the governor and confirmed by the senate, with no more than two from any single profession or occupation. The board was instructed by the law to meet jointly with the state regents during the months of October, November, and December of 1980 in order to effect a smooth transition of governance of OCOMS. Appointed to this new governing board were Jeanne Smith Roush, retired nursing home owner-administrator; Leona Hagerman Limon, nursing home owner-administrator; Simon Parker, retired public school superintendent; Fannie Hill, director of a retired senior volunteer program; Barbara Walter, editor of a rural newspaper; Thomas J. Carlile, osteopathic physician; and Walter L. Wilson, osteopathic physician.[24]

The auxiliary to the Oklahoma Osteopathic Association chose Founders Day ceremonies on March 6, 1980, to present a seventeen-foot tall sculpture by Steve McGuire. It would grace the courtyard just outside the main entrance to the college. The sculpture, called *Affinity*, represents the goals of the profession—holistic health care and family

The Oklahoma College of Osteopathic Medicine and Surgery Board of Regents governed the college from January 1981 to July 1988. Pictured during a board meeting in the administrative office are (*from left*) Regents Leona H. Limon, Jeanne S. Roush, and Walter L. Wilson, D.O., and President John Barson, the college's first president.

medicine. It is symbolic of the family unit with father, mother, and child figures portraying strength, unity, and warmth.[25]

By 1981, the curriculum was expanded to a four-year program with summers off. Currently, the first year of study is designed to bring all students to desired levels of competence in the biomedical sciences and preliminary clinical knowledge. During the second year there is an emphasis on the interdisciplinary study of the structure and function of body systems. Students are introduced to osteopathic clinical care and medical procedures. There is a continuation of the interdisciplinary study and osteopathic principles and practices during the first half of the third year. Students spend their final sixteen months in major and community hospitals, clinics, and offices of private physicians where they observe patients on a daily basis under physician-faculty supervision. The student rotates through primary care services including general practice, surgery, obstetrics-gynecology, pediatrics, internal medicine, and emergency medicine.

Students graduate from the four-year program with a D.O. degree. Following graduation, students are required by the American Osteopathic Association to complete an approved one-year rotating internship. Those who wish to specialize enter a residency program following the internship. They are eligible to be licensed to practice as soon as they complete the internship. On July 1, 1988, the college began to administer a residency program in general practice—the college's first residency program in general practice. A $525,000 postdoctoral training grant, authored by L. D. Cherry, D. O., from the Health Resources and Services Administration of the Public Health Service funded the development and initiation of this residency program.

The college is divided into academic affairs and administrative services. Administrative services is in charge of all nonacademic areas, including the library, accounting and budgeting, campus facilities, personnel services, audio-visual services, and data processing.

Academic affairs administers all research and education-related programs. These areas include research, sponsored programs, and service; clinical education which generally covers the practice of medicine; preclinical education which encompasses the basic science courses; student affairs; and postdoctoral education which administers the internship and residency programs.

The institution has received national recognition for several programs over the years. From 1976 to 1982 Richard A. Wansley pioneered work in the area of neurological disorders, including new methodology in biofeedback treatment of epilepsy and other seizure disorders, as well as in headache and pain. Richard Bost continues the work as a clinical service in biofeedback. In 1985 the National Institutes of Health (NIH) awarded Michael H. Pollak a three-year grant to study cardiovascular response to stress. The project compared heart rate data collected in a controlled laboratory situation to data collected from subjects during a typical day. In the fall of 1988, the NIH funded another of Pollak's projects in which blood pressure will be compared from a controlled

Classrooms at the College of Osteopathic Medicine are equipped with state of the art electronic equipment and audio-visual aids to facilitate medical instruction.

situation to a typical environment. Also in the fall of 1988, J. C. Doggett received a $200,000 grant from the United States Department of Health and Human Services to develop a coalition of health professionals concerned with reducing risk factors associated with the onset of diabetes among the people of the Cherokee Indian tribe.

Through the years the osteopathic college has contracted with the Oklahoma Department of Mental Health on more than forty different community programs, including substance abuse and child abuse prevention. The college has also participated in talk-back television, funded by the Oklahoma State Regents for Higher Education and broadcast throughout the state. Physicians who watch the programs and complete the pre- and post-tests are eligible for continuing medical education credits. In remote and rural areas, this program is essential, providing health professionals with the opportunity to earn required credits for their profession. In addition, the college has initiated a videotape borrowing program in which participants can earn credits for continued licensure by viewing videos of seminars which were held earlier.

The College of Osteopathic Medicine also serves as the headquarters of the Oklahoma Area Health Education Center Program, a federally funded project that provides health care professionals and students with educational opportunities. A variety of programs are offered in geographically remote regions of the state or in medically underserved areas. The programs are regionally coordinated through community-based Area Health Education Centers: Rogers State College in Claremore (northeast), Carl Albert Junior College in Poteau (southeast), and Cameron University in Lawton (southwest). A center for the northwest part of the state is slated to open at the Enid Memorial Hospital.

As with any college or university, it is the student body which makes the institution grow and thrive. Students participate in a variety of organizations, including the Undergraduate American Academy of Osteopathy, the American College of General Practitioners-Undergraduate Chapter, Student Associate Auxiliary (for spouses of students), Delta Omega (sorority of women D.O.s), Christian Medical Society, Sigma Sigma Phi (honorary society), Student Osteopathic Medical Association, Society for the Advancement of Osteopathic Medicine, the Osteopathic Sports Medicine Society, Atlas Fraternity (social fraternity), Geriatric Medicine Club, Minority Student Organization, Inter-Club Council, and the Student Senate (student governing body). By 1988 the college had graduated 770 D.O.s. Sixty percent of these physicians practice in Oklahoma primarily in rural areas outside of Tulsa and Oklahoma counties.[26]

In September 1984 Dr. Barson submitted his resignation to the board, and Rodney Houlihan (Ph.D., University of California-Davis), who was vice president of research and development under Dr. Barson, was named acting president. He had come to OCOMS with Dr. Barson from Michigan State University in 1974 and had served as professor of physiology and as an administrator throughout the life of the college. Dr. Houlihan was named president in 1985 and served in this capacity for two years before his retirement on June 1, 1987.[27]

When newly-elected Governor Henry Bellmon took office in January 1987, he was faced with budget shortfalls of mammoth proportions. He offered ways to economize in state government, but in every case these suggestions were opposed by those who would be adversely affected. Not the least of Governor Bellmon's proposals was to close the Oklahoma College of Osteopathic Medicine and Surgery, the University Center at Tulsa, and the Tulsa Junior College. In their place would be a single four-year, tax-supported university which would take over the OCOMS campus. As might be expected, the strongest resistance came from those interested in the osteopathic college—that is the Oklahoma Osteopathic Association. Objections were raised throughout the state, especially from the rural communities where OCOMS-trained D.O.s had established practices. Within weeks it was obvious that there would be sufficient resistance in the legislature to kill the governor's proposal to close the osteopathic college.[28]

Talk of closing the Oklahoma College of Osteopathic Medicine and Surgery did not prevent Clyde B. Jensen (Ph.D., University of North Dakota) from applying for the job to become the college's third president. Dr. Jensen, a former member of the OCOMS teaching faculty, claims the distinction of giving the very first lecture ever at the college.

COLLEGE OF OSTEOPATHIC MEDICINE

Scott Orbison (*left*), member of the Oklahoma State Regents for Higher Education, and President Rodney T. Houlihan are all smiles at Dr. Houlihan's retirement reception. Dr. Houlihan was vice president of research and development under President John Barson and then served as president from September 1984 to June 1987.

He and the students contended with carpenters who were putting the finishing touches on the renovated building at Ninth and Cincinnati. Dr. Jensen had been named president of a new School of Osteopathic Medicine in West Virginia in 1981, six and one-half years after coming to OCOMS as assistant professor of pharmacology. At the time of his appointment in West Virginia he was only thirty-two, making him one of the youngest presidents of a medical school in the United States. Dr. Jensen's appointment as president of OCOMS was made official by the board of regents on April 7, 1987. He credited his former experience at OCOMS with his success in West Virginia, and by the same token was sure that his experience there would make him a better president of OCOMS.[29]

In early April 1988 Governor Bellmon persisted in his challenge to OCOMS by writing a letter to Avalon B. Reece, chairman of the Oklahoma State Regents for Higher Education, in which he made other suggestions. He proposed that there should be ways "of strengthening the cooperative relationships between the Oklahoma Osteopathic College and the Tulsa Medical College." He further charged the state regents to make a concrete proposal on future organizational arrangements for state-supported medical education. This proposal was requested by October 1, in time to seek legislative action during the next session of the legislature.[30] The tone of the letter seemed threatening to some 700

COLLEGE OF OSTEOPATHIC MEDICINE

On July 1, 1988, the Oklahoma College of Osteopathic Medicine and Surgery became the College of Osteopathic Medicine of Oklahoma State University. President Clyde B. Jensen and OSU mascot Pistol Pete celebrate the occasion by hoisting the OSU flag at the Tulsa campus practicing D.O.s in Oklahoma, especially those who could remember the California "merger" of 1961.[31]

Within one year after Jensen reported to his new duty assignment as president, the Oklahoma College of Osteopathic Medicine and Surgery was merged with Oklahoma State University. The measure effecting the change passed both houses of the legislature and was signed into law by the governor in a single day—April 19, 1988. According to Senate President Pro Tempore Robert Cullison who sponsored the legislation in the senate, it was Bob Jones, executive director of the Oklahoma Osteopathic Association, who suggested the merger. Speaker Jim Barker sponsored the bill in the house of representatives.

The action caught many by surprise and evoked criticism from some for having been rushed through the legislative process where speed is not the rule. Actually the merger was at least eight years in the making. Oklahoma State University has sought opportunities to increase its presence in Tulsa for many years. There was some discussion of a merger of OCOMS with OSU in 1980 when the Oklahoma State Regents for Higher Education wished to be relieved of the governing responsibility for OCOMS. Again in 1983, during troubled times for OCOMS, OSU President Lawrence L. Boger proposed that the two institutions would complement each other by joining forces. President Boger had come from Michigan State University where he had known both President Barson and Vice President Houlihan. A list of ways each institution would benefit was circulated among key members of the OOA, but enough of its members resisted the idea to cause no action to be taken. The list was preserved, however, and resubmitted without change to the OOA in 1988, at which time it was favorably received.

With the approval of the OSU administration, the OCOMS administration, and the OOA, all roadblocks had been removed to effect the change. The law providing for the merger effective July 1, 1988, changed the name of OCOMS to the College of Osteopathic Medicine of Oklahoma State University.[32] President Boger, who retired from the OSU presidency in June of 1988, said: "This is probably the biggest thing to happen during my eleven years at OSU."[33] Time will tell if this is true.

Endnotes

1. *Tulsa World*, 20 April 1988, pp. 1C, 8C.

2. Eric I. Williams, *A History of the Oklahoma State University College of Veterinary Medicine* (Stillwater: Oklahoma State University, 1986), p. 26; Oklahoma City *Daily Oklahoman*, 26 September 1982, p. 23A; Nestor Gonzales, "OSU Gets Osteopathic College," *Oklahoma State University Outreach*, vol. 59, no. 4 (Summer 1988), p. 13.

3. Gonzales, p. 12.

4. Norman Gevitz, *The D.O.'s: Osteopathic Medicine in America* (Baltimore, MD: The Johns Hopkins University Press, 1982), pp. 6, 7.

5. Gevitz, p. 14.

6. Gevitz, p. 18.

7. Gevitz, p. 19.

8. Gevitz, p. 43.

9. Gevitz, p. 61.

10. Gevitz, p. 85.

11. Gevitz, p. 115.

12. Bob E. Jones, *The Difference a D. O. Makes* (Oklahoma City, OK: Times-Journal Publishing Company, 1978), p. 41.

13. Lawrence W. Mills, *A Feasibility Study for the Establishment of a College of Osteopathic Medicine and Surgery in the Tulsa Area* (Oklahoma City, OK: Legislative Council of the State of Oklahoma, 1971), p. 20.

14. Author interview with E. T. Dunlap, 13 September 1988, Oklahoma City, Oklahoma.

15. Dunlap interview.

16. Dunlap interview.

17. Author interview with Bob Jones, 13 September 1988, Oklahoma City, Oklahoma.

18. "A Permanent Home for a New College and the Oklahoma Osteopathic Profession," *Oklahoma DO: The Journal of the Oklahoma Osteopathic Association* (October 1974), pp. 14-20.

19. *Inaugural Commencement Program, The Oklahoma College of Osteopathic Medicine and Surgery, Tulsa*, 14 August 1977, Personal Files of the Author.

20. *Tulsa Daily World*, 11 December 1975.

21. *Oklahoma Higher Education Report*, 29 December 1976, p. 3, 26 September 1978, p. 2; *Tulsa Tribune*, 20 April 1977, p. 1D.

22. Author interview with Edward A. Felmlee, 8 September 1988, Tulsa, Oklahoma; Author interview with James R. Routsong, 8 September 1988, Tulsa, Oklahoma.

23. *Tulsa Tribune*, 28 October 1976, p. 9B; *Daily Oklahoman*, 8 May, 1983, p. 5A; *Oklahoma Higher Education Report*, 25 June 1980, p. 3.

24. "OCOMS to be Governed by New Board of Regents," *Oklahoma DO: The Journal of the Oklahoma Osteopathic Association* (June 1980), p. 8; *Tulsa County News*, 18 September 1980, p. 1.

25. "OCOMS Celebrates Founders' Day," *Oklahoma DO: The Journal of the Oklahoma Osteopathic Association* (March 1980), p. 14.

26. Linda S. Plemons, compiler, "Notes on the College of Osteopathic Medicine," Personal Files of the Author; *Daily Oklahoman*, 1 July 1982, p. 5; *Tulsa Tribune*, 8 February 1984, p. 10C; Gonzalez, p. 13.

27. *Tulsa World*, 8 September 1984, p. 1E, 24 May 1987, p. 14A; *Tulsa Eastside Times*, 8 September 1986, p. 1.

28. *Daily Oklahoman*, 22 January 1987, p. 2A, 15 March 1987, p. 17A; *Tulsa Tribune*, 13 March 1987, p. 1A.

29. *Tulsa Tribune*, 10 April 1987, p. 1D; *Tulsa World*, 17 January 1981, p. 1; Author interview with Clyde Jensen, 8 September 1988, Stillwater, Oklahoma.

30. Henry L. Bellmon to Avalon B. Reece, 4 April 1988, Personal Files of the Author.

31. "1988-89 Annual Directory," *Oklahoma DO: The Journal of the Oklahoma Osteopathic Association* (August 1988), pp. 30-55.

32. Oklahoma State University *Daily O'Collegian*, 20 April 1988, p. 1; Author interview with J. H. Boggs, 7 September 1988, Stillwater, Oklahoma; Jones interview; Jensen interview.

33. *Daily O'Collegian*, 20 April 1988, p. 1.

Appendices

Appendix 1

Oklahoma A. and M. College Extension Professionals
1890-1957

William S. Abbott, Assistant Director, Agricultural-Industrial Development Service, 1950-1957

Ashley Alexander, Director of Student Entertainers, 1956-1957

J. E. Arendel, Associate Professor, Educational Extension, 1942-1957

W. M. Bamburge, Supervisor of Farm Agents, 1908-1914

Walter D. Bentley, Supervisor of Farm Agents, 1908-1914

Lucius W. Burton, Director, Correspondence School, 1927-1929

J. R. Campbell, Director, Correspondence School, 1921-1924

Harry Canup, Director, Business Extension, 1953-1957

Ruth Cox, Director, Correspondence School, 1924-1927

A. L. Crable, Director, Correspondence School, 1929-1936

M. W. Darlington, Educational Extension Instructor, 1941-1943

E. F. Dowell, Staff, Agricultural-Industrial Development Service, Circa 1950

Charles Evans, Director, Educational Extension, 1921-1925

John Fields, Principal of Short Courses, Circa 1900

Robert C. Fite, Director, Arts and Sciences Extension, 1956-1957

J. C. Fitzgerald, Director Audio-Visual Department, 1946-1957

Claude Gatewood, Chemistry Teacher Circuit Rider, 1957-1957

A. D. Hanry, Audio-Visual Technician, 1946-1957

A. C. Hartenbower, Principal of Short Courses, Circa 1913

L. M. Hohstadt, Associate Professor, Educational Extension, 1937-1957

Randall T. Klemme, Director, Agricultural-Industrial Development Service, 1950-1952

Bradford Knapp, Director of Short Courses, Circa 1915

L. F. Sheerar, Director, Engineering Extension, 1953-1957

Ancil D. Simpson, Staff, Agricultural-Industrial Development Service, Circa 1950

Bob Spears, Staff, Agricultural-Industrial Development Service, Circa 1950

Gerald T. Stubbs, Director, Public School Services, 1945-1957

Roy R. Tompkins, Director, Educational Extension, 1936-1956

Appendix 2

University Extension Professionals
1957-present

George A. Abshier, Director, Community Programs, 1967-1975

D. A. Ahrens, Interim Director, Educational Television Services, 1986-1987

Marshall E. Allen, Director, Educational Television Services, 1967-present

L. L. Ballew, University Extension Representative, Oklahoma City, 1986-present

W. H. Beckham, County Extension Director, 1973-1975

Bobby G. Bennett, Audio-Visual Specialist, 1973-1974

D. E. Bigbee, Engineer, Educational Television Services, 1986-present

Ward Blocker, Director of Extension Finance, 1967-1975

Rosanne Brown, Extension Representative, Tinker Air Force Base, 1977-1980

A. Harold Casey, Director of Extension Personnel, 1967-1973

W. E. Crane, Instructor, Educational Television Services, 1980-1984

J. G. Delucia, Television Engineer, 1986-1987

S. H. Duer, Assistant Director, Educational Television Services, 1986-present

D. H. Duroy, Audio-Visual Service Specialist, 1986-1987

Marvin Edmison, Interim Director, University Extension, 1974-1975

R. G. Elston, Producer/Director, Educational Television Services, 1986-present

Jean C. Evans, Vice President, University Extension, 1965-1974

S. K. Fairchild, Coordinator, National University Teleconferencing Network, 1986-present

Charles E. Feasley, Director of Correspondence Study, 1980-present

J. P. Feuquay, Programmer/Analyst, 1979-1980

Robert C. Fite, Director, Programs for Professionals, 1968-1980

J. C. Fitzgerald, Director, Continuing Education, 1957-1969

M. S. Foutz, University Extension Representative, Tinker AFB, 1982-1983

Peggy Gardner, Director, Correspondence Study, 1977-1980

R. H. George, District Extension Director, 1986-1987

T. A. Grant, Technical Specialist, Photography, 1983-1984

J. O. Grantham, Director, University Extension, 1973-present

Edward Gregory, University Extension Representative, Oklahoma City, 1979-1985

Mark Gregory, Assistant Director Extension Projects, 1975-1979

Michael Hannah, University Extension Representative, Oklahoma City, 1973-1982

A. D. Hanry, Audio-Visual Technician, 1957-1961

Woodfin G. Harris, Director, Audio-Visual Department, 1967-1986

C. M. Hartmann, Extension Assistant, Tinker Air Force Base, 1979-1980

C. E. Henderson, Rural Development Specialist, 1965-1966

Mike Hopkins, Administrative Assistant, 1976-1978

John M. Jobe, Coordinator, Correspondence Study, 1975-1977

S. L. Keating, Coordinator, Teleconference Programs, 1986-present

T. L. Kelly, Coordinator, Extension Programs, 1986-present

R. A. Kennedy, County Extension Director, 1974-1975

J. R. Kinser, Producer/Director, Educational Television Services, 1986-present

Gerald Knutson, Director, Educational Services, 1969-1975

J. J. Kopecky, Technical Specialist, Photography, 1984-1985

J. A. Labow, Television Production Manager, 1986-present

Tom W. Lee, Extension Accounting, 1974-1975

J B LeMaster, Conference Coordinator, 1977-1978

T. R. Livsey, Photography Specialist, 1986-present

Floyd A. Loftiss, Audio-Visual Specialist, 1973-1980

Phyllis Luebke, Associate Director, Correspondence Study, 1979-present

L. B. McClure, County Extension Director, 1973-1975

Paul McCrary, Director, Photographic Services, 1957-1978

Gladys McGaugh, Director, Correspondence Study, 1957-1975

A. L. McNew, Conference Coordinator, 1972-1982

William J. Meehan, University Extension Representative, Tulsa, 1973-1978

L. M. Miller, Assistant Director, Correspondence Study, 1978-1980

Max L. Minor, University Extension Representative, Tulsa, 1980-present

Jack R. Monks, Program Coordinator, Engineering Extension, 1977-1978

S. C. Morgan, Television Engineer, 1983-1984

J. E. Moton, County Extension Director, 1975-1982

Jim C. Nelson, Extension Accounting, 1973-1975

J. D. Netherton, Director, Extension Personnel, 1973-1975

Sharon Nivens, Associate Director, University Extension, 1975-present

H. N. Nye, University Extension Representative, Tinker Air Force Base, 1980-1982

E. Marie Oberle, Director, National University Teleconferencing Network, 1986-present

Ron Payne, Director, Audio-Visual Department, 1986-present

David W. Perrin, Extension Project Coordinator, 1981-1985

R. W. Poole, Vice President, University Extension, 1974-present

Gene L. Post, Audio-Visual Specialist, 1961-1965

J. D. Pricer, Data Control Technician, 1986-1987

Guy Pritchard, Director, Audio-Visual Department, 1957-1965

B. Reinschmiedt, Television Producer/Director, 1980-1984

J. R. Sallee, District Extension Director, 1981-1982

G. L. Spivey, Director, Family Living Programs, 1972-1975
Paul S. Sund, KOSU News Reporter, 1986-present
R. W. Tinnell, Instructor, Industrial Arts, 1960-1961
Myra A. Traynor, Coordinator, National University Teleconferencing Network, 1986-present
Eugene Williams, Director, Youth Programs, 1972-1975

Appendix 3

College of Arts and Sciences Extension Professionals
1957-present

Rickey W. Adams, Grants and Contracts Officer, 1982-1983
George E. Arquitt, Associate Professor of Sociology, 1976-present
Jerry A. Bayless, Assistant Director, Arts and Sciences Extension, 1973-1974
Craig C. Beeby, Adjunct Instructor, Journalism and Broadcasting, 1981-1982
Edward Behrens, Contract and Grant Specialist, 1974-1980
David M. Billeaux, Assistant Professor, Political Science, 1987-present
Paul Bischoff, Assistant Professor, History, 1977-1983
W. A. Blanchard, Research Associate, Geography, 1983-1984
Barrie Blunt, Assistant Professor, 1982-1984
A. C. Bodine, Grants and Contracts Officer, 1980-1981
W. F. Bourns, Extension Coordinator, 1978-1983
Bradley Brauser, Atomic World Exhibits Manager, 1968-1969
Anthony E. Brown, Associate Professor, Political Science, 1983-1984
Don N. Brown, Professor, Sociology, 1974-1987
Larry T. Brown, Professor, Psychology, 1985-present
R. J. Brown, Nurse, Cardiac Rehabilitation, 1983-1984
L. H. Bruneau, Professor, Biology, 1959-1960
D. L. Bruyr, Teaching Associate, 1964-1965
M. O. Buchholz, Assistant Professor, Journalism and Broadcasting, 1982-1983
Jack E. Bynum, Professor, Sociology, 1982-1983
James R. Choike, Professor, Mathematics, 1981-present
Paul R. Couey, Assistant Professor, Journalism and Broadcasting, 1982-1983
Jerry J. Crockett, Director, Arts and Sciences Extension, 1968-1976
Jerry D. Croft, Associate Professor, Geography, 1985-1986
Jerry A. Davis, Assistant Professor, Political Science, 1983-1984
J. L. Davis, Associate Professor, Theatre, 1977-1978
Stanley M. Dunham, Extension Programs Specialist, 1980-1985
Paul F. Duvall, Professor, Mathematics, 1983-1984
R. P. Ebersole, Grants and Contracts Officer, 1981-1982
B. W. Eissenstat, Professor, History, 1977-1978
R. E. England, Assistant Professor, Political Science, 1983-1985

Denman C. Evans, Instructor, Arts and Sciences Extension, 1957-1965

Donald D. Fisher, Professor and Head, Computer Science, 1986-1987

Robert C. Fite, Director, Arts and Sciences Extension, 1957-1968

Robert D. Freeman, Coordinator, Chemistry, 1977-1979

R. B. Garner, Assistant Professor, Journalism and Broadcasting, 1985-present

M. J. Folk, Associate Professor, Computer Science, 1983-1984

Claude W. Gatewood, Arts and Sciences Extension Specialist, 1961-1962

J. I. Gelder, Associate Professor, 1987-present

Gerald K. Goff, Teaching Associate, Mathematics, 1963-1964

R. E. Graalman, Visiting Assistant Professor, 1983-1984

Stanley D. Green, Director, Arts and Sciences Extension, 1976-present

Mark S. Gregory, Research Associate, Remote Sensing, 1983-1984

R. N. Habiby, Professor, Political Science, 1980-1981

Paul Hagle, Coordinator, Geography, 1973-1977

H. F. Hampton, Teaching Associate, Arts and Sciences Extension, 1964-1965

Billye S. Harmon, Assistant Professor, Theatre, 1982-1983

Paul D. Harper, Coordinator, Speech, 1976-present

Keith D. Harries, Coordinator, Geography, 1977-1980

A. B. Harrison, Director, Fitness Program, 1976-1986

Bob Helm, Associate Professor, Psychology, 1985-present

J. G. Henry, Coordinator, Journalism and Broadcasting, 1976-1979

J. Steven Hill, Administrative Assistant, Health, Physical Education, and Leisure, 1979-1980

J. P. Huckabay, Teaching Associate, Arts and Sciences Extension, 1963-1964

Lawrence Hynson, Associate Professor, Sociology, 1976-1986

B. H. Jacobson, Assistant Professor, Health, Physical Education, and Leisure, 1987-present

John M. Jobe, Teaching Associate, Mathematics, 1963-1965; Professor, Mathematics, 1987-present

Jerry A. Johnson, Professor, Mathematics, 1977-1980

Katie Johnson, Extension Program Coordinator, 1977-1980

L. Wayne Johnson, Professor and Head, Mathematics, 1965-1966

Claude F. Jones, Assistant Director, Arts and Sciences Extension, 1960-1968

Frank A. Kulling, Assistant Professor, Health, Physical Education, and Leisure, 1985-present

Leonard Laskowski, Atomic World Exhibits Manager, 1971-1972

James J. Lawler, Professor, Political Science, 1981-1987

J. Ben Leake, Teaching Associate, Arts and Sciences Extension, 1964-1965

Merlin E. London, Extension Specialist, Health, Physical Education and Leisure, 1980-1987

J. A. Marks, Instructor, Speech Pathology, 1986-present

G. C. Matthews, Coordinator, History,1979-1983

Gayle E. Maxwell, Cartographer, 1980-1984

Wayne McCray, Atomic World Exhibits Manager, 1969-1971

M. L. McCrory, Director, Fitness Center, 1981-present

Vicki L. McKeeman, Assistant Professor, Health, Physical Education and Leisure, 1985-1986

E. M. Meissinger, Associate Professor, Art, 1980-1986

Helen C. Miller, Associate Professor, Zoology, 1982-1983

L. D. Miller, Manager, KOSU, 1978-1981

Jack E. Moore, Assistant Professor, Geography, 1963-1965

Wayne E. Muller, Coordinator, Music, 1973-present

John D. Naff, Associate Professor, Geology, 1961-1963

Joyce Nichols, Manager, Extension Programs, 1987-present

Robert E. Norris, Coordinator, Geography, 1976-1977

M. H. Paradis, Research Administrative Assistant, 1984-1986

Michael Parle, Assistant Professor, Political Science, 1983-1984

Lise Patton, Extension Coordinator, 1987-present

P. E. Paulin, Assistant Professor, Journalism and Broadcasting, 1973-1977

V. W. Pearson, Manager of Extension Programs, 1985-1987

Jack Phelps, Teaching Assistant, Arts and Sciences Extension, 1963-1965

James L. Phillips, Professor and Head, Psychology, 1982-1984

R. B. Purdie, Manager, Cardiac Rehabilitation, 1984-present

Lavon Richardson, Temporary Director, Arts and Sciences Extension, 1967-1968

C. J. Roberts, Extension Recreation Specialist, 1976-1977

James H. Rogers, Coordinator, Health, Physical Education, and Leisure, 1976-present

R. C. Rohrs, Coordinator, History, 1978-1979

Harold V. Sare, Regents Professor, Political Science, 1982-1987

R. S. Schlottmann, Professor, Psychology, 1983-1984

Leon Schroeder, Professor, Physics, 1979-1982

P. O. Shull Jr., Associate Professor, Noble Research Fellow, 1986-present

D. H. Shumavon, Assistant Professor, Political Science, 1978-1980

Ray L. Six, Associate Professor, Geology, 1960-1961

James M. Smallwood, Associate Professor, History 1985-present

B. J. Smith, Associate Professor, Art 1982-1983

Michael M. Smith, Associate Professor, History 1979-1980

R. M. Spaulding, Associate Professor, History 1980-1982

Robert L. Spurrier, Professor and Associate Director, Arts and Sciences Extension, 1980-present

Michael Stano Jr., Associate Professor, Speech, 1982-1987

Julia Starr, Extension Specialist 1984-present

William R. Steng, Associate Professor, Journalism and Broadcasting, 1982-1983

Gary F. Stewart, Professor, Geology, 1974-1982

William Stewart, Assistant Professor, Statistics, 1982-1983

James H. Stine, Coordinator, Geography, 1977-1979

Joseph A. Stout, Associate Professor, History, 1982-1983

H. H. Susky, Coordinator, Sociology, 1978-1981

J. W. Swain, Coordinator, Political Science, 1979-1982

J. A. Sylvester, Associate Professor, History, 1983-1985

R. L. Tennison, Teaching Associate, Arts and Sciences Extension, 1963-1964

Fred Tewell, Professor, Speech, 1983-1984

Dale W. Toetz, Coordinator, Biological Science, 1977-1980

Mary L. Turner, Assistant Director, Arts and Sciences Extension, 1974-1977

Stephen Tweedie, Coordinator, Geography, 1980-1984

J. K. Varnum, Physical Fitness Analyst 1980-1985

John D. Vitek, Coordinator, Geography 1979-1883

Franz Von Sauer, Associate Professor, Political Science, 1985-1986

D. F. Wade, Cartographer, 1976-1980

L. N. Walker, Assistant Professor, Political Science, 1976-1978

Steve J. Walsh, Coordinator, Remote Sensing, 1978-1985

L. B. Walters, Coordinator, Teleconferencing, 1987-present

William D. Warde, Associate Professor, Statistics, 1982-1983

Thomas L. Warren, Associate Professor, English, 1981-1982

Gordon A. Weaver, Professor, English 1986-1987

J. B. Weaver, Financial Coordinator, Arts and Sciences Extension, 1984-1987

Robert Wegener, Assistant Professor, Journalism and Broadcasting, 1978-1983

Jerry Wilhm, Professor and Head, Zoology, 1976-1981

S. D. Wilson, Extension Specialist, 1979-1980

Timothy M. Wilson, Assistant Director, Arts and Sciences Extension, 1977-1984

Shella A. Wisherd, Assistant Professor, Journalism and Broadcasting, 1983-1987

Harry S. Wohlert, Professor, Foreign Languages, 1985-present

Hildegund Wohlert, Instructor, Foreign Languages, 1986-present

James H. Zant, Professor, Mathematics, 1960-1961

Appendix 4

College of Business Administration Extension Professionals
1957-present

John T. Bale Jr., Business Extension Specialist, 1967-1968

Donald Bumpass, Director, Economic Education, 1987-present

Bruce A. Cook, Business Extension Specialist, 1969-1972

Robert D. Erwin, Director, Business Extension, 1960-1961

Julie Flasch, Extension Program Coordinator, 1986-present

Jill Fremont, Manager, Extension Programs, 1981-1987

B. Curtis Hamm, Director, Business Extension, 1974-1980

Karen Hawthorne, Temporary Program Coordinator, 1987-1988

James G. Hromas, Director, Business Extension, 1970-present

Lana Ivy, Program Coordinator, 1984-1986

Janet P. Kimbrell, Teaching Associate, 1975-1976

Pauline Kopecky, Assistant Director, Economic Education, 1967-1973

J B LeMaster, Assistant Director, Business Extension, 1958-1966

Bernard W. Luster, Business Extension Specialist, 1966-1969

L. Lee Manzer, Associate Professor, Marketing, 1975-1982

Clayton Millington, Director, Economic Education, 1961-1982

Kent W. Olson, Director, Economic Education, 1985-1987

Norman Ringstrom, Director, Business Extension, 1958-1960

Brenda Roberts, Extension Program Specialist, 1977-1979

H. Walter Shaw, Manager, Extension Programs, 1978-present

Mark Vincent, Extension Program Coordinator, 1975-1982

Karen Ward, Assistant Program Coordinator, 1976-present

Larkin Warner, Director, Economic Education, 1982-1985

Lynda Wimmer, Assistant Director, Economic Education, 1979-present

Devon Yoho, Assistant Director, Economic Education, 1975-1978

Appendix 5

College of Education Extension Professionals
1957-present

Deborah P. Allen, Coordinator, Extension Programs, 1986-present

Carl R. Anderson, Associate Professor, Education Extension, 1977-1982

James Appleberry, Associate Professor, Education, 1972-1973

L. K. Arney, Assistant Professor, Education, 1985-1986

John L. Baird, Associate Professor, Occupational and Adult Education, 1984-1986

Gerald R. Bass, Assistant Professor, Educational Administration and Higher Education, 1986-present

J. T. Benjamin, Temporary Professor, Education, 1979-1981

Garry Bice, Associate Professor, Occupational and Adult Education, 1987-present

Ralph A. Brann, Associate Professor, Assistant to Dean of Education, 1972-1973

Linda K. Burks, Counselor, Psychology, 1978-1980

H. S. Caldwell, Associate Professor, Education, 1977-1978

Judith E. Dobson, Professor, Applied Behavorial Studies in Education, 1982-1983

Russell L. Dobson, Professor, Curriculum and Instruction, 1975-1985

Patrick Forsyth, Assistant Professor, Educational Administration and Higher Education, 1979-1981

John J. Gardiner, Associate Professor, Educational Administration and Higher Education, 1984-1985

B. D. Hoover, Instructor, Education, 1977-1978

Waynne B. James, Assistant Professor, Occupational and Adult Education, 1978-1981

Wilbur D. Johnson, Associate Professor, Educational Administration and Higher Education, 1976-present

Thomas D. Johnsten, Professor, Curriculum and Instruction, 1975-1980

Richard P. Jungers, Professor and Director, Education Extension, 1963-1979

C. M. Lawry, Associate Director, Education Extension, 1982-present

Wayne N. Lockwood, Assistant Professor, Occupational and Adult Education, 1975-1978

Kenneth McKinley, Professor and Director of Research, 1974-present

Ronald Miller, Instructor, Curriculum and Instruction, 1979-1981

Ted J. Mills, Professor, Curriculum and Instruction, 1977-1980

J. A. Nichols, Teleconference Program Coordinator, 1987-present

Robert E. Nolan, Assistant Professor, Occupational and Adult Education, 1987-present

Bruce A. Petty, Associate Professor, Curriculum and Instruction, 1983-1984

Milton D. Rhoads, Associate Professor, Curriculum and Instruction, 1985-1986

R. S. Schlottmann, Associate Professor, Psychology, 1980-1982

William C. Scott, Associate Professor, Psychology, 1975-1977

James M. Seals, Professor, Applied Behavorial Studies in Education, 1976-present

William E. Segall, Professor, Curriculum and Instruction, 1985-present

H. Gene Smith, Assistant Professor, Occupational and Adult Education, 1978-1979

Thomas J. Smith, Professor and Director, Education Extension, 1979-1988

Robert L. Spinks, Instructor, Education Extension, 1979-1981

James K. St. Clair, Professor, Educational Administration and Higher Education, 1973-present

Kenneth A. Stern, Assistant Professor, Educational Administration and Higher Education, 1982-1985

Gerald T. Stubbs, Professor and Director, Education Extension, 1957-1963

William R. Venable, Associate Professor, Occupational and Adult Education, 1985-1987

Linda M. Vincent, Associate Professor, Occupational and Adult Education, 1980-1986

Kenneth E. Wiggins, Professor, Research Foundation, 1974-1975

Appendix 6

College of Engineering Extension Professionals
1957-present

Kenneth Anderson, Extension Specialist, 1972-1973

Dan D. Ashcraft, Assistant Professor, Technology, 1981-1982

Edward M. Barnes, Assistant Project Director, 1962-1965

D. D. Basore, Coordinator, Extension Programs, 1982-1985

D. Jack Bayles, Assistant Professor, Technology, 1978-1980

Kenneth Bell, Professor, Chemical Engineering, 1977-1986

W. J. Bentley, Professor and Head, Industrial Engineering, 1960-1965

B. D. Berger, Instructor, Technology, 1979-1980

Larry Borgelt, Associate Professor, Technology, 1981-1985

James E. Bose, Professor and Director Technology 1981-1982

Jerrold Bradley, Associate Professor, Technology, 1981-1985

Pat D. Brock, Associate Professor, Technology, 1981-1985

E. K. Buchholz, Professor, Technology, 1982-1985

Kenneth Case, Professor, Industrial Engineering, 1986-1987

W. G. Chamberlain, Professor, Architecture, 1978-1979

J. R. Cleveland, Associate Professor, Technology, 1979-1984

G. F. Collington, Coordinator, Extension Programs, 1986-present

Bill L. Cooper, Director, Engineering Extension, 1970-present

R. C. Davidson, Instructor, Fire Protection, 1960-1962

C. L. Echols, Engineering Extension Specialist, 1978-1980

Hamed K. Eldin, Professor, Industrial Engineering, 1972-1973

Earl J. Ferguson, Assistant Professor, Industrial Engineering, 1960-1965

R. W. Gose, Extension Specialist, 1976-1977

Quintin Graves, Professor, Civil Engineering, 1960-1965

D. E. Griffith, Director, Engineering Extension, 1979-1981

Gary G. Hansen, Professor, Technology, 1979-1985

John E. Harvey, Assistant Professor, Technology, 1979-1980

R. L. Heiserman, Professor, Technology, 1980-1985

Robert L. Janes, Associate Professor, Civil Engineering, 1964-1965

H. M. Johnson, Associate Professor, Technology, 1978-1986

T. L. Johnston, Research Associate, Architecture 1981-1982

L. D. Jones, Associate Professor, Technology, 1980-1983

R. K. King, Fluid Power Research Center, 1978-1979

Shirley M. Kirk, Extension Specialist, 1979-1986

S. I. Kraemer, Assistant Professor, Technology, 1980-1982

Monroe W. Kriegel, Director, Engineering Extension, 1964-1978

L. G. Lee, Assistant Professor, Technology, 1981-1982

Dan D. Lingelbach, Professor, Computer Engineering, 1965-present

C. C. Linville, Editor, Engineering Publications, 1964-1965

J. P. Lloyd, Associate Professor, Civil Engineering, 1979-1980

M. E. Long, Manager, Technical Information, 1979-1980

R. L. Lowery, Professor,Mechanical Engineering, 1979-1982

D. H. Magruder, Extension Specialist, 1976-1977

Phillip G. Manke, Assistant Professor, Civil Engineering, 1961-1962

J. G. Mayberry, Assistant Professor, Technology, 1980-1984

G. R. McClain, Associate Professor, Technology, 1981-1985

Perry R. McNeill, Professor, Technology, 1980-1982

Faye C. McQuiston, Professor, Mechanical Engineering, 1978-present

Joe H. Mize, Regents Professor, Industrial Engineering, 1975-1986

J. R. Monks, Assistant Professor, Technology, 1974-1979

R. F. Neathery, Associate Professor, Technology, 1979-1980

H. W. Newton, Teaching Associate, Technology Extension, 1985-1986

F. D. Norvelle, Associate Professor, Mechanical Engineering, 1985-1986

G. L. Orgain, Associate Professor, Fire Protection, 1960-1962

J. D. Parker, Professor, Mechanical Engineering, 1978-1979

Samuel O. Powers, Associate Professor, Technology, 1980-1982

J. M. Price, Manager, Extension Programs, 1983-present

Joann Proppe, Supervisor, Architecture Extension, 1979-1986

Karl N. Reid, Professor and Head, Mechanical Engineering, 1977-1983

R. C. Reininger, Assistant Professor, Electrical Engineering, 1984-1985

Mary E. Reynolds, Manager, Extension Programs, 1980-present

R. P. Rosecrans, Coordinator, Extension Programs, 1979-1985

Glenn Rucker, Associate Professor, Engineering Extension, 1957-1964

L. F. Sheerar, Director, Engineering Extension, 1957-1965

J. K. Shelton, Assistant Professor, Technology, 1979-1983

Scott D. Sink, Associate Professor, Industrial Engineering, 1981-1984

A. H. Soni, Professor, Mechanical Engineering, 1976-1982

D. L. Spurrier, Teleconference Specialist, 1978-present

R. L. Swaim, Professor and Associate Dean, 1986-1987

Robert F. Tanner, Assistant Director, Engineering Extension, 1976-1978

K. A. Teague, Assistant Professor, Computer Engineering, 1987-present

M. R. Tiger, Supervisor, Technology Extension, 1979-1980

Wayne C. Turner, Professor, Industrial Engineering, 1976-1987

R. B. Weaver, Manager, Extension Programs, 1980-present

King D. White, Assistant Director, Engineering Extension, 1972-1973

Neal A. Willison, Associate Professor, Technology, 1982-1983

Appendix 7

College of Home Economics University Extension Professionals
1967-present

Ann Basford Benes, Temporary Professor, Family Resource Center, 1987-1988; Coordinator, Family Resource Center, 1988-present

Baker Bokorney, Director, Hotel and Restaurant Administration, 1985-present

Lora B. Cacy, Director, Home Economics University Extension, 1967-1975

Dorothy Carpenter, Conference Coordinator, Center for Community Service and Volunteerism, 1985-1988

Lara Cochran, Temporary Technical/Paraprofessional, 1988-present

Dorothea Danel, Associate Director, Home Economics University Extension, 1980-present

Mary Domnick, Project Director, Stillwater Young Volunteers in ACTION, 1985-1985

Charlene Douglas, Newsletter Editor, Center for Community Service and Volunteerism, 1986-present

Patrick Fitzgerald, Visiting Assistant Professor, 1978-1982

Linda Good, Director, Center for Apparel Marketing and Merchandising, 1986-present

Kathryn Greenwood, Director, Center for Apparel Marketing and Merchandising, 1982-1986

Maxine Hall, Child Care Specialist, 1979-1980; Project Director, Oklahoma Training for Child Care Careers, 1980-1988

Beulah Hirschlein, Director, Home Economics University Extension, 1975-present; Director, Center for Community Service and Volunteerism, 1982-present

Mike Hopkins, Public Service Specialist, 1978-present

William Johnston, Director, Center for Consumer Services, 1977-1987

Robert Kiel, Adjunct Instructor, 1980-1981

Norma Sue Knight, Assistant Professor, 1982-1982

Bernice Kopel, Associate Professor, 1979-1984

B. Anne Labow, Coordinator, Teleconference Program Development, 1986-1987

R. Kay Lambert, Temporary Professional, Stillwater Young Volunteers in ACTION, 1987-1987; Coordinator, Stillwater Young Volunteers in ACTION, 1987-present

Nancy Lowry, Coordinator, Family Resource Center, 1983-1985

Stan Mitchell, Consumer Specialist, 1977-1978

Betty B. Mize, Coordinator, National Consumer Affairs Intern Program, 1988-present

David P. O'Brien, Visiting Assistant Professor, 1987-1987

Claudia Peck, Associate Professor, 1987-present

Eileen Pye, Adjunct Instructor, 1983-present

Verna Lou Reid, Assistant Professor, Adjunct Career Coordinator, 1977-1981

La T. Simmons-Webb, Coordinator, Stillwater Young Volunteers in ACTION, 1985-1986

Harold Snyder, Publications Specialist, 1987-present

Betty Stratton, Director, Oklahoma Training for Child Care Careers, 1988

Deborah Strickland, Coordinator, Extension Programs, 1982-1986

Carol Toews, Temporary Coordinator, Retired Senior Volunteer Program, 1985-1986; Coordinator, Retired Senior Volunteer Program, 1986-1986

Sue Williams, Energy Management Specialist, 1977-1979

Cheryl Wilson, Program Specialist, 1987-1988

Appendix 8

Traveling Science Teachers
College of Arts and Sciences
1957-61

Ava Lee Allsman, Traveling Science Teacher, 1959-1960

Jesse Arriaga, Traveling Science Teacher, 1959-1960

Grover M. Barham, Traveling Science Teacher, 1960-1961

Frederick Bischof, Science Materials Specialist, 1960-1961

Dale Bremmer, Physics Teacher Circuit Rider, 1958-1959

Frank Brewster, Traveling Science Teacher, 1960-1961

Alice Brooks, Traveling Science Teacher, 1959-1960

Edward F. Bryan, Science Materials Specialist, 1960-1961

Rich Calvird, Traveling Science Teacher, 1959-1960

Joe A. Cardenas, Science Materials Specialist, 1960-1961

Katherine Chambers, Science Materials Specialist, 1960-1961

Charles Compton, Traveling Science Teacher, 1959-1960

Charles Cook, Traveling Science Teacher, 1960-1961

Hampton Crowder, Science Materials Specialist, 1960-1961

LeRoy Estergard, Traveling Science Teacher, 1959-1960

Denman C. Evans, Chemistry Teacher Circuit Rider, 1958-1959

Robert C. Fite, Director, Traveling Science Programs, 1957-1961

Jack Folmar, Traveling Science Teacher, 1959-1960

Edward Freeman, Traveling Science Teacher, 1960-1961

Dean D. Gamble, Traveling Science Teacher, 1960-1961

Claude Gatewood, Chemistry Teacher Circuit Rider 1957-1958; Science Demonstration Lecturer, 1958-1959; Assistant Director, Traveling Science Teacher Program 1959-1961

Lloyd E. George, Traveling Science Teacher, 1960-1961

Jessie Jean Gill, Traveling Science Teacher, 1959-1960

William Harlan, Traveling Science Teacher, 1959-1960

Donald Harvey, Traveling Science Teacher, 1959-1960

Claude F. Jones, Traveling Science Teacher, 1959-1960

William Kinniell, Science Materials Specialist, 1960-1961

Joe Landry, Traveling Science Teacher, 1959-1960

Kaye H. Martin, Science Materials Specialist, 1960-1961

Walter McGuire, Traveling Science Teacher, 1959-1960

Dewey H. Miner, Science Materials Specialist, 1960-1961

Richard F. Osner, Traveling Science Teacher, 1960-1961

Lee Roy Pace, Traveling Science Teacher, 1960-1961

Frank Patti, Traveling Science Teacher, 1959-1960

Lawrence Przekop, Science Materials Specialist, 1965-1967

W. C. Robinson, Traveling Science Teacher, 1959-1960

Jack E. Roy, Traveling Science Teacher, 1960-1961

Edward H. Seifert, Traveling Science Teacher, 1960-1961

Glenn H. Sharpe, Traveling Science Teacher, 1960-1961

John Shinpoch, Traveling Science Teacher, 1959-1960

Wendall Spreadbury, Traveling Science Teacher, 1960-1961

Joseph Struthers, Science Materials Specialist, 1960-1961

Ben Thaxton, Traveling Science Teacher, 1959-1960

James F. Thompson, Science Materials Specialist, 1960-1961.

Edward J. Vaughn, Science Materials Specialist, 1960-1961

John Wagner, Traveling Science Teacher, 1959-1960

Charles E. Wall, Traveling Science Teacher, 1960-1961

Norman Watley, Traveling Science Teacher, 1959-1960

Samuel Williams, Traveling Science Teacher, 1959-1960

Appendix 9

Fire Service Training Professionals
College of Engineering
1936-present

Jess Andrews, Fire Service Training Specialist, 1986-present

David E. Ballenger, Fire Service Training Specialist, 1978-1978

Michael Conley, Fire Service Training Specialist, 1985-1988

Gary M. Courtney, Fire Service Training Specialist, 1985-present

Raymond Davidson, Fire Service Training Specialist, 1956-1978

R. J. Douglas, Director, Fire Service Training, 1938-1941; Director, Fire Service Training, 1951-1962

Dennis DuMontier, Fire Service Training Specialist, 1979-1981

Cynthia L. Finkle, Fire Service Training Specialist, 1972-present

Jack R. Gardner, Fire Service Training Specialist, 1980-1986

Joseph A. Gorman, Fire Service Training Specialist, 1979-1985

Hugh Graham, Fire Service Training Specialist, 1982-1985

Jack P. Haltom, Fire Service Training Specialist, 1982-present

Eric Haussermann, Fire Service Training Specialist, 1980-present

Fred Heisler, Fire Service Training Specialist, 1934-1951

Everett Hudiburg, Fire Service Training Specialist, 1936-1938

A. Tom Jones, Fire Service Training Specialist, 1971-1980

Wayne Lehew, Fire Service Training Specialist, 1985-present

Harold R. Mace, Director, Fire Service Training, 1969-present

Bill Morris, Fire Service Training Specialist, 1951-1955

J. Fred Myers, Fire Service Training Specialist, 1982-present

Larry Navarrette, Fire Service Training Specialist, 1972-1978

George Orgain, Fire Service Training Specialist, 1945-1968

Glenn A. Pribbenow, Fire Service Training Specialist, 1982-present

Gaylord Sartain, Director, Fire Service Training, 1964-1970

Donald L. Seelig, Fire Service Training Specialist, 1940-1942

A. J. Smith, Fire Service Training Specialist, 1940-1942

N. J. Trench, Manager, Fire Service Training, 1976-present

Robert Weldon, Fire Service Training Specialist, 1982-present

Appendix 10

Aerospace Education Services Project
College of Education
1969-present

George Allison, Aerospace Education Specialist, 1979-1983

Dennis Ammon, Aerospace Education Specialist, 1974-1975

Charles Anderson, Aerospace Education Specialist, 1984-present

William Anderson, Aerospace Education Specialist, 1979-1983

Lloyd H. Aronson, Aerospace Education Specialist, 1969-1982

Sophia Ashley, Aerospace Education Specialist, 1972-1974

Richard Athey, Aerospace Education Specialist, 1969-1975

Martha Balog, Aerospace Education Specialist, 1980-1981

David Balter, Aerospace Education Specialist, 1973-1975
John R. Bannister, Aerospace Education Specialist, 1969-present
Fred M. Bell, Aerospace Education Specialist, 1969-1973
Patterson B. Biggs, Aerospace Education Specialist, 1983-present
Larry Bilbrough, Aerospace Education Specialist, 1970-1980
James M. Boyle, Aerospace Education Specialist, 1969-1975
Robert Brandeberry, Aerospace Education Specialist, 1972-1974
Dale Bremmer, Aerospace Education Specialist, 1984-present
Jerry D. Brown, Aerospace Education Specialist, 1985-1986
Armistead D. Burks, Aerospace Education Specialist, 1971-1972
Sandra Burton, Aerospace Education Specialist, 1987-present
Richard Byrne, Aerospace Education Specialist, 1983-1985
Angelo Casaburri, Aerospace Education Specialist, 1982-present
Benito Casados, Aerospace Education Specialist, 1969-1972
Michael Caterina, Aerospace Education Specialist, 1983-present
Harmon Chesser, Aerospace Education Specialist, 1985-1986
Dennis Christopher, Aerospace Education Specialist, 1987-present
Don E. Clarkson, Aerospace Education Specialist, 1969-1975
Thomas B. Clausen, Aerospace Education Specialist, 1983-present
Rodney Collins, Aerospace Education Specialist, 1981-1983
Lawrence Costanzo, Aerospace Education Specialist, 1970-1974
Richard V. Coup, Aerospace Education Specialist, 1969-1975
Gregory Crosby, Aerospace Education Specialist, 1983-1985
Louis De La Vina, Aerospace Education Specialist, 1969-1975
Luther Doyle, Aerospace Education Specialist, 1973-1974
Steve Dutczak, Aerospace Education Specialist, 1980-1981
Frank Eckhart, Aerospace Education Specialist, 1983-1984
Jeffrey Ehmen, Aerospace Education Specialist, 1983-1984
Nelson J. Ehrlich, Aerospace Education Specialist, 1970-present
William S. Elliott, Aerospace Education Specialist, 1970-1971
Gordon Eskridge, Aerospace Education Specialist, 1985-present
Gary Ferrell, Aerospace Education Specialist, 1982-1985
Craig Friedrick, Aerospace Education Specialist, 1982-1987
Leslie Gold, Aerospace Education Specialist, 1984-present
Doris K. Grigsby, Aerospace Education Specialist, 1984-1986
Joe E. Hartsfield, Aerospace Education Specialist, 1969-1975
John W. Hartsfield, Aerospace Education Specialist, 1970-present
George Hastings, Aerospace Education Specialist, 1973-1975
Ronald Haybron, Aerospace Education Specialist, 1981-1983
Robert D. Helton, Aerospace Education Specialist, 1969-1975
Harry B. Herzer, Aerospace Education Specialist, 1970-present
Thomas Hill, Aerospace Education Specialist, 1969-1975
Rodney Hisken, Aerospace Education Specialist, 1969-1973
Mark T. Horn, Aerospace Education Specialist, 1985-present

William S. Horvath, Aerospace Education Specialist, 1980-1985
Duane E. Houston, Aerospace Education Specialist, 1971-1975
George Johnson, Aerospace Education Specialist, 1971-1974
Paul Kelter, Aerospace Education Specialist, 1984-1986
William Kenney, Aerospace Education Specialist, 1971-1972
William J. Lockyer, Aerospace Education Specialist, 1980-1983
Clarice Lolich, Aerospace Education Specialist, 1979-present
John Lowerison, Aerospace Education Specialist, 1987-present
Steven Marks, Aerospace Education Specialist, 1979-present
James G. Marlins, Aerospace Education Specialist, 1971-present
Louis B. Marshall, Aerospace Education Specialist, 1982-present
Janifer Mayden, Aerospace Education Specialist, 1987-present
Bob E. Mayfield, Aerospace Education Specialist, 1983-present
R. Wesley McCoy, Aerospace Education Specialist, 1983-1987
James W. McMurtray, Aerospace Education Specialist, 1982-present
Harold E. Mehrens, Aerospace Education Specialist, 1972-1975
James Miracle, Aerospace Education Specialist, 1974-1975
Gary Moen, Aerospace Education Specialist, 1973-1975
James Mosby, Aerospace Education Specialist, 1979-1981
Phillip K. Murphy, Aerospace Education Specialist, 1980-1985
Robert Neal, Aerospace Education Specialist, 1979-present
Timothy O'Connell, Aerospace Education Specialist, 1969-1975
Janet O'Donnell, Aerospace Education Specialist, 1985-1987
George O'Neal, Aerospace Education Specialist, 1985-1987
Minot Parker, Aerospace Education Specialist, 1969-present
Malcom V. Phelps, Aerospace Education Specialist, 1986-present
Norman O. Poff, Aerospace Education Specialist, 1981-present
James Poindexter, Aerospace Education Specialist, 1969-1975
George E. Pope, Aerospace Education Specialist, 1969-1975
Jim Pruitt, Aerospace Education Specialist, 1973-1975
Allen Rajala, Aerospace Education Specialist, 1969-1972
Ransom S. Ritter, Aerospace Education Specialist, 1969-present
William Robertson, Aerospace Education Specialist, 1985-present
Edward A. Robinson, Aerospace Education Specialist, 1969-1971
Edward Romans, Aerospace Education Specialist, 1982-1984
Christian Romero, Aerospace Education Specialist, 1970-1972
Thomas J. Sarko, Aerospace Education Specialist, 1985-1987
Richard Sinclair, Aerospace Education Specialist, 1969-1970
Robert Smith, Aerospace Education Specialist, 1987-present
Theodore Stohr, Aerospace Education Specialist, 1971-1972
Garland Tillery, Aerospace Education Specialist, 1979-1981
Jim R. Tilley, Aerospace Education Specialist, 1973-1975
John Ulrich, Aerospace Education Specialist, 1985-present
Thomas Vallilee, Aerospace Education Specialist, 1982-1984

Gregory L. Vogt, Aerospace Education Specialist, 1979-present
Kenneth L. Watkins, Aerospace Education Specialist, 1971-1972
J. Scott West, Aerospace Education Specialist, 1969-1975
Earl White, Aerospace Education Specialist, 1980-1983
Kenneth E. Wiggins, Director, Aerospace Education Project, 1969-present
Robert E. Wilson, Aerospace Education Specialist, 1969-1983
Ralph Winrich, Aerospace Education Specialist, 1982-present

Center for Local Government Technology Professionals
College of Engineering
1974-present

W. H. Beitl, Extension Engineer, 1976-1981
Gary M. Brown, Local Government Specialist, 1979-1981
Charlie Burns, Rural Development Specialist, 1975-1976
Bill D. Collins, Local Government Specialist, 1974-1975
Bill Cooper, Supervisor, Technical Extension, 1974-1976
Jim Day, Extension Specialist, 1975-1976
Leroy Folks, Professor, Statistics, 1975-1976
R. W. Gose, Extension Specialist, 1977-1978
D. E. Griffith, Director, Engineering Extension, 1979-1980
M. D. Harnly, Local Government Specialist, 1985-present
J. M. Hart, Extension Specialist, 1982-1983
G. W. Holland, Coordinator, Extension Programs, 1987-present
J. L. Hopkins II, Local Government Specialist, 1973-present
K. D. Imel, Industrial Laboratory Technician, 1976-1978
S. K. Iyengar, Engineering Research Project, 1977-1978
A. Jalali-Yazdi, Research Associate, Industrial Engineering, 1976-1977
L. A. Macuila, Local Government Specialist, 1977-1979
C. G. Maule, Assistant Director, Center for Local Government Technology, 1978-present
G. R. McClain, Associate Professor, Technology, 1975-1980
Joe H. Mize, Professor and Head, Industrial Engineering, 1977-1978
J. D. Paden, Local Government Specialist, 1973-present
S. W. Patterson, Research Industrial Engineer, 1977-1979
S. A. Phelps, Extension Specialist, 1983-1984
J. E. Shamblin, Director, Center for Local Government Technology, 1974-present
Michael Tunks, Local Government Specialist, 1978-1979
W. C. Turner, Associate Professor, Industrial Engineering, 1977-1978
S. S. Viner, Coordinator, Extension Programs, 1983-present

R. Dean Weston, Local Government Specialist, 1982-present
W. D. Whitney, Extension Engineer, 1979-1982
D. A. Willett, Senior Agriculturalist, 1987-present
D. A. Wright, Local Government Specialist, 1984-present

Appendix 12

Oklahoma Cooperative Extension Directors
1914-present

Frank H. Baker, Dean of Agriculture and Director, 1974-1979

Walter D. Bentley, Director and State Agent, 1914-1916

William D. Bentley, Director of Extension, 1925-1926

Luther H. Brannon, Director of Extension, 1957-1964

Shawnee Brown, Director of Extension, 1941-1956

Charles Browning, Dean of Agriculture and Director, 1979-present

William A. Conner, Director of Extension, 1921-1922; 1923-1924

Jean C. Evans, Dean of Extension and Director, 1965-1967; Vice President of Extension and Director, 1967-1974

Edward A. Miller, Director of Extension, 1922-1923

Ernest E. Scholl, Director of Extension, 1935-1941

Dover P. Trent, Director of Extension, 1926-1935

James A. Wilson, Director and State Agent, 1916-1921

Appendix 13

College of Osteopathic Medicine*

ADMINISTRATIVE STAFF

Larry D. Cherry, D.O., Assistant Dean of Clinical Education, 1977

Tom E. Denton, D.O., Clinic Director, 1985

Dean R. Fullingim, D.O., Chairman of the Department of Radiology, 1982

Jim L. Hashbarger, Director of Accounting and Budgeting, 1988

Clyde B. Jensen, Ph.D., President, 1987

Paul P. Koro, D.O., Chairman of the Department of Surgery, 1976

Loren G. Martin, Ph.D., Director of Continuing Medical Education, 1981

Sue McKnight, Director of Personnel Services, Affirmative Action, and Risk Management, 1973

William E. Moore, D.O., Director of Clerkships, 1985

Daniel E. Overack, Ph.D., Assistant Dean of Students, 1976

Thomas R. Pickard, D. O., Chairman of the Department of General Practice and Interim Assistant Dean of Postdoctoral Education, 1985

Michael H. Pollak, Ph.D., Acting Director of the Center for Behavioral Medicine, 1981

Robert C. Ritter, Ph.D., Associate Dean of Preclinical Education, 1974

Kenneth W. Roberts, Director of Campus Facilities, 1976

Linda L. Roberts, College Librarian, 1974

Richard C. Staab, D.O., Chairman of the Department of Medicine, 1980

Melvin J. Van Boven, D.O., Chairman of the Department of Pathology, 1984

Richard A. Wansley, Ph.D., Assistant Dean of Research, Sponsored Programs, and Service, 1976

Gary H. Watson, Ph.D., Director of Research, 1985

Jack R. Wolfe, D.O., Dean of Academic Affairs, 1980

Jan G. Womack, Ph.D., Vice President of Administrative Services, 1986

FACULTY

Martin W. Banschbach, Ph.D., Professor of Biochemistry, 1980

Richard H. Bost, Ph.D., Associate Professor of Behavioral Sciences, 1982

George M. Brenner, Ph.D., Professor of Pharmacology, 1976

Larry D. Cherry, D.O., Professor of General Practice, 1977

Robert S. Conrad, Ph.D., Professor of Microbiology, 1974

Tom E. Denton, D.O., Associate Professor of General Practice, 1985

Robert F. Distefano, D.O., Assistant Professor of Pathology, 1988

J. C. Doggett, Ph.D., Professor of Behavioral Sciences, 1976

William Stephen Eddy, D.O., Associate Professor of General Practice, 1984

Richard A. Felmlee, D.O., Associate Professor of General Practice, 1977

Warren E. Finn, Ph.D., Associate Professor of Physiology, 1975

Susan K. Geiss, Ph.D., Assistant Professor of Behavioral Sciences, 1982

Kenneth E. Graham, D.O., Associate Professor of General Practice, 1982

James L. Howard, D.O., Assistant Professor of General Practice, 1987

Robert E. Irvin, D.O., Associate Professor of General Practice, 1988

Kirby L. Jarolim, Ph.D., Professor of Anatomy, 1974

William R. Kennedy, D.O., Associate Professor of Pediatrics, 1983

Gerald R. Kirk, Ph.D., Professor of Anatomy, 1975

Rosalie J. Lawson, Ph.D., Associate Professor of Behavioral Sciences, 1981

Loren G. Martin, Ph.D., Professor of Physiology, 1981

William D. Meek, Ph.D., Assistant Professor of Anatomy, 1985

Dianne K. Miller-Hardy, Ph.D., Professor of Pathology, 1985

Mark A. Mitchell, Ph.D., Assistant Professor of Pharmacology, 1985

William E. Moore, D.O., Professor of Surgery, 1985

Daniel E. Overack, Ph.D., Professor of Anatomy, 1976

Thomas R. Pickard, D.O., Assistant Professor of General Practice, 1985

Michael H. Pollak, Ph.D., Associate Professor of Behavioral Sciences, 1981

Joseph A. Price, III, Ph.D., Associate Professor of Microbiology/Immunology, 1985

Robert C. Ritter, Ph.D., Professor of Microbiology, 1974

William G. Robertson, Ph.D., Professor of Physiology, 1974

M. Jean Root, D.O., Associate Professor of General Practice, 1983

James F. Routsong, D.O., Assistant Professor of General Practice, 1982

Charles G. Sanny, Ph.D., Associate Professor of Biochemistry, 1985

Ortwin W. Schmidt, Ph.D., Assistant Professor of Microbiology/Virology, 1985

James F. Taylor, Ph.D., Professor of Anatomy, 1975

Richard A. Wansley, Ph.D., Associate Professor of Behavioral Sciences, 1976

Gary H. Watson, Ph.D., Assistant Professor of Biochemistry, 1985

Jack R. Wolfe, D.O., Professor of General Practice, 1980

PROFESSIONAL STAFF

Don Anderson, Associate Director, Oklahoma Area Health Education Center, 1989

James D. Bloch, D.O., Director of Medical Education, 1988

Terry R. Boucher, Coordinator of Physician Placement and Alumni Affairs, 1981

Donald G. Casto, Coordinator of Anatomy Laboratory, 1988

Esther L. Davis, Data Processing Manager, 1986

Howard L. Eubanks, Assistant Director of Campus Facilities, 1976

Dan H. Fieker, D.O., Director of Medical Education, 1979

Joseph F. Fusco, Ed.D., Assistant to the Dean of Academic Affairs and Instructional Developer, 1987

Janice L. Giacomo, Coordinator of Continuing Medical Education, 1985

Robert L. Gray, Senior Accountant, 1980

Christian S. Hanson, D.O., Licensed Physician Educator, 1985

Barbara A. Johnson, Purchasing and Contracts Officer, 1977

Jacqueline D. Johnson, Registrar and Coordinator of Admissions, 1988

Dixie Jurney, Coordinator of Physician Placement, 1980

Janna L. Kraft, Coordinator of College Relations, 1986

G. Diane Landrum, Executive Assistant to the President, 1981

John C. Loose, Jr., Coordinator of Payroll and Employee Benefits, 1981

Gail A. Maercklein, Research Associate, 1982

George David Money, Assistant Librarian, 1978

Victoria M. Noe, Business Office Coordinator, 1981

Wennette Pegues, Ed.D., Associate Director, Oklahoma Area Health Education Center, 1989

Linda S. Plemons, Coordinator of Publications, 1987

Brian T. Raber, Electron Microscopist, 1986

William D. Roettger, Clinic Business Office Manager, 1986

James F. Routsong, D.O., Coordinator of Career Opportunities in Osteopathic Medicine, 1982

Anita K. Schell, Clinical Education Coordinator, 1986

Wynema Scott, Project Coordinator, Cherokee Health Coalition Project, 1988

Bruce A. Singer, Clinical Associate, 1981

Kenneth Slade, Research Associate, 1985

H. C. Snook, Financial Aid Officer, 1981

Ellen L. Stockton, Coordinator of Graphic Arts and Photography, 1980

Anita K. Sutrick, Assistant Librarian, 1979

Randy L. Taylor, Coordinator of Audio-Visual Services, 1980

John A. Voorhees, D.O., Director of Medical Education, 1980

*This list includes only those faculty and staff members at the College of Osteopathic Medicine of Oklahoma State University as of February 1, 1989.

Selected Bibliography

In addition to the specific items listed, other sources include innumerable letters, memos, programs, brochures, notes, reports, informal interviews and conversations, and other miscellaneous sources of information.

ARTICLES

Abbott, William S. "Is the World Becoming our Campus?" *Oklahoma State Alumnus Magazine*, vol. 7, no. 7 (September-October 1966), pp. 44-46.

"Aggieland Roundup." *Oklahoma A. and M. College Magazine*, vol. 28, no. 2 (October 1956), pp. 10-11.

"Around the Campus." *Oklahoma A. and M. College Magazine*, vol. 8, no. 7 (April 1937), p. 10.

"Arts and Sciences Extension: A College Within a College." *Oklahoma State Alumnus Magazine*, vol. 6, no. 2 (February 1965), p. 20.

"Business Vice-Dean Acts as Labor Dispute Arbitrator." *Oklahoma State Alumnus Magazine*, vol. 6, no. 5 (May l965), p. 31.

Caldwell, Richard M. "The Okmulgee Branch College." *Oklahoma A. and M. College Magazine*, vol. 18, no. 3 (December 1946), pp. 8-9.

"Campus and Faculty News.' *Oklahoma A. and M. College Magazine*, vol. 26, no. 8 (April 1955), pp. 20-22.

"CBA Extension Covers Three Major Areas." *Oklahoma State University Outreach*, vol. 15, no. 4 (April 1974), pp. 30-31.

"Clay Potts Serves in Nation's Capitol." *Oklahoma A. and M. College Magazine*, vol. 22, no. 1 (September 1950), p. 13.

"Coeds Entertain Troops for USO." *Oklahoma State Alumnus Magazine*, vol. 3, no. 9 (March 1968), pp. 12-14.

Duning, Becky. "Reaching Out with NUTN." *Teleconference Magazine*, vol. 6, no. 1 (January-February 1987), pp. 16-21.

"Dunlap Appointed Chancellor of Higher Education." *Oklahoma State Alumnus Magazine*, vol. 2, no. 2 (February 1961), p. 21.

Ellis, Bill. "Candid Campus' Educational Services." *Oklahoma State University Outreach*, vol. 14, no. 8 (November 1973), pp. 6-7.

"Engineering and Industrial Extension: A Tradition of Service." *Oklahoma State Alumnus Magazine*, vol. 6, no. 3 (March 1965), p. 27.

"Engineering Extension Programs are Varied." *Oklahoma State University Outreach*, vol. 15, no. 4 (April 1974), pp. 34-35.

"ESMWT Courses Offered." *Oklahoma A. and M. College Magazine*, vol. 14, no. 5 (February 1943), p. 6.

"Evans Is Chosen as Director of OSU Extension." *Oklahoma State Alumnus Magazine*, vol. 6, no. 2 (February 1965), p. 19.

Evans, Jean C. "Extension is Expanding." *Oklahoma State Alumnus Magazine*, vol. 7, no. 7 (September 1966), pp. 26-27.

Evans, Jean C. "University Extension Covers Wide Range of Activities." *Oklahoma State University Outreach*, vol. 15, no. 4 (April 1974). pp. 4-6.

"Everlasting Service." *Oklahoma State Alumnus Magazine*, vol. 2, no. 6 (June 1961), p. 9.

"Extends a Helping Hand in Community Problems." *Oklahoma State University Outreach*, vol. 15, no. 4 (April 1974), pp. 10-11.

"Extension Administrative Personnel Action." *Oklahoma State Alumnus Magazine*, vol. 9, no. 6 (June-July 1968), p. 19.

"Extension Centers Plan Open House." *Oklahoma State Alumnus Magazine*, vol. 10, no. 5 (May 1969), p. 5.

"Extension Service Reorganized by University Regents." *Oklahoma State Alumnus Magazine*, vol. 6, no. 7 (September-October 1965), p. 17.

"Extension Teaching by Long Distance Hookup." *Oklahoma State Alumnus Magazine*, vol. 9, no. 5 (May 1968), p. 30.

"Eyes, Ears, Wheels and Wings." *Oklahoma A. and M. College Magazine*, vol. 26, no. 1 (September 1954), pp. 10-13.

"Faculty Changes." *Oklahoma A. and M. College Magazine*, vol. 8, no. 2 (October 1936), pp. 10, 15.

"The Flying Aggies—Color Them Silver." *Oklahoma State University Outreach, vol. 14, no. 7 (September-October 1973), pp. 18-19.*

Gonzales, Nestor, "OSU Gets Osteopathic College," Oklahoma State University Outreach, vol. 59, no. 4 (Summer 1988), pp. 12-13.

Grantham, J. O. and Poole, Richard W. "New Technology for a Traditional Land Grant Mission." *Oklahoma State University Outreach*, vol. 56, no. 3 (Spring 1985), pp. 52-54.

"Helping with Family Living Needs." *Oklahoma State University Outreach*, vol. 15, no. 4 (April 1974), pp. 7-9.

"In Pursuit of Knowledge." *Oklahoma State Alumnus Magazine*, vol. 1, no. 9 (October 1960), pp. 4-7.

Kriegel, Monroe W. "Attacking Technical Obsolescence." *Chemical Engineering*, vol. 70, no. 9 (29 April 1963), pp. 134-138.

"Laboratories on Wheels." *Oklahoma State University Magazine*, vol. 2, no. 4 (October 1958), pp. 16-18.

"Long Arm of Service." *Oklahoma State Alumnus Magazine*, vol. 6, no. 1 (January 1965), p. 31.

"Maestro of Aggieland Student Entertainment Talent." *Oklahoma A. and M. College Magazine*, vol. 28, no. 3 (November 1956), pp. 5-6.

"1988-89 Annual Directory." *Oklahoma DO: The Journal of the Oklahoma Osteopathic Association* (August 1988), pp. 30-55.

"Nuclear Science for the Student." *Oklahoma State Alumnus Magazine*, vol. 2, no. 4 (April 1961), pp. 8-11.

"OCOMS Celebrates Founders' Day." *Oklahoma DO: The Journal of the Oklahoma Osteopathic Association* (March 1980), p. 14.

"OCOMS to be Governed by New Board of Regents." *Oklahoma DO: The Journal of the Oklahoma Osteopathic Association* (June 1980), p. 8.

"Operations College Education: By Invitation Only." *Oklahoma A. and M. College Magazine*, vol. 28, no. 5 (January 1957), p. 9.

"OSU Ambassador H. Clay Potts Dies at Age 72." *Oklahoma State Alumnus Magazine*, vol. 8, no. 1 (January 1967), p. 26.

"OSU Institute for Budding Scientists." *Oklahoma State University Magazine*, vol. 1, no. 3 (September 1957), pp. 12-13.

"OSU Plans Summer Science Program." *Oklahoma State Alumnus Magazine*, vol. 4, no. 4 (April 1963), p. 47.

O'Toole, Lela. "Strengthening of Family Life." *Oklahoma State Alumnus Magazine*, vol. 3, no. 4 (April 1962), p. 25.

Perdue, Phil. "Short Courses." *Oklahoma A. and M. College Magazine*, vol. 8, no. 3 (December 1936), p. 6.

"A Permanent Home for a New College and the Oklahoma Osteopathic Profession." *Oklahoma D.O.: The Journal of the Oklahoma Osteopathic Association* (October 1974), pp. 14-20.

"Potts Sets a Good Table." *Oklahoma A. and M. College Magazine*, vol. 19, no. 2 (November 1947), p. 7.

Scroggs, Schiller. "Cooperation for Defense." *Oklahoma A. and M. College Magazine*, vol. 13, no. 5 (February 1942), pp. 3-4, 12-13.

"Serving the Needs of Business." *Oklahoma State University Magazine*, vol. 2, no. 9 (March 1959), pp. 4-7.

"Specialists Play Major Role in Ag Extension." *Oklahoma State University Outreach*, vol. 15, no. 4 (April 1974), pp. 26-27.

Turner, Mary L. "Changing Times are Challenge to Extension." *Oklahoma State University Outreach*, vol. 15, no. 4 (April 1974), pp. 28-29.

"A Venture into Radio's Educational Broadcasting." *Oklahoma State University Magazine*, vol. 2, no. 11 (May 1959), pp. 16-17.

"Veterinary Medicine's Role in Extension." *Oklahoma State University Outreach*, vol. 15, no. 4 (April 1974), p. 36.

"Your College Extension Program." *Oklahoma A. and M. College Magazine*, vol. 18, no. 5 (February 1947), pp. 8-10.

Zant, James H. "Revolutionizing the Math Curriculum." *Oklahoma State Alumnus Magazine*, vol. 3, no. 9 (October 1962), pp. 16-17.

AUTHOR INTERVIEWS

Allen, Marshall E., 15 December 1987, Stillwater, OK.

Boggs, J. H., 7 September 1988, Stillwater, OK.

Cacy, Lora B., 14 October 1987, Stillwater, OK.

Conway, Russell V., 28 September 1987, Stillwater, OK.

Cooper, Bill L., 15 October 1987, Stillwater, OK.

Crockett, Jerry, 21 September 1987, Stillwater, OK.

Dunlap, E. T., 13 September 1988, Oklahoma City, OK.

Feasley, Charles E., 15 December 1987, Stillwater, OK.

Felmlee, Edward A., 8 September 1988, Tulsa, OK.

Fitzgerald, J. Conner, 28 January 1986, Stillwater, OK.

Grantham, J. O., 22 July 1986 and 14 December 1987, Stillwater, OK.

Green, Stanley D., 12 October 1987, Stillwater, OK.

Hirschlein, Beulah M., 14 January 1988, Stillwater, OK.

Hromas, James G., 13 October 1987, Stillwater, OK.

Jensen, Clyde, 8 September 1988, Stillwater, OK.

Jones, Bob, 13 September 1988, Oklahoma City, OK.

Jungers, Richard, 22 July 1986, Stillwater, OK.

Kamm, Robert B., 29 September 1987, 28 March 1988, Stillwater, OK

Kriegel, Monroe W., 24 July 1986, Stillwater, OK.

Luebke, Phyllis J., 23 January 1986, Stillwater, OK.

Malle, Albert L., 27 September 1987, Stillwater, OK.

McCollom, Katherine, 24 January 1986, Stillwater, OK.

McGaugh, Gladys S., 24 January 1986, Stillwater, OK.

Millington, Clayton, 25 July 1986, Stillwater, OK.

Oberle, E. Marie, 17 December 1987, Stillwater, OK.

Poole, Richard W., 12 October 1987, Stillwater, OK.

Pritchard Guy M., 27 January 1986, Stillwater, OK.

Richardson, Lavon P., 18 September 1987, Stillwater, OK.

Routsong, James R., 8 September 1988, Tulsa, OK.

Sheerar, L. F. "Mike," 27 February 1986, Stillwater, OK.

Smith, Thomas J. Jr., 12 October 1987, Stillwater, OK.

Thedford, Thomas R., 14 October 1987, Stillwater, OK.

Wiggins, Kenneth E., 21 September 1987, Stillwater, OK.

BOOKS

Conference of Academic Deans. *Evaluation of Student Achievement: The Twelfth Yearbook of the Annual Summer Conference of Academic Deans*. Stillwater: Oklahoma State University, 1958.

Fite, Robert. *The Transfer of Environmental Information via the Cooperative Extension Service: A Report to the U.S. Environmental Protection Agency*. Stillwater: Oklahoma State University, January 1978.

Gevitz, Norman. *The D.O.'s: Osteopathic Medicine in America*. Baltimore, MD: The Johns Hopkins University Press, 1982.

Gill, Jerry Leon. *The Great Adventure: Oklahoma State University and International Education*. Stillwater: Oklahoma State University Press, 1978.

Jones, Bob E. *The Difference a D. O. Makes*. Oklahoma City, OK: Times-Journal Publishing Company, 1978.

Kincaid, William M. Jr. *A History of the Oklahoma State University College of Business Administration*. Stillwater: Oklahoma State University Press, 1987.

Mills, Lawrence W. *A Feasibility Study for the Establishment of a College of Osteopathic Medicine and Surgery in the Tulsa Area*. Oklahoma City, OK: Legislative Council of the State of Oklahoma, 1971.

Oklahoma A. and M. College General Catalog, 1922; 1924; 1926; 1928; 1938.

Oklahoma State University Student Handbook, 1957-58.

Roberts, Edd, editor. *History of Oklahoma State University Extension*. Stillwater: Oklahoma State University, Omicron Chapter, Epsilon Sigma Phi, [1970].

Rulon, Philip Reed. *Oklahoma State University—Since 1890*. Stillwater: Oklahoma State University Press, 1975.

Williams, Eric I. *A History of the Oklahoma State University College of Veterinary Medicine*. Stillwater: Oklahoma State University, 1986.

COLLECTIONS

Bound Volume of Letters from Friends and Professional Associates Presented to Roy Tompkins on His Retirement from Oklahoma A. and M. College. In the personal possession of Katherine Tompkins McCollom, Stillwater, Oklahoma.

Office of University Extension, Oklahoma State University, Stillwater, Oklahoma:

Annual Reports, Oklahoma State University Extension, 1977-1986.

Office of the Vice President for University Relations and Extension, Oklahoma State University, Stillwater, Oklahoma:

Files.

Special Collections, Edmon Low Library, Oklahoma State University, Stillwater, Oklahoma:

Board of Regents for the Oklahoma Agricultural and Mechanical Colleges Minutes.

NUTN Annual Report, 1986-87.

Oklahoma State Board of Agriculture Minutes.

Transcript of Vernon Parcher interview with L. F. "Mike" Sheerar, 23 July 1983, Stillwater, OK.

NEWSPAPERS

Kansas City Star, 27 April 1958.

Oklahoma City Daily Oklahoman, 5 October 1958; 27 September 1959; 15 January 1965; 18 July 1965; 13 August 1965; 9 October 1965; 20 March 1970; 1 July 1982; 26 September 1982; 8 May 1983; 22 January 1987; 15 March 1987; 22 September 1988.

Oklahoma State University Student Newspapers:

Oklahoma A. and M. College Mirror, 1895-1898.

College Paper, 1899-1907.

Brown and Blue, 1908.

Orange and Black, 1908-1924.

O'Collegian, 1924-1927.

Daily O'Collegian, 1927-1988.

Stillwater Advance-Democrat, 22 November 1917; 6 June 1923.

Stillwater Gazette, 6 September 1918; 25 September 1925; 6 December 1929; 10 May 1957; 18 October 1957.

Stillwater NewsPress, 8 May 1936; 11 September 1939; 22 November 1957; 26 June 1958; 9 March 1959; 11 July 1961; 18 July 1965; 12 June 1966; 5 February 1967; 7 October 1974; 12 January 1975; 25 June 1978; 11 January 1981; 23 August 1981; 6 December 1981; 11 April 1982; 3 April 1983; 29 January 1986; 15 January 1988.

Stillwater Payne County News, 8 May 1936.

Tulsa County News, 18 September 1980.

Tulsa Eastside Times, 8 September 1986.

Tulsa Tribune, 1 January 1943; 28 October 1976; 20 April 1977; 8 February 1984; 13 March 1987; 10 April 1987.

Tulsa World, 24 August 1982; 11 December 1975; 17 January 1981; 8 September 1984; 24 May 1987; 20 April 1988.

Index

B

Bacon, Charles: 108.
Baker, E. C.: 21.
Baker, Frank: 101.
Baker, J. N.: 50.
Bamburge, W. M.: 12.
Band Clinic: 72.
Barker, Jim: 144.
Barrett, Dick: 44.
Barson, John: 136, 138, 139, 141, 142, 144.
Bartlett, Dewey: 83.
Bayless, Jerry: 83.
Bellmon, Henry: 73, 79, 118, 129, 142, 143.
Bendix Award: 59.
Bennett, Henry G.: 23, 24, 29, 32, 33, 34, 35, 37, 38, 39, 41, 42, 43, 44, 48, 49, 51, 52, 55, 56.
Bentley, W. D.: 12, 13.
Bentley, Wilson: 62.
Berg, Milton: 47, 70.
Bernstein, Jim: 122.
Birchard, Ralph: 47.
Bittenbender, H. A.: 8.
Bivins, Richard: 120.
Boger, Lawrence L.: 5, 107, 108, 123, 144.
Boll Weevil: 12.
Bone, John H.: 11.
Bose, Jim: 110.
Bost, Richard: 140.
Boyd, E. P.: 23.
Brannon, Luther: 57, 66.
Bremmer, Dale: 68.
Brennan, Charles F.: 43.
Broadway Plays: 120.
Brobst, Harry K.: 48, 61.
Brown, Don: 121.
Brown University: 121.
Brumbaugh, Norma: 67.
Bruneau, Herbert: 70, 71.
BSCS Biology: 70.
Buck, Richard: 58.
Bumpass, Donald: 115.
Bureau of Narcotics and Dangerous Drugs: 84.
Bureau of Tests and Measurements: 48.
Burris, Edward C.: 64, 65.
Burton, Lucius W.: 19.
Business Extension: 46, 47, 60, 61, 64, 87, 88, 102, 114, 115, 116.
Butler, Ellen: 37.

C

Cable Television: 5.
Cacy, Lora: 89, 90, 116.

California College of Medicine: 133.
California Medical Association: 133.
California Merger: 144.
California Osteopathic Association: 133.
California State University at Chico: 83, 112.
Cameron University: 141.
Campbell, James R.: 18.
"Candid Campus": 96, 107, 108.
Cantwell, James W.: 14.
Canup, Harry: 46, 47, 60, 64.
Carl Albert Junior College: 141.
Carlile, Thomas J.: 138.
Carnegie Foundation: 45.
Carnegie Music Library: 45.
Caskey, Raymond: 47.
Cavett, Debbie: 91.
Center for Apparel Marketing and Merchandising: 117.
Center For Community Services and Voluntarism: 117.
Center for Local Government Technology: 104, 105.
Central Airlines: 50.
Challenger: 113.
Chamberlain, Wilt: 59.
Chandler, Emma A.: 7.
Chandler, Philip: 57.
CHEM Chemistry: 70.
Cherokee Indian Tribe: 141.
Cherry, L. D.: 139.
Cheese Festival: 66, 80.
CHIME: 113.
Choike, Jim: 124.
Civil Defense Work Shop: 72.
Civil War: 130, 132.
Civilian Conservation Corps: 26.
Clark, Edward F.: 6.
Code of Ethics: 132.
Coleman, Nina: 46.
College of Agriculture: 4, 18, 31, 36, 78, 80, 97, 118.
College of Arts and Sciences: 4, 18, 31, 34, 36, 45, 46, 52, 55, 61, 78, 80, 82, 102, 107, 108, 119, 121, 123.
College of Business Administration: 4, 18, 31, 34, 36, 46, 47, 52, 55, 65, 78, 79, 81, 102, 114.
College of Education: 4, 31, 36, 46, 52, 55, 59, 61, 78, 81, 86, 94, 102, 111, 112.
College of Engineering, Architecture and Technology: 4, 18, 31, 36, 37, 46, 52, 55, 61, 78, 81, 104.
College of Home Economics: 4, 31, 34, 36, 67, 78, 80, 89, 116, 117.
College of Osteopathic Medicine of Oklahoma State University: 130, 135, 136, 140, 141, 144.

College of Osteopathic Physicians and
  Surgeons: 133.
College of Veterinary Medicine: 4, 78, 90,
  118, 129.
Combs, Denny: 44.
Committee on Science and Engineers: 57.
Communications Satellite: 5.
Community Development Institute: 86.
Community Development Program: 49.
Community Education: 111.
Community Education Center: 86, 111,
  112.
Condry, Russell J.: 36.
Conference for Academic Deans: 65.
Conger, Napoleon: 38.
Continuing Education: 45, 52, 55, 56, 59,
  77, 78, 80, 125.
Conway, Russell: 90, 91, 107.
Continental Classroom: 72.
Cooper, Bill: 89, 109, 110.
Cooperative College School Science
  Program: 71, 82, 87.
Cooperative Extension Service: 4, 13, 17,
  23, 27, 31, 32, 62, 67, 77, 78, 87, 89,
  96, 97, 98, 101, 102, 116, 118, 129.
Coordinator of Conferences: 66.
Correspondence Courses: 14, 18, 20, 36,
  106.
Couey, Paul: 121.
Council on Educational Outreach: 109,
  111, 114, 117.
Counseling Clinics: 72.
County Agent. See County Extension
  Director.
County Extension Director: 78, 85.
County Home Demonstration Agent. See
  Extension Home Economist.
Covell, L. K.: 42.
Cox, Ruth: 18, 19, 20.
Cox, Wayne: 44.
Crable, A. Lawrence: 19, 20, 29.
Crabtree, Beverly: 116.
Crockett, Jerry: 81, 83, 102, 119.
Croft, Jerry: 120.
Cullison, Robert: 144.
Cunningham, Thomas: 89.

D

Danel, Dorothea: 117.
Daniels, Dorothy: 37.
Darlington, Meredith W.: 31.
Darlow, Al: 57.
Davis, Jerry: 120.
Deal, Roy: 69.
Deering, Ferdie: 44.
Defense Classes: 33.
Demonstration Train: 9.
Department of Radio Services: 37.
Department of Radio-TV: 59

Depression: 17, 24, 26.
Dermer, Otis: 71.
Developmental Economic Education
  Program: 87.
Diplomates in Osteopathy: 131.
Director of Short Courses: 24, 51, 65.
Division of Agriculture. See College of
  Agriculture.
Division of Commerce and Marketing. See
  College of Business Administration.
Division of Engineering. See College of
  Engineering, Architecture and
  Technology.
Division of Home Economics. See College
  of Home Economics.
Dobson, Judith: 109.
Dobson, Russell: 109.
Doctor of Osteopathy: 131, 132, 133, 134,
  135, 136, 138, 141, 142, 144.
Doggett, J. C.: 141.
Donnell, Philip S.: 50.
Douglas R. J.: 63.
Dowell, C. T.: 23.
Dowell, E. F.: 48.
Downlink: 108, 123.
Driver Education: 84.
Dudley, Eldon: 44.
Dunlap, E. T.: 109, 136, 137.
Dunlap, Milan: 37.
Dust Bowl: 17, 24, 29.
Dutreau, Frances: 83, 120.
Dyess, Ben C.: 20.

E

Earth Sheltered Housing: 110.
Economic Opportunity Act: 74, 86.
Edmison, Marvin: 58. 97.
Education Extension: 60, 61, 62, 102,
  111, 113.
Education for the Space Age: 111.
Educational Extension: 22, 29, 31, 34, 42,
  46, 47, 56.
Educational Television: 5, 30, 59, 95.
Educational Television Services: 5, 107,
  118, 123, 124.
Eisenhower, Dwight: 57, 74.
Eissenstadt, Bernard: 120.
Elburz Mountains: 49.
Elderhostel: 120.
Electronic University Network: 106.
Engineering and Industrial Extension: 46,
  60, 62, 63, 86, 88, 89, 102, 104, 109,
  110.
Engineering Extension. See Engineering
  and Industrial Extension.
Engineering, Science, and Management
  War Training: 35.
Enid Memorial Hospital: 141.
Environmental Institute: 86.

Environmental Quality Conference: 83.
Erwin, Robert: 58, 64.
Eskridge, James R.: 17, 21.
Evans, Charles: 21, 30.
Evans, Denman: 68.
Evans, Jean C.: 67, 78, 79, 87, 88, 96, 97, 101, 103.
Explorer I: 58.
Extension Agent: 3, 7, 13.
Extension Courses: 21, 31, 36, 41, 43, 78, 80, 87.
Extension Faculty Award: 108.
Extension Home Economist: 78.

F

Fairs: 11, 12, 17, 36.
Family Medicine: 138, 139.
Farm and Home Week: 35.
Farmers' Institute: 6.
Farmers Week: 11.
Faust, H. G.: 45.
Feasley, Charles E.: 105, 106.
Featherly, Charles A.: 137.
Featherly, H. I.: 71.
Fedderson, Don: 44.
Federal Aid for Education: 74.
Federal Emergency Relief Administration: 26.
Federal Highway Administration: 84.
Feeders Day: 35, 80.
Felmlee, Edward A.: 136, 138.
Ferguson, Felicia: 5.
Fields, John: 10, 11.
Finn, Warren E.: 137.
Fire Service Training: 89, 110.
Firefighting Manuals: 110.
Fischer, Ruth Helen: 37.
Fisher, Hoover: 73.
Fite, Robert C.: 46, 59, 67, 68, 69, 70, 71, 82, 83, 84, 103, 104.
Fitzgerald, J. Conner: 41, 42, 47, 52, 56, 57, 59, 61, 78, 84.
Flight School: 32, 33, 43, 59, 92.
Flying Aggies: 44, 59, 92, 105.
Flying Farmers: 43, 44, 67.
Food and Agriculture Organization: 5.
Ford Foundation: 49, 57.
Ford, Gerald R.: 94.
Ford, Ronald: 97.
"Foxhole University": 36.
Frank, Gerald: 121.
Freeman, Orville L.: 88.
Frisco Railroad: 8.
Frontiers of Science Foundation of Oklahoma: 55, 68, 83.
Fry, Floyd: 50.
Fry, Mrs. Floyd: 50.
Fulbright Fellowship: 81.

G

Gallagher Hall: 72.
Gardner, Peggy: 105, 106.
Gates, Byron E.: 47.
Gatewood, Claude: 68.
Gee, Lynn: 71.
Gerber, Ruth: 71.
Geriatric Medicine Club: 141.
G. I. Bill of Rights: 38.
Gillson, R. G.: 136.
Girod, Raymond: 52, 72.
Glass, Bryan: 71.
Glazier, Henry E.: 11.
Glennan Hospital: 42.
Godfrey, Max: 37.
Good, Linda K.: 117.
Governor's Conference: 83, 122.
Graduate College: 55, 86.
Graduate School. *See* Graduate College.
Graham, Herb: 44.
Grantham, J. O.: 5, 62, 63, 86, 87, 98, 101, 102, 103, 108, 109, 122, 124, 125.
Great Society: 90.
Gregory, Doris: 37.
Green, Stanley: 73, 119, 121.
Greenwood, Kathryn: 117.
Gregory, Mark: 110, 111.
Gries, George: 102, 108, 121.
Griffith, Dean: 109, 110.
Grondzik, Walter: 110.
Grover Loening Award: 92.
Gumm, Robert: 96.
Guthrie, Al: 32, 33, 34, 42, 44.

H

Hall, David: 136.
Halley, Bill: 108.
Hamilton, James: 135.
Hamilton, O. H.: 71.
Hamm, B. Curtis: 88, 102, 115, 116.
Hanry, A. D.: 42.
Hansen, Walter: 71.
Hargrave, George: 135.
Harley Thomas Ford Agency: 66.
Harrington, Harold: 71.
Harris, Fremont: 71.
Harris, Tom N.: 34, 37, 45, 73.
Harris, Woodfin: 85, 105.
Harrison, A. B.: 121.
Hartenbower, A. C.: 8, 10.
Hawkins, Glenn B.: 49.
Hawkins, Jean: 73.
Head Start Program: 89.
Health Care Cost Containment: 122.
Health Resources and Services Administration: 139.
Heath, Harry: 108.
Helt, Dwight: 91.

Henry, Hiram: 45, 73.
Hickman, LaMoyne: 136.
Higher Education Act: 74.
High School and College Relations: 22, 27, 91, 107.
High School Institute: 46, 74.
Higher Education Alumni Council: 107.
Highways: 50, 59.
Hill, Fannie: 138.
Hirschlein, Beulah: 116, 118.
Hodnett, Ernest: 71.
Hoffer, Josephine: 89.
Hoffman, C. E.: 69.
Hofler, Pat: 108.
Hohstadt, L. M.: 31, 42.
Holistic Health Care: 138.
Holt, Smith: 121, 123.
Holter, George L.: 6.
Home Demonstration Agent: 17.
Home Economics Day: 89.
"Home Economics on Parade": 67.
Home Economics University Extension: 89, 109, 116, 118.
Hopkins, Michael: 117.
Houlihan, Rodney: 141, 142, 144.
House Resolution 3420: 77.
Howard, Gene: 135.
Hromas, James: 115, 116.
Hudiburg, Everett: 63.
Humphrey, Hubert: 86.
Hunt, DeWitt: 33, 34, 50.

I

Imperial Ethiopian College of Agriculture and Mechanical Arts: 49, 57, 67, 73, 93.
"Independence Hall": 118.
Independent and Correspondence Study: 105. *See also* School of Correspondence Study.
Individual-Opportunity-Achievement Ranch: 50.
Industrial Editors' Short Course: 72.
International Business Machines: 88.
International Cooperative Education: 120.
International Teacher Development Program: 72.
Interscholastic Contests: 14, 17, 36, 44.
Iowa State University: 64.
Irey, Karen: 92.

J

Jackson, Ben: 93.
Jeffery, D. B.: 57.
Jensen, Clyde B.: 142, 143, 144.
Jobe, John: 105, 109, 124.
Johnson, Elmer: 63.
Johnson, L. Wayne: 70, 71.
Johnson, Lyndon: 74, 79, 90.
Johnson, Robert: 59.

Johnson Space Center: 82, 116.
Johnson, W. D.: 86, 111.
Johnson, William: 109, 117.
Jones, Bob: 136.
Jones, Claude: 82.
Jones, Fred L.: 19.
Jones, Hilton I.: 22.
Jones, Roy W.: 71.
Jungers, Richard: 60, 61, 62, 85, 102, 111.

K

KAMC Radio: 58.
Kamm, Robert B.: 80, 81, 92, 93, 96, 97, 101, 107.
Kelley, Garland: 44.
Kellogg Foundation: 118.
Kennedy, John F.: 74.
Kerr, Robert S.: 37, 38, 51, 66.
Keso, Edward E.: 68.
KETA Television: 59, 96.
Klemme, Randall T.: 48, 49.
Knapp, Bradford: 10, 22, 23.
Knapp, Seaman A.: 10, 12, 13.
Knight, James: 110.
Knowles, Malcolm: 61.
Knutson, Gerald: 85.
KOED Television: 96.
Kolshorn, Henrietta: 8.
KOSU-FM Radio: 108.
Kriegel, Monroe W.: 64, 88, 89, 102, 109, 110.
KVOO Radio: 23, 35.
KVRO Radio: 58.

L

Lacy, Robert: 59.
Lane, W. C.: 22.
Langston University: 114.
Lapsley, Tiner: 59.
Laughlin, Glenn: 47.
Lawry, Connie: 113.
"Laying on of Hands": 131.
Legislative Council: 134, 135.
LeMaster, J B: 48, 64.
Lesher, Richard L.: 106.
Levin, Alfred: 47.
Lewis Field: 66.
Limon, Leona Hagerman: 138, 139.
Lingelbach, Daniel D.: 94, 95.
Linklater, W. A.: 8.
Little, Everett: 57.
Lohmann, M. R.: 79.
Long, J. K.: 44.
Loomis, C. B.: 49.
Low, Edmon: 45.
Luebke, Phyllis: 105.
Lynch, R. W.: 31.

M

Mace, Harold: 110.
MacVicar, Robert: 55, 70.
Maleev, V. L.: 21.
Malle, Albert L.: 90.
Manipulative Therapy: 131.
Manning, Irma: 90.
Manzer, Lee: 109.
Marland, E. W.: 29.
Martin, A. Frank: 26, 34, 37, 45, 73.
Martin, Archie O.: 34.
Martin, Don: 37.
Martin, Quintin: 44.
Materia Medica: 130, 133.
Matthews, Irma: 8.
McAuliffe, Christa: 113.
McCollom, Katherine Tompkins: 29.
McCormick, Robert: 112.
McCrary, Paul: 46, 47, 57.
McCullough, Robert D.: 136.
McElroy, Clarence H.: 8.
McElroy, William D.: 83.
McGaugh, Gladys: 46, 47, 56, 105.
McGuire, Steve: 138.
McNamara, Dave: 44.
Medearis, Robert: 135.
Medical Doctor: 129, 130, 131, 132, 133, 134.
Meeks, Geron: 136.
Mendenhall, H. S.: 71.
Men's Glee Club: 45.
Michigan State University: 64, 78, 136.
Mid America Assembly: 87.
Military Medical Corps: 133.
Miller, Dave: 44.
Miller, Franklin: 93.
Miller, Larry: 108.
Miller, Vergil: 102.
Millington, Clayton: 64, 87, 88, 115.
Mitchell, Max: 45.
Mobile Chemistry Project: 68.
Mobile Physics Laboratory: 68.
Monk, John: 52.
Moon, Jeff: 121.
Moore, George: 71.
Moore, Norman F.: 65.
Mooring, D. C.: 10.
Morgan, Barbara: 112, 113.
Morgan, Clayton: 62.
Morrill Act: 5.
Morrow, George E.: 6, 11.
Moss, George D.: 18.
Mott Foundation: 111.
Movable School: 9.
Muerman, John C.: 24, 25, 32.
Murdaugh, Edmond D.: 6.
Murphy, H. F. "Pat": 34.
Murray, Anne: 137.

Musculoskeletal System: 131, 132, 134.

N

National Aeronautics and Space Administration: 82, 83, 112, 113.
National Broadcasting Company: 72.
National Defense Education Act: 61.
National Institutes of Health: 140.
National Intercollegiate Flying Association: 105.
National Mail Carriers Association: 65.
National Science Foundation: 50, 56, 63, 68, 69, 70, 71, 74, 82, 83, 87.
National University Continuing Education Association: 109, 117.
National University Extension Association: 42, 52.
National University Teleconferencing Network: 4, 5, 122, 123, 124, 125.
National Youth Administration: 26, 36.
New Deal: 26, 36.
Newman Club: 49.
Nivins, Sharon: 108.
Northeastern Oklahoma State University: 114.
Northern Institute of Osteopathy: 132.
Northern Natural Gas Company: 63, 86.

O

Oak Ridge Associated Universities: 82.
Oberle, Marie: 122, 124.
Office of Economic Opportunity: 89.
Office of Naval Research: 56.
Oklahoma Academy of Science: 71, 82.
Oklahoma Adult Education Association: 52.
Oklahoma Agricultural and Mechanical College: 3, 41, 43, 55, 57, 59, 129.
Oklahoma Area Health Education Center: 141.
Oklahoma Center for Economic Education: 115.
Oklahoma City Technical Institute: 57.
Oklahoma Coalition for Clean Air: 83.
Oklahoma College of Osteopathic Medicine and Surgery: 129, 135, 137, 138, 139, 142, 143, 144.
Oklahoma College of Osteopathic Medicine and Surgery Board of Regents: 138, 139, 143.
Oklahoma College Public Relations Association: 107.
Oklahoma Council on Economic Education: 64, 65, 87, 88.
Oklahoma Court of Criminal Appeals: 37.
Oklahoma Department of Education: 59.
Oklahoma Department of Highways: 63, 89.

Oklahoma Department of Mental Health: 141.
Oklahoma Department of Public Safety: 59.
Oklahoma Education Association: 91.
Oklahoma Educational Television Authority: 59.
Oklahoma Geographic Information Retrieval System: 110.
Oklahoma Indian Affairs Commission: 87.
Oklahoma Junior Academy of Science: 71, 82.
Oklahoma Legislature: 59, 83, 84, 113, 129, 134, 135, 138, 143, 144.
Oklahoma Osteopathic Association: 136, 142, 144.
Oklahoma Osteopathic Hospital: 135, 136, 137.
Oklahoma Planning and Resources Board: 46.
Oklahoma State Board of Agriculture: 23, 29, 33, 38.
Oklahoma State Chamber of Commerce: 122.
Oklahoma State Regents for Higher Education: 60, 94, 109, 111, 113, 117, 119, 134, 135, 136, 137, 141, 142, 143, 144.
Oklahoma State University: 57.
Oklahoma State University Board of Regents: 38, 57, 77, 80, 94, 96, 97, 102.
Oklahoma State University Development Foundation: 58, 64.
Oklahoma State University Energy Conservation Committee: 108.
Oklahoma State University Filmathon: 120.
Olson, Kent: 115.
Opera House: 36, 44, 81,
"Operation Alternatives": 84.
Operation Bootstrap: 47, 52, 68.
Orbison, Scott: 142.
Osner, Richard: 71.
Osteopathic Oath: 136.
Osteopathic Sports Medicine Society: 141.
Osteopathy: 130, 131, 132, 133.
OSU Days for Women: 89.

P

Pacific School of Osteopathy: 132.
Package Library: 45.
Parker, Simon: 138.
Parris, Joe: 48.
Patterson, Herbert: 23.
Payne County Sheltered Workshop: 92.
Payne, Ron: 105.
Peabody College: 29.
Pearl Harbor: 33.

Pegues, Wannette: 113.
Penton Learning Systems: 115, 116.
Perkins, Larry: 121.
Perkins, L. N. "Cy": 45, 73.
Peterson, Elmo G.: 50.
Phillippi, E. J.: 13.
Phillips, Leon C.: 37.
Phillips Petroleum Company: 86, 95.
Photographic Services: 57, 78.
Pittuck, B. C.: 8.
Plant Disease Diagnostic Laboratory: 80.
Point Four Program: 49, 57.
Pollak, Michael H.: 140.
Poole, Richard W.: 5, 65, 79, 87, 94, 97, 102, 103, 107, 125.
Posey, Vance: 52.
Potts, Henry Clay: 23, 24, 30, 31, 34, 35, 50, 51, 65, 66.
Powers, M. L.: 46.
President's Science Advisory Committee: 70.
Price, Robert: 67.
Prinkley, C. H.: 7.
Pritchard, Guy: 47, 56, 85.
Privett, Rex: 134.
Przekop, Lawrence R.: 72.
PSSC Physics: 70.
Public Broadcasting Service: 5.
Public Health Service: 139.
Public School Services: 47, 61.
Purdue University: 78, 108.

R

Radio: 14, 22, 23, 27, 35, 37, 39, 58.
Railroads: 7.
Raper, Jean: 46.
Readers Digest Foundation: 94.
Reece, Avalon B.: 143.
Reger, Buddy: 44.
Remote Sensing Laboratory: 110.
Research Foundation: 58, 82, 97.
Reserve Officers Training Corps: 35, 36.
Residence Halls Association: 106.
Residency Program: 139.
Reynolds, T. H.: 32.
Rhoads, Milton D.: 84.
Rhoads, Ralph: 122.
Richardson, Lavon: 82.
Richter, Elsie Mae: 37.
Ringstrom, Norman H.: 64.
Roads: 1, 6, 9, 14.
Roaring Twenties: 17.
Roberts, C. J.: 122.
Roberts, Mary: 116.
Robinson, Donald: 102.
Rogers, Murl: 107.
Rogers State College: 141.
Rollins, Peter: 120.

Roney, Maurice: 94.
Roosevelt, Franklin D.: 33.
Roosevelt, Theodore: 18.
Ross, O. Burr: 77, 78.
ROTC Rifle Team: 50.
Rouk, Hugh F.: 94.
Roush, Joanne Smith, 138, 139.
Routsong, James F.: 136.
Rucker, Glenn L.: 32, 43, 63, 64.
Rural and Urban Population Shift: 87.
Rural Development Subcommittee: 86.
Russell, Roy: 44.
Rutledge, Lee: 69.

S

Sanders, J. T.: 23.
Sandhu, Harjit: 109.
Sandmeyer, Robert: 114.
Santa Fe Railroad: 8.
Savage, Herbert: 44.
Schmidt, Arlo: 71.
School of Agriculture. See College of
  Agriculture.
School of Arts and Sciences. See College
  of Arts and Sciences.
School of Commerce and Marketing. See
  College of Business Administration.
School of Correspondence Study: 17, 18,
  19, 20, 21, 27, 29, 31, 36, 47, 56, 78,
  105. See also Independent and
  Correspondence Study.
School of Education. See College of
  Education.
School of Engineering. See College of
  Engineering, Architecture and
  Technology.
School of Home Economics. See College
  of Home Economics.
School of Navy Language: 36.
School of Science and Literature. See
  College of Arts and Sciences.
School of Technical Training at Okmulgee:
  42, 57, 94.
School of Technology: 89.
Schreiner, Jerry O.: 81.
Schweitzer, Marjorie: 120.
Science and Mathematics Teachers'
  Conference: 71.
Science Materials Project: 82.
Science Teaching Center: 82.
Scott, J. W.: 23.
Scroggs, Schiller: 25, 34, 45, 65, 67, 68.
Seals, James: 109.
Searcy Airport: 33.
Segall, William: 108.
Self-help Industries: 25.
Shamblin, James E.: 104.
Shearer, John: 87.
Sheerar, L. F. "Mike": 46, 60, 62, 88.

Short Courses: 9, 10, 14, 15, 22, 24, 31,
  32, 34, 51, 65, 80.
Short Winter Courses: 10.
Shull, Peter: 124.
Simpson, Ancil D.: 48.
Simpson, Gary: 121.
Smallwood, James: 121.
Smith, Finis: 134, 135, 138.
Smith, Ladora: 90.
Smith, Rose Ann: 37.
Smith, Tom: 111, 113.
Smith-Lever Act: 13, 15.
Smithsonian Institution: 124.
SMSG Mathematics: 70.
Society for the Advancement of
  Osteopathic Medicine: 141.
Soil Testing Laboratory: 80.
Sorenson, Helmer: 94.
Southeastern State Teachers College: 30.
Southwest Center for Safety Education:
  84.
Southwest Regional Adult Education
  Association: 49, 52.
Southwestern State Teachers College: 18.
Soviet Union: 55.
Space Science Education Project: 83.
Spacemobiles: 83.
Speakers Bureau: 57.
Spears, Bob: 48.
Specialized Training Acceptance and
  Reclassification School: 35.
Spivey, Grace: 90.
Spreadbury, Wendell: 72.
Spurrier, Robert: 123.
Stapley, Edward R.: 35.
State Department of Public Instruction: 19.
"State Is Our Campus": 97, 111.
State Technical Services Act: 79.
Staten, Hi: 57.
Statewide Campus: 47.
Still, Andrew Taylor: 130, 131, 132.
Stillwater Rotary Club: 42.
Stillwater Tutoring Educational Project: 92.
Stratton, Dale: 122.
Stubbs, Gerald T.: 47, 48, 52, 61, 62.
Student Army Training Corps: 14.
Student Association: 92.
Student Entertainers: 36, 37, 45, 73, 91,
  92, 105.
Student Osteopathic Medical Association:
  141.
Student Union: 65, 86, 87.
Study Centers: 20.
Study Tours: 42.
Sub-state Planning Districts: 97.
Sullivan, Mike: 135.
Summer Institutes: 50, 70.
Suzuki String Program: 81.
Swearingen, Eugene L.: 64, 65, 87.

WESTAR 1 Satellite: 108.
Whatley, James A.: 97.
White, George H.: 31, 47,
White, Harvey E.: 72.
Wiggins, Kenneth: 82, 112, 113.
Wilbanks, Charles: 37.
Wilkinson, John W.: 8.
Will Rogers Council of the Boy Scouts of America: 42.
Willham, Oliver S.: 52, 56, 57, 79, 80.
Willis, William P.: 135.
Wilson, James A.: 8.
Wilson, Walter L.: 136, 138, 139.
WKY Television: 59.

Wohlert, Harry: 120, 121, 123, 124.
Women Appointed for Voluntary Emergency Service: 35, 36.
Works Progress Administration: 33.
World Food Day: 125.
World Neighbors, Inc.: 94.
World War I: 9, 13, 15, 17.
World War II: 32, 38, 39, 41, 42, 43, 47, 50, 58, 67, 133.
Wright, Betty: 37.

XYZ

Young Men's Christian Association: 19.
Zant, James H.: 50, 70, 71.

A History of
Oklahoma State University
Extension and Outreach

is a specially designed volume of the Centennial Histories Series.

The text was composed on a personal computer, transmitted by telecommunications to the OSU mainframe computer, and typeset by a computerized typesetting system. Three typefaces were used in the composition. The text is composed in 10 point Melliza with 2 points extra leading added for legibility. Chapter headings are 24 point Omega. All supplemental information contained in the endnotes, charts, picture captions, appendices, bibliography, and index are set in either 8 or 9 point Triumvirate Lite.

The book is printed on a high-quality, coated paper to ensure faithful reproduction of historical photographs and documents. Smyth-sewn and bound with a durable coated nonwoven cover material, the cover has been screen-printed with flat black ink.

The Centennial Histories Committee expresses sincere appreciation to the progressive men and women of the past and present who created and recorded the dynamic, moving history of Oklahoma State University, the story of a land-grant university fulfilling its mission to teach, to research, and to extend itself to the community and the world.